Speak of the Devil

Speak of the Devil

How The Satanic Temple Is Changing the
Way We Talk About Religion

JOSEPH P. LAYCOCK

OXFORD
UNIVERSITY PRESS

OXFORD
UNIVERSITY PRESS

Oxford University Press is a department of the University of Oxford. It furthers the University's objective of excellence in research, scholarship, and education by publishing worldwide. Oxford is a registered trade mark of Oxford University Press in the UK and certain other countries.

Published in the United States of America by Oxford University Press
198 Madison Avenue, New York, NY 10016, United States of America.

CIP data is on file at the Library of Congress
ISBN 978-0-19-094849-8

9

Printed by Integrated Books International, United States of America

For my alma mater St. Stephen's Episcopal School,
where I learned sympathy for the devil.

Contents

Prologue   ix

1. The Day Satan Came to Oklahoma   1

2. Origins and History of The Satanic Temple   27

3. Satanic Schisms   61

4. The Satanic Reformation: How The Satanic Temple Is
   Changing the Way We Talk About Satanism   83

5. Religion or Trolls?: How The Satanic Temple Is Changing the
   Way We Talk About Religion   103

6. Satanic Bake Sales: How The Satanic Temple Is Changing
   the Way We Talk About Evil   131

7. "Taking Equality Too Far": How the Satanic Temple Is Changing
   the Way We Talk About Pluralism   155

8. Conclusion: Speak of the Devil: *The Satanic Temple as American
   Counter-Myth*   187

Notes   197
Bibliography   243
Index   251

Prologue

I am not now, nor have I ever been, a Satanist. But people have accused me of being one—both as a middle schooler for playing D&D (Dungeons and Dragons) and doodling monsters in notebooks and as a scholar for writing a book about self-identified vampires. (Most vampires are not Satanists, but anti-Satanists have little use for nuance.) Perhaps it is because of these accusations that I was so interested when a group of Satanists offered to erect a statue of the devil next to a monument of the Ten Commandments. I have covered The Satanic Temple (TST) for *Religion Dispatches* and other news outlets since 2013. It wasn't that TST lacked for headlines—in the age of "click bait," online media is madly in love with TST. But most of the coverage was and remains shallow, sensationalistic, and uninformed. Few outlets understood the constitutional issues at stake (or else grossly distorted them), and fewer still had any theoretical framework to think about TST's assertion that they are, in fact, a *religion*.

TST grew so fast and did so much in its first six years that it took patient observers to keep track of what was happening. The canard that TST members are "just trolls" has, in part, served as a convenient way of shirking the hard work of sorting out just what this group does and why. Amazingly, even when lawsuits filed by TST began to move into circuit courts and I started receiving calls from attorneys and prison chaplains asking me to explain what TST is, some persisted in telling me that the whole thing was "obviously" just a PR stunt.

While the future of TST is far from clear, I think there are several reasons why it is worth understanding this group, its arguments, and its history better. First, as a professor of religious studies, TST is "good to think with." Their provocations provide almost ideal case studies for classroom discussions precisely because they problematize our assumptions about religion and religious freedom. I have several colleagues who have asked their students to analyze TST for just this reason.

Second, TST is eliciting similar conversations—in a less organized and productive fashion—on a national scale: the more their provocations are discussed, condemned, or even dismissed, the more "unsettled" previous assumptions about religion and religious freedom become. These are strange times: while exploring the discourse surrounding TST, I encountered skeptics professing a newfound appreciation for the value of religious ritual and community and conservative American Catholics openly denouncing the idea of religious freedom.

Third, TST seems to have played a major role in a global renaissance of religious Satanism. Since 2013 new Satanic organizations have formed throughout the United States, Europe, Australia, New Zealand, and South Africa. There are also rumors of groups forming in South America and the Middle East. Some of these emerging forms of Satanism are allied with TST and some are not; some reject supernaturalism as TST does, and some do not. But many of these groups have emulated TST in seeking a public platform and a degree of social engagement that is largely unprecedented in the history of religious Satanism. A decade ago, Satanists marching in gay pride parades, adopting highways, or running donation drives to aid the homeless would have been considered an absurdity. Today, such activities occur around the world.

This book, therefore, seeks to do two things. First, there is a need for a detailed history of TST. This history is short but far more complicated than the casual observer may suspect. The media has reported sporadically on TST, providing arresting headlines for their campaigns and provocations, but little context. I have already seen a number of legal and theoretical arguments put forward regarding TST, but without an understanding of what TST is or where it came from these arguments will be counterproductive. I have attempted to provide a history that is comprehensive if not exhaustive that includes details that might otherwise have been lost and arranges them into a coherent narrative.

Second, I hope to show how TST's provocations are affecting our national conversation about important issues. TST punches above its weight due to its ability to draw media attention, its creative use of the legal system, and its tactical manipulation of its opponents' rhetoric. Due to these factors, TST has a real effect on how we talk about "religion," morality, and what a religiously plural democracy ought to look like. There is already a body of scholarly literature on religious Satanism, but I think TST shows why Satanism has wider implications and should be taken more seriously by religion scholars.

Researching this book took far longer than any project I have previously done. In order to see the full range of discourse surrounding TST, I set up a daily news alert for the word "Satanic." Each morning I went through all the local news segments, blog entries, and editorials discussing TST. Working over a period of years, I created an archive of over 2,600 news items.

I did ethnographic observation with TST chapters in San Marcos and Austin, Texas, as well as in Salem, Massachusetts, and Little Rock, Arkansas. I also conducted research interviews with over fifty people spread across fifteen states as well as the United Kingdom and Australia. With many of these individuals there were second and even third interviews. Many people interviewed for this book use pseudonyms for safety reasons. I have tried as much as possible to protect the identities and privacy of my informants. Because TST often requires its leaders to sign non-disclosure agreements (NDAs), I should mention that I never signed an NDA and was never asked to do so.

Several months into the ethnographic phase of my research, TST went through a major schism and several chapters left to become independent. As a scholar of new religious movements, it was an interesting experience to watch a religious group splinter before my eyes. While witnessing this was exciting from a pure research perspective, it was very painful for everyone involved. Several of my interview subjects exhibited signs of anxiety and depression, and at times I felt depressed myself. Some approached me for follow-up interviews about how they were feeling, and at times I felt more like a confessor than an ethnographer.

Unfortunately, the schism affected my relationship with my research subjects as some saw this book as an opportunity to "set the record" straight about what had happened. It is said that history is written by the victors, but bending the ear of the historians is itself a form of victory. I have tried to be as neutral as possible and to respect the experiences described by my informants. At any rate, this book is meant to be the first word in a scholarly conversation about the history of TST, not the last.

I would like to thank everyone who was interviewed for this book including TST's co-founders and executive ministry, Malcolm Jarry and Lucien Greaves (Doug Mesner); early collaborator David Guinan; Greg Stevens, Amber Saurusrex, Sadie Satanas, Chalice Blythe, and Sebastian Simpson from TST's National Council; Shiva Honey, TST's Director of National Events; Stu de Haan, legal counsel for TST; Satanic activist and artist Jex Blackmore; Hofman A. Turing, Emma Story, and Belle Phomet from LORE:SCNYC (League of Rebel Eve: Satanic Collective of NYC); Salome DeMeur of FAUST; David Suhor and Nelcitlaly from TST-West Florida; Seraphina from TST-NYC; Chris Turvey from TST-Colorado; Christopher

Paul from TST-Atlanta; Lex Manticore and Lux Armiger from TST-Chicago; Jill, Jesse, and Brandon from TST-Boston; Daniel Walker and Simone from Satanic Bay Area; Bel Citoyen of HelLA; Damien Ba'al of United Aspects of Satan; Mara Gorgo and and Damien Blackmoor from TST-Indiana; Rose Vespiria and Marius Omnes from the Crossroads Assembly; Lilith Starr from TST-Seattle, Michelle Shortt and Jack Matirko from TST-Arizona; Cara Jeanne in Philadelphia; Steve Hill in Los Angeles; High Cardinal Zeke Apollyon of Global Order of Satan; F. Felix Fortunado in Dallas, Jon and Laura Winningham from TST-Houston; Donny from TST-Springfield; Dex Desjardins and Sekhmet Solas from TST-Albany; Koren Walsh (Jezebel Pride) of The Minnesota Left-Hand Path Community; Artemis Pine and Sutekh of Satanic Australia; Lanzifer Longinus and Lilim Camus from TST-San Marcos; Brian Valencia from TST-San Antonio; Alex from TST-Austin; Evyn and Thom of Satanhaus; filmmaker Joy Davenport (Erin Morningstar); attorney James McNaughton; actor Michael Weiner; Dianne Post of the Freedom from Religion Foundation; and Francis X Clooney, SJ, of Harvard Divinity School. I would also like to thank everyone who supported me in thinking through and executing this project including Evan Derkacz at *Religion Dispatches,* James R. Lewis and David Bromley for their guidance as peers, author Don Webb for his insights into the Left-Hand Path and its history, Jeffrey Sanchez for his needed assistance with preparing this manuscript, and my patient wife Natasha Mikles who tolerated her husband being out late fraternizing with Satanists.

1

The Day Satan Came to Oklahoma

Even if they mock Judeo-Christian-Islamic values, even if they ridicule everything most of us hold dear, devil-worshippers (if there are any) are entitled to practice their religion, so long as they break no constitutionally valid law.

—Carl Sagan, *The Demon-Haunted World*[1]

Now these Satanists are *abusing* this loophole. That . . . is so Satanist.

—Stephen Colbert on The Satanic Temple (May 6, 2014)

When people asked me, "what I was working on," and I answered, "The Satanic Temple," I would often be met with looks of befuddlement. That is, until I said, "You know, those guys who wanted to put a statue of the devil up at the Oklahoma state capitol." After I said that, *everyone* knew whom I was talking about. The Satanic Temple (TST) is a political and religious movement that advocates progressive values and the separation of church and state. Although they reject supernaturalism, they argue that they have a sincere religious commitment to Satanism as evidenced by a shared ethos, symbols, and rituals. Satan, for TST, is a symbol of rebellion rather than a literal force of evil. I have been following the dizzying growth and activity of TST since December 2013 when the group announced its intention to donate a monument of Satan to the Oklahoma state capitol. Although the offer was initially regarded as a joke, the statue—entitled *Baphomet with Children*—has become a reality and has traveled across the country from Salem, Massachusetts, to Detroit, Michigan, to Little Rock, Arkansas. Baphomet has become a sort of metonymy not only for TST but also for a cultural moment defined by social polarization and the ongoing erosion of political norms. But to understand how this situation arose and why I think TST is significant to the study of religion and American culture, it is necessary to back up several years.

Speak of the Devil. Joseph P. Laycock, Oxford University Press (2020). © Oxford University Press.
DOI: 10.1093/oso/9780190948498.001.0001

In 2009 the Oklahoma legislature enacted the Ten Commandments Monument Display Act that mandated the construction of a Ten Commandments statue on the grounds of the state capitol. Although the US Supreme Court has made some creative exceptions, in principle, erecting a monument to a set of religious laws at a site where a secular state government writes laws is a violation of the Constitution's establishment clause. The reason for this is obvious: a religious symbol at the state capitol sends a message that the state of Oklahoma favors a particular religion and that its legislators intend to pass laws that privilege the interests of this religion to the exclusion of others.

Proponents of such monuments often claim that the Ten Commandments are "the foundation of American law." It is true that three of the prohibitions in the Ten Commandments (against lying, killing, and stealing) are congruent with American law. However, these simple prohibitions have been traced through the earliest versions of English Common Law and back to Germanic tribes from before they were Christianized.[2] Meanwhile other commandments (restricting which gods can be worshipped, what kinds of images can be constructed, and mandatory observance of religious holy days) directly contradict the freedoms guaranteed in the First Amendment.

The Oklahoma legislature sought to circumvent the establishment clause by exploiting a loophole. In 2005, the Supreme Court decided two similar cases on the same day: *Van Orden v. Perry* concerned the constitutionality of a Ten Commandments monument at the Texas state capitol, and *McCreary County v. ACLU of Kentucky* concerned displaying framed copies of the Ten Commandments in court houses and public schools. In two 5-4 decisions, the Kentucky display was struck down but the Texas monument was permitted. The "swing vote" was Stephen Breyer. Breyer felt the Texas monument was different from the Kentucky displays for two reasons: First, it had already been standing for forty years without controversy. Second—and important for future cases—it was located alongside other monuments around the state capitol. This context, Breyer reasoned, showed that the religious content was part of a "broader moral and historical message."[3] This kind of hairsplitting is common when the Supreme Court is asked to assess whether religious monuments and holiday displays on government property are constitutional. One lower court judge commented, "The endorsement test makes judges render decisions that are more like interior decorating than Constitutional law."[4]

HB1330, the 2009 Oklahoma bill sponsored by state representative Mike Ritze that proposed the Ten Commandments Monument Display Act, relied heavily on the precedent set by *Van Orden v. Perry*:

> The Ten Commandments monument shall use the same words used on the monument at issue in Von [*sic*] Orden v. Perry, that the United States supreme court ruled constitutional. . . . The placement of this monument shall not be construed to mean that the state of Oklahoma favors any religion or denomination thereof over others, but rather will be placed on the Capitol grounds where there are numerous other monuments.[5]

In the logic of the bill, the presence of other monuments at the capitol grounds is the primary factor at stake in determining whether a Ten Commandments monument amounts to a state endorsement of religion. Strangely, the bill also attempts to legislate how individuals may interpret symbolic expression, prohibiting any interpretation that views the monument as unconstitutional.

HB1330 justifies the monument by invoking a particular view of history that arguably resembles religious belief rather more than historical fact:

> That the Ten Commandments represent a philosophy of government held by many of the founders of this nation and by many Oklahomans and other Americans today, that God has ordained civil government and has delegated limited authority to civil government, that God has limited the authority of civil government, and that God has endowed people with certain unalienable rights, including life, liberty, and the pursuit of happiness.[6]

The belief that the God of Israel (the God referred to in the Ten Commandments) has ordained civil government, delegated and limited its authority, and endowed people with rights is described as a "philosophy of government," but it could also be described as a religious creed. An atheist would not, and could not, be persuaded by these claims. The same could be said about people of many religions, including Christians who believe civil government was invented by humans rather than God.

HB1330 does not explicitly endorse these claims about God, but it does emphasize that these claims were believed by the nation's founders as well as "many Oklahomans and other Americans today." It then explains that the monument is necessary so that the people of the United States and Oklahoma "may understand and appreciate" that these claims about God were believed by so many people. The monument is necessary because the people "need to identify the Ten Commandments, one of many sources, as influencing the development of what has become modern law."[7] The claim that a particular set of beliefs about a particular God has so much historical importance that the government must erect monuments to impress the significance of these beliefs on the public certainly seems like a government establishment of religion. The stated purpose for building the monument is clearly more relevant to its constitutionality than whether or not there are any other monuments nearby.

HB1330 was signed into law, and in March 2012 a monument was installed on the capitol grounds. Mike Ritze's family paid $10,000 to build it so that no tax dollars were used in its construction. In the summer of 2013, Baptist pastor Bruce Prescott complained that the monument's location violated the state constitution and filed a lawsuit with the help of the ACLU. In June 2015, the Oklahoma Supreme Court ruled 7-2 in *Prescott v. Oklahoma Capitol Preservation Commission* that the monument violated article 2, section 5 of the state's constitution, which forbids the use of public money or property for religious uses, either "directly or indirectly." The court ruled that *Van Orden v. Perry* was irrelevant because this case concerned state law rather than federal law. The court was also dubious of the distinction implied in the language of HB1330 between endorsing religious truth claims and endorsing the historical significance of religious truth claims. The court's opinion explained, "Prohibiting uses of public property that 'indirectly' benefit a system of religion was clearly done to protect the ban from circumvention based upon mere form and technical distinction. . . . As concerns the 'historic purpose' justification, the Ten Commandments are obviously religious in nature and are an integral part of the Jewish and Christian faiths."[8] Justice Steven Taylor added that the Ten Commandments are not mentioned in the Federalist Papers, the Declaration of Independence, or the Constitution, were not mentioned during the Philadelphia Constitutional Convention, and have never been invoked by the Supreme Court as a source of law. In October the monument was removed late at night under guard at the cost of $4,700 to the city.

While the Oklahoma Supreme Court addressed the issue at stake with the Ten Commandments monument and its stated purpose of informing the public about a particular religion's historic significance, the contours of this argument were not explained in news coverage of the decision. I found virtually nothing in sources like CNN and *USA Today* explaining *why* the legislature thought the monument was constitutional or why the court ruled it was not. This is par for the course in discussions of constitutional law: most press coverage of the Supreme Court only explains who won or lost and makes no attempt to explain why. Because the underlying legal principles were not explained, it was easy for politicians such as Oklahoma representative Bobby Cleveland to frame the controversy over the monument as a case of Christianity under attack by "political correctness" rather than a principled ruling by a court.[9] TST's intervention was significant not because it led to the removal of the Ten Commandments monument, but because it changed the narrative around the controversy.

On November 17, 2013, while the ACLU's suit was still in litigation, TST's two founders, using the pseudonyms Malcolm Jarry and Lucien Greaves, sent a formal letter to the State Capitol Preservation Commission offering to construct a monument to Satan that would accompany the Ten Commandments monument. Their letter stated, "We are aware that there is currently a legal dispute over the presence of the Ten Commandments monument. Granting us permission to make our donation would certainly reinforce the arguments being made by Oklahoma City in defense of the current monument."[10] The proposal had been Jarry's idea although as the story became national news, Greaves stepped forward as TST's official spokesperson. Greaves explained to CNN, "They said they wanted to be open to different monuments and this seems like a perfect place to put that to the test." Greaves approached the Oklahoma Capitol Preservation Commission, obtained the required forms for proposing a new monument, and set to work designing a statue of Satan that would meet the Commission's standards. Greaves stated, "We want something big and bold that will be able to stand up to the weather or whatever other kinds of assaults. . . . My favorite idea right now is an object of play for children. We want kids to see that Satanism is where the fun is."[11]

No one knew what to make of Jarry's proposal. One representative remarked, "I think it is a joke."[12] Cleveland, apparently asked whether TST was also attacking Christianity out of political correctness, responded, "I think these Satanists are a different group. You put them under the nut category."[13] Brady Henderson, the legal director of the ACLU's Oklahoma chapter, seemed uncertain whether TST was an ally. He was initially supportive of the Satanists' intervention, stating:

We would prefer to see Oklahoma's government officials work to faithfully serve our communities and improve the lives of Oklahomans instead of erecting granite monuments to show us all how righteous they are. But if the Ten Commandments, with its overtly Christian message, is allowed to stay at the Capitol, the Satanic Temple's proposed monument cannot be rejected because of its different religious viewpoint.[14]

However, in a subsequent interview, Henderson stated, "Their basis for saying we have [a] right to have this on the Capitol lawn is inconsistent with our case. The state shouldn't have a religious monument at all."[15]

Nevertheless, the Baphomet proposal led to some interesting consequences. Despite the mention of other monuments in HB1330, it seems clear that the Oklahoma legislature was not actually interested in creating a diversity of monuments, but rather in trying to replicate the conditions of the *Van Orden v. Perry* decision to justify a Ten Commandments monument. By "calling their bluff," TST created doubt about this argument. Days after TST's offer, the Pastafarians—a satirical "parody" religion—offered to build a monument to their object of worship, the Flying Spaghetti Monster. The Universal Society of Hinduism, based in Nevada, offered to erect a statue of the monkey deity Lord Hanuman. People for the Ethical Treatment of Animals (PETA) proposed a monument as well. In response, the Oklahoma Capitol Preservation Commission declared a moratorium on new monument proposals.[16]

The moratorium put pressure on the Oklahoma legislature to give a rationale—other than state endorsement of Christianity—as to why the Ten Commandments were being prioritized and other monuments were not even being considered. The ready-made answer was that the Ten Commandments have historical significance while the other religious symbols do not. Representative Paul Wesselhöft explained:

> What will disqualify them [The Satanic Temple] has really nothing to do with Satan, as such. It's that it has no historical significance for the State of Oklahoma. The only reason why the Ten Commandments qualified is because at the Capitol, what we do is we make laws. We are lawmakers. Well, one of the earliest laws we have are the Ten Commandments. So therefore, it has historical significance.[17]

Mike Reynolds, another state representative, went even further, claiming that the Satanic monument was being proposed for religious purposes while the Ten Commandments monument was put up for historical purposes.[18] But Lucien Greaves countered that Satan is also a significant figure in the history of jurisprudence:

Satanism is a fundamental component at the genesis of American liberty. Medieval witch-hunts taught us to adopt presumption of innocence, secular law, and a more substantive burden of proof. Today, we are rightly offended by the notion of blasphemy laws and divine fiats. Acknowledging wrongful persecutions has helped shape the legal system that preserves the sovereignty of our skeptics, heretics, and the misunderstood. It has shaped a proud culture of tolerance and free inquiry. This is to be a historical marker commemorating the scapegoats, the marginalized, the demonized minority, and the unjustly outcast.[19]

Since getting to know Greaves, I do not think he is being entirely facetious here. In line with skeptics like Carl Sagan, Greaves sees tolerance and free inquiry as core American values that were hard won by freethinkers who challenged the religious establishment of their day. More importantly, by mirroring the Oklahoma legislature's argument back at them, Greaves revealed its disingenuousness: if many religious symbols can be framed as having historical significance, it seems that the real reason the legislature chose the Ten Commandments was to designate Christianity as privileged by the state. Reynolds's claim that one religious symbol is "actually religious" in purpose while another is merely historic only highlights how arbitrary and politically motivated these distinctions are.

TST also attempted to reframe who the aggressor was in this situation. Political theorist Corey Robin argues that conservatives have a tendency to "play victim and victor" by advancing their privilege while framing their actions as a restoration of some damage perpetrated by subversive forces.[20] This dynamic is especially at play in debates surrounding Ten Commandments monuments at courthouses and state capitols. Often the politicians who propose these monuments find themselves in a "win/win" situation. If their monument goes unchallenged, they have proven their credentials as a Christian politician. On the other hand, if such proposals are defeated in court, this is not seen as evidence that proposing them was a bad idea or that the legislator is ignorant about constitutional law; rather, the legislator can claim to be the victim of political correctness and anti-Christian persecution. Either way, a conservative Christian base will be energized. The narrative that opponents of such monuments are hostile to Christianity in general is an extremely effective diversion from the more nuanced constitutional issues at stake. This narrative is also so entrenched that contradictory evidence is often ignored. For example, almost no one noticed that it was a Baptist pastor who first filed suit against the Oklahoma monument.

TST attempted to derail this narrative by emphasizing that their offensive proposals are only possible because Christian politicians have damaged an arrangement that had been beneficial to everyone. Greaves said of Mike Ritze, "He's helping a satanic agenda grow more than any of us possibly could. You don't walk around and see too many satanic temples around, but when you open the door to public spaces for us, that's when you're going to see us."[21] The narrative of Christian persecution became even more untenable during a panel discussion of the monument that aired on Fox News's *Don Imus in the Morning* on January 9, 2014. Bernard McGuirk, the show's executive producer, opined, "They should be able to put the statue up and then they should be shot right next to it." Legal counsel for TST responded with a letter to Fox News demanding an apology, stating: "Advocacy of the murder of American citizens based on their religious beliefs is intolerable and sickening. For [Fox News] to disseminate such a position as part of a televised debate on a national network strikes at the heart of this country's founding principles and potentially places the Temple's members in imminent danger." McGuirk responded with an on air apology, stating: "My comments were rooted in ignorance. Satanists do not promote evil a la Charles Manson or Hitler. Regardless, I don't want to see anybody shot, that's the truth of the matter, so I do apologize unequivocally. I apologize for those comments and certainly, certainly withdraw them."[22]

The longer the conversation about TST's monument went on, the more assumptions that had gone largely unstated began to bubble to the surface. In a moment of honesty that undermined claims that the Ten Commandments monument was not religious, Representative Earl Sears expressed his opinion that "this is a faith-based nation and a faith-based state." "Faith," in this context was code for Protestantism symbolized by a monument with the Protestant version of the Ten Commandments. Sears added, "I think it is very offensive they would contemplate or even have this kind of conversation."[23] The fact that the *conversation* is deemed offensive is telling: it is not the statue itself, but the discussion of it that is disruptive because it unsettles assumptions.

Important insights into how the public understood the controversy were uncovered when TST filed a Freedom of Information Act request with the Oklahoma Capitol for any communications concerning their statue. They were given a sizable archive of emails and voicemails from citizens who were alarmed over the proposed statue, which they shared with me. Most of these messages demonstrated only a partial understanding of the situation: a caller from Florida had been told by his pastor that the Satanic statue was in response to a private citizen erecting a Ten Commandments monument on his own property; a woman from Oklahoma wanted to know if the governor was in favor of or opposed to erecting a statue of the devil; several callers seemed to think the Satanic statue had been put up to a popular referendum. The most striking voicemail was a tearful, rambling message pleading not to erect the statue. The caller, who identified herself as a Christian, explained how she had used peyote and read Nietzsche in the 1960s before invoking the plight of crack babies and genocide in Africa as evidence of why the statue must not be erected. She was still weeping when the allotted space of three minutes ran out and the voicemail was cut off. Significantly, this caller *did* understand the underlying principal of the establishment clause. At one point she stated:

> I am gonna beg this community not to put that Satanic crap on the lawn of our White House—our state building—whatever, where the governor lives. It can't be done and if they're combatting that just to get us to take the Ten Commandments down, then take the damn Ten Commandments down. Don't put something for Satan on the lawn![24]

This response suggests that TST was at least somewhat successful in persuading the public that the establishment clause is good for everyone.

The most significant political ramification of TST's proposal came in the aftermath of *Prescott v. Oklahoma Capitol Preservation Commission* decision. Only days after this decision, a conservative think tank called the Oklahoma Council of Public Affairs announced a campaign to simply alter the state constitution by repealing article 2, section 5. Rather than presenting themselves as sore losers, they argued that this section of the state constitution had been written in a historical moment of anti-Catholic bigotry. This view is heavily indebted to the work of legal scholar Philip Hamburger.[25] Although the states disestablished their formerly established churches between the 1770s and 1833, Hamburger notes that, in the nineteenth century, Protestants turned to the idea of "separating church and state" as a way of repressing a wave of Catholic immigrants who formed parochial schools to maintain their distinct religion and identity. The Blaine Amendment was a constitutional amendment proposed in 1875 that would have applied the establishment and free exercise clauses to the states and banned the use of tax revenue to fund parochial schools. It was never adopted, but in the fifty years after it was proposed, twenty-two states passed laws blocking funding for parochial schools. These state laws are likewise referred to as "Blaine Amendments" or, often, "Little Blaine Amendments." Hamburger's retelling of the history of the separation of church and state is appealing to conservative groups that oppose separation. It is very unpopular to attack the idea of separation if it is enshrined in the First Amendment. On the other hand, if separation was invented much later as a political cudgel to disenfranchise Catholics, then opposing it can be framed as progressive and even tolerant.

Supporters of the Oklahoma Ten Commandments monument claimed that article 2, section 5 of the Oklahoma constitution was "a Blaine Amendment" and therefore rooted in bigotry. Two justices of the Oklahoma Supreme Court, writing separately, specifically rejected this claim, noting that the 1875 Blaine Amendment would have forbidden only the use of government funds for parochial schools, while article 2, section 5 forbids the use of government funds or property to support any religion.[26] Nevertheless, after the monument was removed, the Oklahoma Council of Public Affairs began soliciting donations for its campaign to "eradicate the bigotry in Oklahoma's Constitution that is the Blaine Amendment."[27]

For some Oklahomans this might have been a compelling argument for amending the constitution: the Christian majority could enjoy a religious symbol at the capitol and simultaneously feel they were correcting an injustice against religious minorities rather than marginalizing them. But some people now saw TST as a credible threat if the separation of church and state were removed. Wayne Green, an editor for *Tulsa World*, opined, "The legislature can pass a lot of laws but they can't repeal the law of unintended consequences." He added that the reform might "open the door to all sorts of crazy things, for example there was a group that wanted to put a Satanic statue on the grounds of the state capitol. I think the chances of that become much greater if you just take out article 2, section 5."[28] TST's "stunt" had made them a factor in the state's political calculus.

The Wandering Baphomet

When CNN first reported on the proposed monument to Satan at the Oklahoma capitol, the article noted rather mockingly that TST had created an Indiegogo page to fund the statue, which had only raised $150 toward its $20,000 goal.[29] But by the time the fundraising ended, the public had contributed $30,000 to the project.[30] By some estimates, the final product—an 8-foot-6-inch bronze statue weighing one and half tons—cost over $100,000.[31] It seemed that no one—including TST—had anticipated how much interest there would be in such a project. When I interviewed Lucien Greaves in December 2013, I asked him whether he would really create a monument to Satan. He explained they were quite serious, and anyway they had no choice because the project had been crowd-funded: there was no way to return the money, and TST was obligated to use it for its stated purpose. In fact, the founders of TST ended up paying much of the cost from their own pockets.

As the plan developed, Greaves decided to make an image of Baphomet. The name "Baphomet" dates back to the fourteenth century when the Knights Templar were suppressed by the French monarchy. The knights were accused of worshipping an androgynous idol named "Baphomet," likely an old French corruption of the name "Muhammad."[32] In 1856 occultist Eliphaz Levi published an image of Baphomet as "the goat of the sabbath." Levi's illustration showed a goat-headed entity with feathery wings, female breasts, and a caduceus in its lap suggesting a phallus. Levi's Baphomet was not meant to portray an evil entity but rather to symbolize the reconciliation of opposites. This image has been parodied and pastiched by Christian moral entrepreneurs and heavy metal culture alike ever since.

TST's Baphomet is based on Levi's illustration, although it lacks breasts and the phallic wand (in order to meet the standards of the Oklahoma Capitol Preservation Commission). Jarry wanted to design the statue so that visitors could sit in Baphomet's lap for "contemplation and introspection." He also added a cherubic boy and girl that stand on either side of the creature reverently gazing up at its face. Jarry's friend, David Guinan, began researching construction costs. The statue could be constructed cheaply using spray-on cement, but everyone agreed it should be made of bronze. Bronze showed this was a serious proposal and it would be more difficult for vandals to destroy. Guinan found New York sculptor Marc Porter. He recalled Porter asking him, "Are you serious about this? Because if you are, I'm going to have to clear my schedule for the next six months." Porter worked for the next six months, using space Guinan found in a vermouth distillery in Brooklyn. Actual children were brought in as models, who had latex casts made of them. Baphomet's rather emaciated torso was modeled on that of punk rocker Iggy Pop. When Porter's sculpture was complete, a mold was taken and the bronze was poured in a foundry in Florida.[33] The mold was also kept so that replacements could be crafted. Greaves joked that if the statue were insured for enough, destroying it would provide the resources to build two more.

TST had always emphasized that their monument was meant as a complement to, and not a replacement for, the Ten Commandments monument. In October 2014, Michael Tate Reed—a self-described "Jesus freak" diagnosed with schizoaffective disorder—destroyed the Ten Commandments monument by crashing his car into it. Greaves released a statement announcing that TST was "appalled" by this act of vandalism. He explained, "To be clear, The Satanic Temple will not seek to erect its monument unless the 10 Commandments is restored."[34] The Baphomet statue was officially unveiled in a ceremony in Detroit held in July 2015. But only a few months later, the Ten Commandments monument was removed from the Oklahoma capitol, leaving Baphomet without purpose.

Unmoored from the conflict in Oklahoma, Baphomet began a series of peregrinations across the country. Currently, Baphomet resides in Salem, Massachusetts, where TST opened its official headquarters in September 2016. As TST formed chapters across the country, local members began lobbying to bring the statue to courthouses and town halls in Indiana and Arizona where religious displays were present. Some suggested sending Baphomet to the Texas capitol, the site of *Van Orden v. Perry* case.

In 2015 a nearly identical controversy began when the Arkansas state legislature passed a bill decreeing the erection of a Ten Commandments monument at their state capitol. Once again, the bill sought to replicate the *Van Orden v. Perry* decision. In October 2016, Greaves traveled to Little Rock and attended a meeting of the Arkansas State Capital Arts and Grounds Commission to discuss bringing Baphomet to the capitol. The Commission treated the proposal seriously and actually discussed possible locations on capitol grounds where Baphomet might be installed. A public hearing for further discussion of the monument was scheduled for May 2017. But in February, TST was informed that their hearing was cancelled because of a new law—that was applied retroactively to their proposal—that the legislature must first approve any monument proposals before they can be considered by the Arts and Grounds Commission. HB1273 even featured a clause declaring the situation to be an emergency and stating the bill would go into immediate effect because it was "necessary for the preservation of public peace, health, and safety."[35]

In response, Stuart de Haan, an attorney and TST member, sent a letter to the deputy secretary of state arguing that applying HB 1273 retroactively was a clear case of religious discrimination. TST and the ACLU began preparing for lawsuits. Undaunted, the legislature installed the Ten Commandments monument on June 18, 2017. But less than twenty-four hours after installation, Michael Tate Reed, a resident of Arkansas, once again destroyed a Ten Commandments monument using his car. This time, Reed filmed himself shouting "freedom!" as he crashed into the monument. He later explained he had committed this act of vandalism to defend the separation of church and state.[36] In response, TST postponed their lawsuit.

Pureflix—an evangelical film company that produced the *God's Not Dead* films—donated $25,000 for a second Ten Commandments monument that was installed on April 26, 2018. This time, the monument featured concrete barriers to deter car attacks. In response, TST announced that it was resuming its religious discrimination lawsuit and would file an "intervenor," merging it with other suits against the monument. The Liberty Institute, a conservative group that defends Christian monuments on government property, pledged to pay for any court costs accrued in defending the monument.

On August 16, 2018, TST took the bold move of loading the Baphomet statue onto a flatbed truck and driving it from Salem to Little Rock, where they parked it in front of the capitol to hold a "rally for religious liberty." A podium was placed on top of the truck, and religious leaders representing atheists, mainline Protestants, evangelicals, and Satanists spoke on the importance of the establishment clause. Afterward the Baphomet was covered in a tarp and returned to Salem.

TST's lawsuit against the state of Arkansas is still pending at the time of this writing. Whether or not Arkansas is forced to take down its Ten Commandments monument, it is a near certainty that no government or municipality will ever accept Baphomet on public property—and any community willing to house TST's statue wouldn't be offered it in the first place. And so the homeless statue remains a perpetual threat, wandering from battlefield to battlefield across America's culture wars.

The Age of Socially Engaged Satanism

The Baphomet controversy is representative of an emerging form of Satanism that is political and *socially engaged*. I use the term "socially engaged Satanism" in the same way Thich Nhat Hanh used the term "socially engaged Buddhism" to delineate a form of activism rooted in a religious tradition.[37] Historically, the accusation of Satanism has been used as a smear for one's political and religious opponents. With some rare exceptions, no one identified as a Satanist until Anton LaVey founded the Church of Satan (CoS) in 1966.[38] While LaVey's Satanists expressed their contempt for Christianity, they shared the assumption of many in the 1960s that Christianity was dying. LaVey sometimes described his vision to improve society, but the CoS was primarily interested in improving themselves: instead of challenging Christianity's political power, they wanted to challenge its ability to inculcate guilt and shame so that they could better enjoy what pleasures the world offered. This project mostly involved creating enclaves of decadence where the morals of "the herd" could be safely mocked or ignored.

By the 1980s, America was deep in the clutches of a Satanic Panic. A coalition of conservative Christian leaders, talk show hosts, credulous law enforcement agents, and therapists presented the public with a conspiracy theory that an organized cult of criminal Satanists was active in America. Some claimed they tortured children and murdered thousands of people a year in human sacrifices. The Satanic Panic was a boon for some politicians. Around the country, bills were introduced that raised the penalty for hurting people or animals if done in a "ritualistic" context. In 1985, conservative leader Jesse Helms proposed an amendment to a bill that would deny tax-exempt status to "any cult, organization, or other group that has as a purpose, or that has any interest in, the promoting of satanism or witchcraft."[39] Of course, there were virtually no actual Satanists performing sacrifices that might object to this legislation. The imaginary threat of the Panic meant politicians could propose anti-Satanism legislation that pleased their constituents with no political consequences.

Occasionally deviant individuals (usually adolescent males) would declare themselves Satanists and carry out the very crimes alleged by the claimsmakers, ranging from vandalism to killing animals (a phenomenon folklorists call "ostension.").[40] Adolescent murderers also found the public was more sympathetic to them if they blamed their crimes on involvement in Satanism. But organized Satanists, to the extent they existed, had no political voice. LaVey complained, "Whenever I got on TV or the radio, I was given a few seconds to say what they desperately needed me for. Someone else who had lost 240 pounds of ugly fat got 20 minutes of air time. A woman who saw Jesus on a tortilla had even more time to recount her experience. If Satanism was so hot, why wasn't I able to talk about it?"[41]

But since 2013, there has been an unprecedented cultural moment in which Satanic speech, symbolism, and ritual have been deployed for political purposes, of which TST is only the most prominent example. Conservative Christian leaders, particularly Catholic ones, have noted this trend with horror. In 2015, after TST sought participation in an "open forum" of holiday displays at the Florida capitol, Catholic League president Bill Donahue exclaimed, "Until two years ago, Satanists were never bothered by the presence of a menorah on public property in Tallahassee."[42] The following year, John Ritchie of the traditionalist Catholic political group The American Society for the Defense of Tradition, Family, and Property described the lawful public actions of multiple Satanic groups as a "Satanic revolution" that was "gnawing at our nation's moral fabric, numbing our culture to the horror of sin, and paving the way for more sordid aberrations."[43]

This new brand of Satanism is being spearheaded by a generation that came of age during the Satanic Panic of the 1980s. The CoS emerged in a decade when many Americans believed Christianity was dying out. By contrast, this new generation perceives core American values of tolerance and free inquiry as under assault by a radical Christian agenda. Satanism—the boogieman presented to them in their youth—is now looked to as a weapon against their enemies and a symbolic expression of their anger.

TST first appeared in January of 2013. Since then they have grown from a handful of people into a national organization with chapters throughout North America, hundreds of chapter members, and thousands of members who support TST's campaigns. TST has initiated dozens of projects addressing issues of church and state, education, reproductive rights, and LGBTQ rights. TST chapters have also engaged a wide variety of philanthropy projects, including cleaning highways and beaches and donation drives to help the homeless and needy—all activities not normally associated with Satanism.

Religion scholars have described Satanism as a "self-religion" in the sense that it holds the self as sacred and regards the demands of society as a hindrance to being one's "authentic" self. In this, Satanism is actually a cousin to the New Age and Human Potential movements.[44] While TST members I interviewed did frame their religion as a celebration of autonomy and self-determination, they also indicated that this project cannot be divorced from political action, social engagement, and community building. As Amber, who is currently a member of TST's National Council, stated, "Publicly identifying as a Satanist *is* a form of political discourse."[45] For Greaves, the mission of TST is about self-sacrifice, not self-cultivation. As he explained it to me in 2018:

> My vision of a happy life is not one in which I'm doing what I'm doing now. What I'm doing now is more in line with my vision of a good death—where I can go out with a certain degree of pride, knowing I took some gambles, knowing I fought the fight, and feeling that I did, in some way, leave a mark and at least help lay out some working methods of achieving a better future.[46]

This does not sound like a self-religion at all, but it does sound like a socially engaged one.

TST is currently the most organized and developed manifestation of this new wave of political Satanism, but not its only expression. In June 2013, pro-life and pro-choice protesters gathered at the Texas capitol over HB 2—a bill (ruled unconstitutional in 2016) that would have severely restricted the number of clinics in Texas that could provide abortion services. While the pro-life demonstrators sang "Amazing Grace," some pro-choice demonstrators appeared to spontaneously start shouting "Hail Satan!" in response. This action delighted conservative Christians, who had long claimed their opponents were in league with the devil, and irritated the CoS. Peter Gilmore, who has led the CoS since 2001, called the chanting "ludicrous and meaningless."[47]

Strategically speaking, the chanters conceded the moral high ground in exchange for the short-term satisfaction of upsetting their opponents. However, implicit in the chant of "Hail Satan!" is a desire to show that Christians do not speak for everyone and that framing a political perspective as "Christian" does not necessarily make it moral. As socially engaged Satanism has developed, it has experimented with a variety of techniques aimed at deploying the symbols of Satan and Satanism to unsettle assumptions about religion and religious freedom. Some of these tactics have been more effective than others.

In 2014 the Supreme Court ruled in *Greece v. Galloway* that town councils could open with prayer invocations provided they did not discriminate against minority faiths. This decision inspired atheist Preston Smith, a middle school English teacher, to request to give a prayer invocation before a meeting of the Lake Worth, Florida, city commission. Smith's request was granted in December, and his prayer invoked numerous deities, including Satan. An outraged local pastor responded that the First Amendment only applies to Christianity and other "accepted" religions and not to "evil" religions like Satanism.[48]

Apparently inspired by Preston, Chaz Stevens of Jupiter, Florida, announced a "Satan or Silence" project. He visited several towns in South Florida that traditionally had Christian prayer invocations before town meetings and demanded the right to give a Satanic prayer invocation. He threatened to sue communities that rejected him, although no lawsuit ever materialized.[49] Several towns suspended prayer invocations in favor of a moment of silence in response to this pressure.[50]

Adam Daniels is another figure known for confrontational public displays of Satanism. Unlike TST, Daniels is not a materialist but describes a belief in literal powers of darkness. Since 2010 he has organized a series of Satanic rituals held at the Oklahoma City Civic Center and invited the public to purchase tickets. Daniels has expressed feeling bullied by Oklahoma's Christian majority with special resentment directed toward the Catholic Church. In a 2010 interview for a local news station, Daniels appeared in a red devil mask boasting, "There's nothing the city can do to stop the group from holding its event at the Civic Center. The city cannot discriminate against any religious group as long as the organization does nothing illegal."[51] The city conceded that Daniels was legally in the right, despite numerous calls and emails from outraged citizens. In 2012 Daniels formed the "Church of Ahriman" with his wife Kelsey. This is described as a "Satanic Church," although Daniel's religion revolves around Ahriman, an evil deity described in ancient Zoroastrian texts, and also incorporates other frightening deities such as Kali.

When Daniels learned of TST's offer to build a monument at the state capitol, he emailed Lucien Greaves and offered his support. Initially an alliance was formed: if TST worked with Daniels, it could no longer be claimed that their monument did not represent the interests of Oklahomans. Kelsey Daniels put her name on the application for the Baphomet monument. However, this alliance quickly dissolved after TST learned Daniels was a registered sex offender and Daniels renounced Greaves as self-aggrandizing.[52]

Although Daniels ceased contact with TST, the national controversy surrounding TST meant that much more attention was paid to his rituals at the Civic Center. In May 2014, TST was scheduled to perform a re-enactment of a "black mass" at Harvard University under the auspices of the Harvard Extension School's Cultural Studies Club. The event drew national headlines, and more than 2,000 Catholics marched in protest. Afterward, Daniels's displays of public blasphemy were suddenly national news. Some conservative Catholics actually seemed eager for a second chance to rally against a Satanic opponent.

Daniels held his own black mass on September 21, 2014, explaining he was holding it in retaliation against the Boston Catholics who had infringed TST's freedom of religion.[53] This time, spectators purchased all eighty-eight tickets available at the venue. In August, Paul S. Coakley, archbishop of Oklahoma City, called for a campaign of spiritual warfare against the black mass and its organizers. All parishes in the diocese were asked to conclude each mass with a prayer to St. Michael though September 29.[54] At one point Daniels stoked this outrage by boasting that he had acquired consecrated hosts from a priest in Turkey that would be desecrated during the ceremony. In response, the archdiocese filed a lawsuit arguing that hosts acquired under false pretenses were the property of the church. Daniels's lawyers returned the host to the archdiocese along with a signed statement that he did not have and would not use a consecrated host.[55] The day of the event 1,600 Catholics gathered for a holy hour led by Archbishop Coakley.[56] Several protestors were arrested for attempting to directly disrupt the event, including one woman who shouted, "Jesus still loves you!"[57] The following morning, Archbishop Coakley visited the Civic Center to offer prayers of exorcism.[58]

This only encouraged Daniels, who held a ritual outside St. Joseph's Old Cathedral on Christmas Eve, 2015, in which he poured costume blood and ashes onto a statue of the Virgin Mary.[59] On August 15, 2016, the Feast Day of Mary's Assumption, he held a ritual at the Civic Center that he claimed would banish the Virgin Mary to hell. Bishop Coakley switched tactics and urged Catholics not to give Daniels more attention.[60] Writing for the conservative Catholic group Tradition, Family, and Property, James Bascom wrote of Daniels's provocations, "The hatred on display in Oklahoma City is not only real, but part of a broader trend, and with a specific purpose. It is the cutting edge of a cultural revolution that seeks to erode Americans' horror for the occult and to banish Christianity from the public square."[61]

Neither TST, nor Stevens, nor Daniels has ever stated that their intention is to "banish Christianity" from the public square. On the contrary, they feel that Christians are using the power of the state to colonize the public square for themselves. Still, this is an interesting cultural moment in America's changing religious landscape: it is striking that multiple people began deploying Satanic images and rituals as a form of political protest at around the same time.

In the summer of 2018, TST underwent a major shift with numerous chapters breaking away to form their own Satanic groups. Such schisms are common in the history of new religious movements, but it is significant that these groups remained interested in Satanism as a progressive religious and political movement. Public political Satanism on this scale is largely unprecedented within the short history of organized religious Satanism. All of this raises the question: Why is this happening now?

Satanism and the Culture Wars

Legal debates about the separation of church and state have long raised hypothetical scenarios involving Satanism. In a letter to the editor, a former evangelical Baptist described debating politics with a teacher at a Christian academy in Houston who was also a Trump supporter. The Trump supporter opposed the separation of church state. The ex-Baptist asked how he would feel if this separation were removed and public schools began promoting a religion other than Christianity. The Trump supporter responded, "I would not like it but if the majority in that area agreed, then I would be OK with my Christian children being taught satanic prayers and rituals in the local public school."[62] It defies credibility that someone who teaches at a Christian academy rather than a public school actually subscribes to this theory of "majority rule" or would be "OK" with his children learning to perform Satanic rituals in public schools. But talk is cheap, especially when the idea of Satanic prayers in public schools seems like an impossibility. However, since 2013, these scenarios involving Satanists that were once hypothetical have become increasingly plausible. It is telling that a Jesuit priest compared TST to a "Comment Box come to life."[63] Now the public is being forced to rethink attitudes about religious freedom and the separation of church and state and to be a bit more honest when discussing these topics.

The unstated arrangement in which Satanists were discrete about their practices was, like many cultural norms, a casualty of America's culture wars. Stephen Prothero describes a "culture war cycle" summarized by the axiom, "After the Right strikes out, the Left strikes back."[64] The cycle begins on the right when some shift in America's social or political structure (immigration, the spread of new religions, recognition of gay marriage, etc.) is experienced as a loss by conservatives. There is a backlash from the right as they attempt to restore society to the way they remember it. The left then responds by defending the change as a positive good or else appealing to the American values of liberty. The culture war cycle is a useful model for thinking about the rise of political Satanism. In most cases, groups like TST represent the "strike back" from the left: the Baphomet statue was a response to a Ten Commandments monument. In turn, the desire to place Christian symbols on public property arises from feelings on the right that America's taken-for-granted status as a "Christian nation" is eroding.

In his book *The End of White Christian America*, Robert Jones points out that 2008—the year America elected its first black president—was also the last year on record in which Protestants represented a majority of the country. By 2014 the religiously unaffiliated made up 22% of the American population, a figure rivaling the percentage of Catholics.[65] Meanwhile, the percentage of Americans who are Christian dropped 8% between 2007 and 2014 and currently hovers around 70%.[66] Demographers have predicted since 2004 that white Americans will no longer be the majority by some time in the mid-twenty-first century. Mark Mather, a demographer for the Population Reference Bureau, said of the projected shift, "No other country has experienced such rapid racial and ethnic change." With these statistics, Jones paints a picture of America at a crossroads between its white Protestant past and its multiracial, religiously plural future. It is a moment celebrated by some and feared by others. As Prothero explains, culture wars are fundamentally about *classification*: What "America" is and who counts as a "real American" are always the questions at the heart of these battles.[67]

Jones argues that recent attempts to strengthen Christian hegemony through legislation paradoxically betray an awareness that white Christian culture is crumbling. As an example he points to bills proposed in Mississippi in 2015 to declare the Bible the official state book. No other state has an official book (although Michigan and Massachusetts have official children's books). Critics of the bill argued that a work of Faulker would surely be more appropriate than the Bible. But for Jones, the critical question is why a state like Mississippi, where Christianity is thoroughly entrenched, would suddenly feel the need for this kind of official state endorsement of a Christian text. He writes:

When leaders feel it is necessary to state explicitly what has always been assumed, they betray their own cultural insecurity. . . . The need to forcefully elevate their Christian status reflects white Christian lawmakers' fear that for an increasing number of citizens the Bible and God are no longer a guiding cultural force. These efforts amount to little more than bargaining beside the deathbed of White Christian America.[68]

Recent attempts to ensconce the Ten Commandments in courthouses and state capitols can likewise be interpreted as a response to a sense of vulnerability and a wish to reverse Christianity's declining cultural influence. Oklahoma's HB1330 stressed the importance of *reminding* people that many Americans have historically believed government is ordained by God and that *the majority still do*. But if this were really true, why would such a reminder be needed?

Where Jones sees an admission of insecurity, secular and atheist groups see an attack on core American values enshrined in the Constitution. By demanding the same privileges as Christians, groups like TST hope to show that attempts to secure Christian hegemony through legislation will come with a heavy price. Predictably, the presence of Satanists in the public square has heightened the insecurities described by Jones. While some have conceded the point TST is attempting to make about the value of separating church from state, many on the right seem to be more energized than ever now that they have an openly Satanic opponent.

This cycle of escalation was repeated with the 2016 election of Donald Trump. After Trump's upset victory over Hillary Clinton, several pundits suggested nostalgia for white, Christian America was a key factor in the election.[69] For some white evangelicals, Trump's campaign slogan of "Make America Great Again" was code for "Take America Back Again."[70] In a January 2016 speech at Dordt College, a Christian liberal arts college in Iowa, Trump stated, "We [Christians] have to strengthen. Because we are getting— if you look, it's death by a million cuts—we are getting less and less and less powerful in terms of a religion, and in terms of a force." He then positioned himself as the answer to the decline of Christian power, declaring, "Because if I'm there, you're going to have plenty of power. You don't need anybody else. You're going to have somebody representing you very, very well. Remember that."[71]

When the left struck back following Trump's victory, some looked to TST. TST reported that in the first thirty-six hours after the election thousands of new members joined in an unprecedented surge. In a speech at Colorado University Boulder, Lucien Greaves said TST was receiving anxious emails and donations to its legal fund faster than the group's staff could respond. "It's crazy," he said, "People have a desperate need for something to rally to right now."[72] TST chapters organized protests of Trump's inauguration on January 20, 2016, and participated in historic women's marches on January 21. For now at least, it seems Satanists will play a significant role in the America's ongoing culture war.

Why The Satanic Temple Matters

Religious Satanism is interesting, and there is a small but adroit group of researchers producing scholarship on this subject. But in general, religious studies relegates Satanism to the margins of the field. New religions scholar James R. Lewis suggests academics ignore Satanism because they regard it as a trivial phenomenon rather than a serious religion.[73] Religion scholar Tim Murphy goes further, suggesting that religious studies tacitly perpetuates a two-tier model of religion with Christianity and other "world religions" at the top and Satanism marking the bottom of the lower tier. In fact, Murphy suggests the study of religion may be "a kind of culture club where scholars go to study 'people like me.' "[74] As the ultimate religious "other," Satanists are kept out of this club.

TST represents a new chapter in the history of religious Satanism. Their campaigns and legal challenges will no doubt force the academy to take research on Satanism more seriously and further challenge the two-tier model of religion described by Murphy. But I am even more interested in how TST is changing our public discourse. Hugh Urban, in his analysis of the history of Scientology, notes that "religion" is a contested category and that such diverse actors as celebrities, the IRS, judges, and even foreign governments all have a role in how this category is ultimately understood.[75] The history of TST is likewise a case study in how the idea of "religion" is being contested in the public square. Satan and Satanism are heady symbols in American culture, especially in politically divisive times. By using these symbols as leverage, TST is forcing a public conversation about where our values lie, what arrangements between government and religious institutions are desirable, and what we mean when we talk about "religion." Culture wars, after all, are wars over classification.

At its best, TST exposes hidden contradictions in the ways we talk about religion. Hegemonic discourse—discourse that works to maintain the power of the dominant group—often operates by presenting the interests of the dominant group as the interests of everyone. These manipulations frequently entail paradoxes and logical contradictions, but hegemonic discourse can effectively conceal these contradictions so that they go unnoticed and unchallenged. Foucault wrote: "Power is tolerable only on the condition that it mask a substantial part of itself. Its success is proportional to its ability to hide its own mechanisms."[76] Thus hegemony goes unchallenged because the public fails to notice its presence or more often simply cannot imagine that things could be another way.

The confrontational style of TST is designed to direct attention to these maneuvers and to bring unstated assumptions into the open where they can be challenged: If a Christian religious symbol on a state capitol does not violate the establishment clause, then why doesn't a Satanic one? If Christian companies can claim a religious exemption to a healthcare law, then why can't Satanists claim a religious exemption to a restriction on abortion? The deployment of shock value is meant to make people reassess arrangements they have taken for granted.

In some cases, TST has driven conservative Christian groups to renounce freedom of religion as a positive good. For example, an article on TST by the conservative Catholic group Church Militant claimed the freedom of religion enshrined in the Constitution is wrong because it goes against Catholic law.[77] Of course, Church Militant is free to condemn religious freedom as incompatible with their religious views. What I find significant about this position is that a contradiction has been uncovered: it is easy to claim that everyone has a right to freedom of religion while simultaneously believing that certain religions are "evil" and should not enjoy the same rights as one's own. But TST created a situation in which maintaining this contradiction became untenable so that their opponent openly condemned the idea of religious freedom. Exposing these kinds of contradictions weakens hegemonic discourse by revealing that the interests of the hegemony are not, in fact, the interests of everyone.

A drawback to employing shock value is that it often backfires. By using the symbol of Satan as a lever to shift the discursive landscape, TST risks strengthening hegemonic discourses instead of weakening them. After all, if Satan is the enemy of all mankind, then aren't those who oppose TST on the side of everyone? TST has received heavy reportage from such conservative news outlets as Fox, Breitbart, and Lifesitenews because their references to Satan are so easily folded into a narrative that progressives and secularists do not have a principled disagreements about social issues but rather are simply "evil."

Another challenge faced by TST is "ignorant familiarity." New religions scholar David Feltmate defines "ignorant familiarity" as "widespread superficial—and often erroneous—knowledge about groups of people that other groups use to facilitate social interaction."[78] Having studied TST for years, I understand more about its history, workings, and culture than almost any outsider and even many of its members. Yet people who have only a passing familiarity with this group routinely inform me that members of TST are "just trolls," that the entire affair is a prank, or that Greaves is a "typical cult leader" motivated only by a desire for sex and money. As a religion scholar, I see TST as an interesting and complicated movement, and I am naturally annoyed by the smugness of people who seem certain they have gotten to the bottom of it so quickly.

My suspicion is that this dismissive attitude goes beyond mere intellectual laziness and actually functions as a defense mechanism: it is a facile way of ducking the challenges that TST poses and preserving the two-tier model of religion described by Murphy in which we do not have to think about Satanists. Paradoxically, I think we dismiss TST because of, and not in spite of, the fact that they have something important to say. Ignorant familiarity represents the inertia that TST must overcome in order to affect our conversation about religion and religious freedom. One reason TST's legal actions are so significant is that courts are a forum where ignorant familiarity can sometimes be circumvented because arguments must be heard and responded to. Legal scholar Marci Hamilton has compared TST to the Jehovah's Witnesses.[79] Although many still regard the Jehovah's Witnesses as an outsider sect, their repeated visits to the Supreme Court in 1940s shaped the contours of American religious freedom.[80] However, it remains to be seen whether TST can have a similar effect under a court system that has heavily shifted to the right under the Trump administration.

The Structure of the Book

This book offers a historical survey of TST before exploring the movement's effects on public discourse. Chapter 2 provides an overview of the movement's somewhat murky origins and its growth into an organized religious movement. As I was writing this book, a major schism affected TST, causing several local chapters to break away. The causes and significance of this schism are discussed in chapter 3.

Chapter 4 analyses how TST is changing the milieu of religious Satanism. The CoS has engaged in a bitter feud with TST, such that some TST members have described the situation as a "Satanic Reformation." I use Ann Swidler's theory of culture as a "toolkit" to analyze how TST is drawing on Romantic literature and other sources to reimagine Satanism and create a tradition distinct from that enshrined in the writings of Anton LaVey and the CoS.

Chapter 5 considers how TST is challenging popular understandings of what religion is, focusing on a series of lawsuits in which TST claimed a religious exemption to restrictions on abortion in the state of Missouri, invoking the state's Religious Freedom Restoration Act (RFRA). TST's critics often claim that it is a political organization that merely mimics the trappings of religion, and often point to satirical elements of TST to make this claim. I invoke Melissa Wilcox's category of "serious parody" to argue that playfulness is not inconsistent with sincerely held religious beliefs and argue that TST can be reasonably classified as a religion. I also argue while TST has shaped the category of religion, this category has likewise shaped TST: that is, invoking religious freedom has caused TST members to think about themselves and their worldview in ways they may not have otherwise.

Chapter 6 explores how TST invokes and complicates popular notions of "evil" to achieve their goals. This chapter, following the work of David Frankfurter, regards evil as a discourse used to justify the social order. By presenting themselves as "good Satanists," TST engages in a maneuver I call "hijacking the discourse of evil," in which powerful categories of social thought are appropriated and confounded. Through this hijacking, which I argue occurred in early modern Europe as well, TST seeks to disrupt prevailing assumptions about the categories of "good" and "evil." The disruption is deployed to corner their opponents and to push people to judge morality by actions rather than group affiliation. The chapter explores three tactics by which TST deploys popular notions of evil and the sinister to advance their agenda: "culture jamming" and performance art that repurposes symbols in unexpected and compelling ways; creating legal scenarios in which public institutions are forced to either tolerate reasonably behaved Satanists or else declare that the public square is secular; and, finally, philanthropy in which

TST disrupts the category of evil by cleaning highways or serving the needy in the name of Satanism.

Chapter 7 explores how TST is changing ideas of religious pluralism. While many American institutions pride themselves on being tolerant toward other religions, critics such as Russell McCutcheon and Tim Murphy have suggested that the language of pluralism actually masks a kind of privilege in which the powerful decide who will be tolerated and on what terms. TST is the first Satanic group to appeal to the idea of religious pluralism on a large scale, attempting to hold a re-enactment of a black mass at Harvard University and demanding the right to hold Satanic prayer invocations in cities across the country. In some cases, responses to these provocations from TST prove the critiques made by McCutcheon and Murphy that many people who claim to endorse religious pluralism do not really tolerate any meaningful religious difference. However, there are also signs that TST may be expanding notions of what religious pluralism could mean and causing a reassessment of where the limits of tolerance lie. In closing, I speculate on the future of TST and its political significance as America continues to undergo a dramatic demographic shift.

2

Origins and History of The Satanic Temple

> The reasonable man adapts himself to the world: the unreasonable one persists in trying to adapt the world to himself. Therefore all progress depends on the unreasonable man.
>
> —George Bernard Shaw, *Man and Superman*[1]

> It didn't start as a prank. It's not a prank.
>
> —Lucien Greaves[2]

The emergence of TST seems simultaneously inevitable and fantastically unlikely. It seems inevitable because organized religious Satanism has been a feature of American culture since 1966 and it was only a matter of time until Satanists began demanding the same privileges as Christians. But it was unlikely that a group of people would come together that not only had the vision, resources, and expertise to make such demands but were also willing to bear the inevitable scorn and death threats that come with such an undertaking. In this way, the two men who came to be known as Malcolm Jarry and Lucien Greaves, are both extraordinary people.

Malcolm Jarry and Doug Mesner (Lucien Greaves) met in 2012 at a function at the Harvard faculty club. Both men hold degrees from Harvard and were living near Cambridge at the time. Mesner recalls being invited to the function by a female friend to serve as her "wingman" while that she chatted with Harvard-educated bachelors. Mesner and his friend were sitting on a couch when Jarry wandered over. Jarry had met a young woman and was locked in a debate with her about public education. They decided to continue their conversation seated and pulled up chairs in front of Mesner's couch. Jarry felt public schools were essentially like prisons; their function was not to educate but to inculcate compliance with authority. The woman objected, explaining that her public school experience had been entirely positive. Mesner, who watched the debate unfold, recalled, "Of course,

Speak of the Devil. Joseph P. Laycock, Oxford University Press (2020). © Oxford University Press.
DOI: 10.1093/oso/9780190948498.001.0001

I *wanted* to agree with the beautiful lady, but Malcolm was clearly right." Mesner finally chimed in, siding with Malcolm and the woman, perhaps feeling outnumbered, made her excuses and walked away. She left Jarry with Mesner, having no comprehension of the chain of events she had just set in motion.

Mesner and Jarry became friends and briefly roommates. Although they came from different backgrounds and did not share all the same interests, they were both alarmed at how the political power of conservative evangelicals had grown during the administration of George W Bush. Jarry and Mesner also shared an irreverent sense of humor and a certain refusal to be shamed. They were unwilling to let conventional notions of respectable behavior prevent them from challenging institutions they regarded as unworthy of respect.

Jarry grew up outside of New York City and has described his religious upbringing as atheistic Judaism. He holds multiple graduate degrees and has taken on numerous projects in whatever area interests him, including Japanese martial arts, writing books and articles, and producing musical albums and films. One of his enduring interests has been education reform. In an essay written the year he met Mesner, Jarry wrote, "On prima facie grounds, it is incomprehensibly absurd to place children in a totalitarian environment for 13 years of their lives and to expect them, upon removal, to be able to fulfill the obligations of citizenry in a democracy. The greatest obligation being to oppose the very same manifestations of tyrannical power to which students are acclimated."[3]

Jarry's interest in Satanism dates to January 2001 when George W. Bush announced his first executive order, creating the White House Office of Faith-Based and Community Initiatives. Among other things, the office gave federal funds to support philanthropy conducted by religious groups. The announcement upset many secularists, including Jarry, who recalls thinking, "They wouldn't allow a Satanic organization to take advantage of this." In fact, Jarry suspected many evangelicals would rather see the entire program shut down before federal funds were given to Satanists. Obama expanded the program further to create the Office of Faith-Based and Neighborhood Partnerships. Jarry was especially upset that this office gave federal funds to "pregnancy crisis centers," that is, Christian centers that often present themselves as abortion providers but actually counsel pregnant women against receiving an abortion—a practice that some medical experts regard as unethical.[4] Jarry was discussing Bush's Office of Faith-Based and Community

Initiatives with his friend and filmmaker David Guinan during an international flight in 2007. They discussed how the public would react if someone demanded federal funding for a "Satanic soup kitchen."[5] Jarry thought about requesting federal funds for a "Satanic youth outreach center for troubled teens" that would bring teenagers off the streets by giving them Ozzy Osbourne and Judas Priest albums. He told me, "I have a way of making things happen when I get a crazy idea like that."[6] Jarry did not have a background in religious Satanism, but Mesner did.

Like Jarry, Mesner is a polymath whose interests include creating art and music, and Japanese martial arts. Greaves was raised in Detroit by a Catholic father and a Protestant mother. He attended both churches and felt he was "exposed to the worst of both." He never experienced anything like abuse, but in his father's church he saw "ignorant and malicious superstition" while in his mother's more politically focused evangelical church he saw a "judgmental and cruel culture."[7] He recalled, especially, attending Sunday school where he was exposed to the song "O Be Careful, Little Eyes" which begins

> O be careful little eyes what you see
> O be careful little eyes what you see
> There's a Father up above
> And He's looking down in love
> So, be careful little eyes what you see

The song proceeds to warn children that their ears, hands, feet, and mouths are likewise being surveilled. Mesner interpreted the song as a warning that he was "being looked upon and judged by [an] ultimate tyrant in the sky."[8] A recording of children singing this song would later be put to eerie effect in TST performances.

Like Jarry and many other TST members, Mesner came of age during the "Satanic Panic" of 1980s. He was in middle school when the infamous 1998 Geraldo special *Exposing Satan's Underground* aired. He remembered teachers and parents speaking about it in hushed tones. Mesner found the panic psychologically interesting: he noticed that people *talked* about allegations of Satanists murdering and eating children as if they took these stories seriously, but they did not *act* as if they believed a nationwide epidemic of child murders was really underway. He also became interested in stories of "Satanic ritual abuse," often based on "recovered memories" obtained through hypnosis. This engendered a lifelong interest in psychology. Before founding TST, Mesner had imagined he might become a science writer, working to educate the public about research on memory and the sociology of moral panic.

Ironically, exploring the claims of Satanic Panic is what led Mesner to religious Satanism. He became interested in the history of the idea of Satanism going back to early modern Europe. He read essays by Anton LaVey and found him "a likable fellow." By the end of high school, he had come to think of himself as a Satanist. He explained that there was never a moment of conversion to Satanism, it was simply the confluence of several factors including his disgust with mainstream religion and a growing appreciation for scientific skepticism.

Mesner began exploring unusual subcultures and made friends in the Church of Satan (CoS), even meeting its leader Peter Gilmore on one occasion. He produced material for Radio Free Satan, an online radio network founded in 2000 and affiliated with the CoS. Describing himself as a "Gonzo reporter," Mesner produced news segments on conspiracy subcultures. He also agreed to illustrate a new edition of *Might Is Right* produced by Satanist Shane Bugbee. *Might Is Right* (1890) is a political screed, parts of which LaVey plagiarized to create *The Satanic Bible* (1969). Despite these connections, Mesner never formally joined the CoS, remarking, "They just didn't have a whole lot going on."[9]

In 2009, Mesner reported on a conference held in Connecticut by a group called SMART—an acronym for "Stop Mind Control And Ritual Abuse Today." The organization was founded in 1995 and serves as a forum for people who believe they have been the victims of mind control and ritual abuse as well as therapists who claim they can aid their recovery. SMART's members include many of the people in the medical and helping professions who worked to legitimize claims of recovered memories and Satanic ritual abuse. Mesner was one of the first people to draw attention to the fact that these individuals are still promoting such ideas, decades after the Satanic Panic supposedly ended. He was shocked to learn there were still people with professional credentials lending official sanction to stories of recovered memories such as being brainwashed to serve as assassins for the CIA or sex slaves for Freemasons. Mesner wrote a scathing article on his blog and was met with a hostile reaction from SMART. He received hate mail accusing him of involvement with a conspiracy of Satanic pedophiles. Mesner has worked to expose SMART ever since, and SMART has retaliated by producing "exposes" of Mesner's activities on their website.

Hail Satan! Hail Rick Scott!

TST began when Jarry decided to respond to a bill signed in March 2012 by Florida governor Rick Scott allowing students to read "inspirational messages of their choosing" at assemblies and sporting events. (Early drafts of the bill used the word "prayer" rather than "inspirational messages.")[10] As someone interested in education, Jarry found the bill especially troubling. Its apparent purpose was to promote Christian messages in public schools by using school resources to give a platform to the Christian majority. But to maintain some semblance of neutrality, the bill stated that students could promote any "inspirational message" they chose, including—in theory—a Satanic one. This inspired Jarry, who had experience as a filmmaker, to undertake a political action: he would travel to Florida and hold a rally in which Satanists praised Rick Scott for turning public schools into a platform from which to spread Satanic ideology. He described his intention behind the rally in an essay entitled, "Educational Mission: A Report and Plan of Action" in which he wrote: "Action is based on the theory that when the rules that are used to subjugate a population are applied to the people who create and enforce those rules, constructive changes occur."[11] Jarry's essay, completed on December 12, 2012, is essentially the birth certificate of TST.

David Guinan thought Jarry's project would be fun and agreed to help. Mesner offered to serve as a consultant on Satanism. Guinan explained, "Doug was our authenticity meter."[12] Mesner felt the project was making an important point and that these kinds of public provocations were exactly what the CoS *should* be doing. Jarry gave their ad hoc Satanic group the rather generic sounding name "The Satanic Temple." This was partly to distinguish the group from the CoS and partly a nod to Jarry's Jewish heritage. A website presented a fictional background and belief system for the group, stating, "In 2012, Neil Bricke, raised in a multigenerational Satanic Temple tradition of worship, decided, with the blessings of his fellow Satanic devotees, to officially found the Satanic Temple." The name "Neil Bricke" appears to have been a barb aimed at Neil Brick, who founded SMART and claims to be to be the survivor of a clandestine government mind-control project.[13] The website also outlined a belief system in which God has abdicated rulership of the physical universe to Satan, who "has the compassion and wisdom of an angel."[14] Jarry later described all this as "some bullshit pretend doctrine."[15]

This literature was also the first appearance of the name "Lucien Greaves," who was listed as a spokesperson for The Satanic Temple. At first this was simply the pseudonym used by the group for answering press inquiries. But Mesner, as the expert on Satanism, rather reluctantly assumed this persona. He explained, "I had to become Lucien. It just became obvious that you're not going to be able to coach somebody on what we think and feel. We couldn't constantly have a feed going into his ear."[16]

Mesner obtained the necessary permits and the trio headed to Tallahassee. To recruit more Satanists, Guinan put out a casting call explaining he was making "a mockumentary about the nicest Satanic Cult in the world," and, "Actors will be required to wear tasteful Satanic garb."[17] The casting call was discovered by *The Miami Herald*, leading the media to proclaim the entire affair was just a hoax. Jarry recalled how he felt upon learning about Guinan's casting call, "I could have killed him! He just undermined everything!"[18] For Jarry, the Florida rally was not a mockumentary, it was a real attempt to effect social change.

When I spoke with Michael Wiener, an actor Guinan hired to play "the high priest" at the rally, he stated simply, "We were making a movie, and then it turned into a real movement."[19] He recalled shooting scenes of his character in New York preparing for his trip to Tallahassee and performing Satanic rituals in a Florida mansion that had been rented for the project. In 2012 Jarry and Guinan visited the American Atheists convention in Washington, DC, where they interviewed American Atheists president David Silverman, activist Jessica Ahlquist, and Richard Dawkins.

Guinan described collecting footage of Dawkins's reaction when they told him that benevolent Satanists were planning to open a soup kitchen. And yet, Guinan conceded he was wrong to describe what they were doing as a mockumentary. He explained, "We didn't know what the fuck it was. We weren't making a documentary so much as doing things we thought needed to be documented."[20]

On January 25, 2013, the group arrived at the capitol steps accompanied by four "minions" wearing black cloaks. They passed out some religious tracts, including two comics Mesner had drawn about the Satanic Panic, parodying the evangelical tracts of Jack Chick.[21] Footage of the rally shows Mesner at a podium in front of a banner that Jarry created that reads, "Hail Satan! Hail Rick Scott!" Mesner introduces himself as Lucien Greaves and gives a short speech condemning the public perception of Satanism as "nothing more than a paranoid conspiracy theory" and praising Rick Scott for the opportunity to dispel these myths and educate children about Satanism. Greaves is replaced by a woman who is introduced as "Cassandra Wagner, a Satanic high school student." Wagner describes how Satanism has been a positive influence in her life and how she has suffered from anti-Satanic stigma. "Wagner" was apparently an actual Satanist from Tallahassee who wanted to get involved with the project.[22]

Finally, Michael Wiener steps forward clad in a cape and a headdress of black horns. He is introduced simply as "the high priest." As he takes the podium he blesses Wagner for her courage, and Wagner replies, "Thank you, my dark eminence." Wiener gives a speech in praise of Rick Scott that presents Satanists as compassionate and misunderstood, yet is punctuated with sinister phrases such as, "We will make you one of us." At one point, a heckler is heard yelling at Wiener that he will go to hell. Weiner concludes by declaring, "We feel confident that Rick Scott has helped initiate the inevitable—opening the gates of hell to unleash a new Luciferean age that will last one thousand years and beyond! Hail Rick Scott! Hail Satan!"[23]

To anyone able to understand what Jarry, Greaves, and Guinan were doing, the rally *was* funny. (I laughed out loud watching the footage.) It is an example of what John Morreal calls the "incongruity theory" of humor. Morreal explains: "We live in an orderly world, where we have come to expect certain patterns among things, their properties, events, etc. We laugh when we experience something that doesn't fit into these patterns."[24] The idea of a Christian Republican passing laws that spread Satanism or Satanists describing their values of compassion creates such a disruption and inspires laughter.

The humorous dimension of the rally, combined with the discovery of Guinan's casting call, led critics to dismiss the entire affair as a prank. Some critics have gone further arguing that everything TST has ever done has been prank. For example, when TST sued the state of Arkansas in 2018, attorneys representing secretary of state Mark Martin filed a response describing TST as "trolling' pranksters" and "beneath the dignity of this Court." The attorneys cited the casting call discovered in 2012 and speculated, "it is entirely plausible that the proposed intervenors intend to use their involvement in the action before this Court as part of their mockumentary."[25]

Such critiques amount to a fallacy of genesis. Martin's suggestion that the entire movement has been an elaborate six-year campaign to collect footage for a mockumentary is entirely *im*plausible. Indeed, district judge Kristine Baker explicitly rejected this argument, noting, "There is no evidence before the Court that the proposed intervenors' actions are not genuinely aimed at procuring favorable government action."[26] Jarry, while clearly amused about how his political action went, rejects the idea that they were "fake Satanists." He points out, "Everything he [Greaves] said in that initial rally is totally consistent with everything TST has done since then."[27] If a filmmaker starts a new religion, how would they begin other than with making a film? While the metaphysical trappings of the rally were discarded, the idea of compassionate Satanism was real—and it became more real as TST continued to evolve.

The Pink Mass

The short history of TST could have ended in January 2013 with the completion of Jarry's experiment. But on April 13, 2013, Dzhokhar and Tamerlan Tsarnaev set off bombs at the Boston Marathon, killing three people. Then the Westboro Baptist Church announced their plans to picket the funerals of the victims. Greaves and Jarry were discussing the impending arrival of the Westboro Baptists to their city over Chinese food, when Jarry got the idea to photograph gay couples kissing over the grave of Catherine Johnston, the mother of the church's founder, Fred Phelps. Initially, he imagined a website where gay couples could upload photos of themselves kissing over Johnston's tombstone. He explained, "I was thinking of something like the Suicide Girls' website. I hoped gay couples could make a pilgrimage there and that it would be empowering for them."[28] The idea appealed to Greaves's and Jarry's sense of humor, but it also represented going on the offensive against the Westboro Baptists. For over a decade, the Westboro Baptist Church had used other people's funerals as opportunities to get attention by deliberately upsetting the friends and families of the deceased. And while their pickets had been met with hostile counter-protesters, no one had ever responded by targeting *their* dead loved ones.

In July, Jarry, Greaves, and Guinan set about their new project. Greaves and Jarry began a long road-trip from Boston to Meridian, Mississippi, the resting place of Catherine Johnston. Guinan flew to New Orleans in search of same-sex couples willing to drive three hours to be photographed kissing over a grave. This task proved more difficult than he had anticipated. When Guinan met a volunteer from Craigslist he was suffering from a large goiter that was deemed too distracting for the project. Another volunteer turned out to be an underaged prostitute. When the group attempted to call him, they reached his mother who thought they were attempting to solicit her son.

Jarry recalled feeling anxious as they drove south. Guinan had not found models for the project, and they were not certain they had the correct location of the grave. But in the end, everything came together. Guinan arrived in a van with two men and two women—all four attractive, consenting adults—and Jarry located Johnston's grave near the front of Magnolia cemetery. Jarry began taking photos of the couples leaning over the grave to kiss, while Greaves, wearing the black horn headdress, posed as an officiant. At some point, Greaves opened his fly and placed his genitals on the tombstone, and a production assistant working with Guinan snapped a picture of it. Afterward, Jarry took everyone to Chili's to celebrate. A black employee noticed them and stopped sweeping the floor to ask what they were doing in Meridian. Greaves replied, "We were just in town to perform a Satanic ceremony over a grave." The employee found this answer hysterical.

Jarry and Greaves began writing a press release, but there was concern that the event lacked a meaningful connection to Satanism. Jarry asked whether they could call it "a black mass," but Greaves explained that this meant something specific in Satanism. Jarry recalls musing, "If it can't be a black mass, could it be a blue mass? An orange mass? A pink mass!" They agreed the "Pink Mass" was the perfect name for the project. The press release stated that the Pink Mass had turned Catherine Johnston gay in the afterlife—an idea loosely adapted from the idea of baptism for the dead practiced by the Church of Latter-day Saints. It added that whenever same-sex couples kiss over her grave, Johnston will be "pleasured" in the afterlife. Jarry said this idea was inspired by the film *It's a Wonderful Life*. In an interview with *Vice*, Greaves stated, "We believe that Fred Phelps is obligated to believe that his mother is now gay in the afterlife. Further, if beliefs are inviolable rights, nobody has the right to challenge our right to believe that Fred Phelps believes that his mother is now gay."[29] He threatened to continue performing pink masses for all of Phelps's ancestors and, eventually Phelps himself. The group briefly registered the website westboro-baptists.com with the intent of posting pictures of gay couples making their own pilgrimage to Johnston's grave. Greaves apparently made a unilateral decision to post the photo with his genitals on Johnston's grave. Jarry and Guinan felt this detracted from the tone of the project. However, the photo contributed to the high volume of press The Pink Mass received.[30]

Greaves was charged with desecration of a grave, even though the grave was unharmed. The charge was unenforceable as Greaves had left Mississippi. He took this as an opportunity for further satire, telling *Vice*:

> I believe it quite possible that I could find myself in a holding cell witnessing the Meridian Police devolve into a sweaty, grunting, savage orgy of uncaged homosexuality . . . all influenced by the idea that they were utterly powerless against my sexual conversion magic. Perhaps they are merely looking for such a scapegoat.[31]

Jarry felt that satire was not only appropriate but also an effective tactic, commenting, "The Westboro Baptist Church feeds on hate. But there's no good reply to people laughing at you, and no one had ever laughed at them before."[32] When I interviewed prominent members of TST, many recalled that the Pink Mass was what first attracted them to TST. Lux Armiger, a co-founder of TST-Chicago, is a gay man who had thought a lot about how to respond to provocations from the Westboro Baptist Church. He described the Pink Mass as "really clever" because it "matched bad speech with good speech instead of silence."[33] Later that summer, Fred Phelps was excommunicated from the Westboro Baptist Church for allegedly breaking ranks and supporting a gay rights group. He died the following March.

In October 2014, Guinan moved with his family to Nigeria to serve as director of television services for a new channel being created by vice president Atiku Abubakar. The region he was staying in faced repeated attacks by the terrorist group Boko Haram, and Guinan did not want to be publicly connected with a Satanic organization. He continued to do "pinch-hitting" for a number of important projects with Jarry and Greaves but could not maintain the same level of involvement.

Jarry remembered the aftermath of the Pink Mass as a decisive moment for TST. Everyone had had a lot of fun, but it was increasingly apparent that this was more than a series of politically motivated pranks. Jarry recalled, "Doug at all times saw this as sincere."[34] Greaves felt that there ought to be an organized Satanic religion fighting for issues that Satanists believe in. The CoS was far and away the most established Satanic organization, but Greaves felt they had become moribund and made no effort to let the public know who they were. The "pretend doctrines" created for the Rick Scott rally were abandoned, and the founders began to think further about what their true convictions were.

Founding a Religion

Initially, Greaves had a vague idea that the group's provocations would inspire others to take similar actions and "be" The Satanic Temple. In an interview, Greaves explained:

> When it began, we didn't have the audacity to think we could start a religious movement organization like we have now. Soon that all changed, however, when we saw just what a need there had been for an actual relevant active Satanist organization because one hadn't existed up until then. So instead of people kind of taking up the banner on their own, they all started coming to us and looking to us for the next activity.[35]

Somehow, Greaves now found himself the spokesperson for an emerging religious movement. Jarry, who once described himself to me as "a tactician," preferred to operate from behind the scenes. Greaves has described himself as "a very private person" and had initially imagined his involvement with TST would consist primarily of writing essays under a pseudonym. But he was the best suited to speak about Satanism, and he had already made public appearances as Lucien Greaves through the Rick Scott rally and the Pink Mass. Jarry felt that Greaves's reluctance to have the spotlight made him a better spokesperson. Greaves also has a corneal scar on his right eye that is sometimes mistaken for a contact lens. In a news milieu of "talking heads" this gave him a striking appearance that some said reminded them of a supervillain. Before long, Greaves was appearing on Fox News to debate household names such as Megan Kelly and Tucker Carlson as well as receiving threats from neo-Nazis and other dangerous groups. In an unguarded moment, I once heard him say, "I wake up horrified that this is my life."[36]

The doctrines used for the Rick Scott rally had to be replaced with something sincere and purposeful, so Jarry wrote "The Seven Tenets" of TST with contributions from Greaves:

1. One should strive to act with compassion and empathy toward all creatures in accordance with reason.
2. The struggle for justice is an ongoing and necessary pursuit that should prevail over laws and institutions.
3. One's body is inviolable, subject to one's own will alone.

4. The freedoms of others should be respected, including the freedom to offend. To willfully and unjustly encroach upon the freedoms of another is to forgo one's own.

5. Beliefs should conform to one's best scientific understanding of the world. One should take care never to distort scientific facts to fit one's beliefs.

6. People are fallible. If one makes a mistake, one should do one's best to rectify it and resolve any harm that might have been caused.

7. Every tenet is a guiding principle designed to inspire nobility in action and thought. The spirit of compassion, wisdom, and justice should always prevail over the written or spoken word.

Jarry explained that the tenets were meant to be simple so that people would not get hung up on individual words. He did not want TST's philosophy to lend itself to authoritarianism. James R. Lewis notes that there are essentially three types of "legitimation strategies" available to new religious movements: charismatic appeals, which often involve claims of revelation or the supernatural; traditional appeals; and rational appeals.[37] The Seven Tenets are an example of a rational appeal—they are presented as self-evident and rooted in common sense rather than any superhuman authority. In interviews, many TST members described the tenets as articulating—and in some cases *sacralizing*—the values they already held. Chris Turvey, a chapter head for TST-Colorado, was raised Christian but became an atheist in college. He recalled, "As soon as I read their tenets it fit immediately with my identity. A year prior I thought I would never be part of a religion again."[38]

When Jarry and Greaves decided to create a bronze statue of Baphomet to stand at the Oklahoma capitol, the fledgling movement gained a symbol as well as a philosophy. Greaves produced sketches of the statue that began to circulate in December 2013. Both Jarry and Greaves recalled there was a great deal of discussion about whether the statue should have breasts, in keeping with Eliphaz Levi's idea that Baphomet symbolizes the reconciliation of opposites. With the sculptor, Greaves discussed adding some sort of toga to cover the breasts, but everyone involved agreed the bronze toga would resemble "crumpled metal" and be aesthetically unpleasing. Some fans of Levi's original design were disappointed. The CoS, which had already become rivals with TST, called the removal of the breasts "transphobic" and even added that the addition of children suggested pedophilia.[39] However, Stu de Haan, who later served as an attorney for TST, saw the sketch of the breastless Baphomet and immediately understood that the changes had been made for legal reasons. He thought, "These guys know exactly what they're doing, and I want to get involved."[40] Media coverage of the Baphomet statue caused people all over America to become interested in TST. Michelle Shortt, who became a spokeswoman for TST recalled, "Seeing action in the real world from a Satanic organization—that was unheard of."[41]

Satanists Protecting Children

While the Baphomet project was underway, Greaves and Jarry began brainstorming new campaigns that used TST's tenets to frame progressive causes in terms of religious liberty. In April 2014, TST announced the "Protect Children Project." Jarry had long known that corporal punishment and isolation were used in public schools across the country. According to the National Center for Education Statistics, .2% of students in public schools were subjected to paddling or other forms corporal punishment during the 2013–2014 school year. This percentage was considerably higher for students who were black or Native American.[42] Greaves had suggested the third tenet declaring that TST members regard their bodies as inviolable. TST's Protect Children Project encourages students threatened with corporal punishment to register for the project through a website. TST then sends a letter to the student's school board—on official TST letterhead featuring TST's logo of a goat skull over an inverted pentagram—declaring that the student (while not necessarily a Satanist) has a deeply held religious conviction that their body is inviolable, and that hitting them, restraining them, depriving them of bathroom access, or subjecting them to solitary confinement constitutes a violation of their religious rights. The letter also specifies that TST is prepared to take legal action if the rights of the letter holder are violated. TST declared May 15 to be "Protect Children Day," encouraging people to do registration drives for the project on this date. The announcement of the campaign earned TST accolades from the women's family website Mommyish.com.[43]

The idea for the project came to Jarry after studying *Ingraham v. Wright* (1977), a Supreme Court case that tested whether the Eighth Amendment, which prohibits cruel and unusual punishment, applies to public school teachers and administrators. Although plaintiff James Ingraham was paddled so badly by his principal he was taken to a hospital for a hematoma, the court ruled the paddling did not violate the Eighth Amendment. However, corporal punishment had never been tested on religious grounds. In an interview, Jarry told me, "So few lawyers have any imagination."[44] So far, the Protect Children Project has not found a plaintiff. However, W. James McNaughton, an attorney who advised TST in drafting the letter, explained, "I see the letter as exhibit A of a complaint."[45]

In March 2017, TST purchased billboards for the Protect Children Project in the small community of Springtown, Texas. The black billboard featured TST's sinister goat-skull and declared "Never Be Hit in School Again: Exercise Your Religious Rights." Springtown was chosen because of a 2012 incident in which a male assistant principal paddled two teenage girls. Spanking students of the opposite sex violated school policy, so the superintendent simply changed the policy to allow this.[46] The incident predated the Protect Children Project, but Greaves explained that the goal was to shame the school district:

> Hopefully, our billboard will serve as a daily reminder to the citizens there that they live in a barbaric backwater town where dysfunctional and possibly sexually disturbed middle-aged men may titillate their depraved impulses by violently spanking teenaged girls. . . . And hopefully the billboard can also serve as a beacon of hope to the youth of Springtown, showing them that they do have recourse to protect themselves against this shameful savagery.[47]

The billboard did bring media attention to the town. Springtown citizens voiced their complaints in a petition to take down the billboard, which they described as "bullying" by interlopers from the East Coast. Messages from signatories included, "Spare the rod, spoil the child! So many children are growing up with no parental guidance. If kids were being spanked more often, there wouldn't be sassy mouthed brats!!" And, "Our kids are bad enough feeling empowered by this will make them monsters."[48] Within a few days, someone ripped the billboard down, but Lamar advertising immediately replaced it.

In October a second billboard was purchased near the small Texas town of Three Rivers after its school district approved paddling for the 2017–2018 school year. This one read, "Our religion doesn't believe in hitting children." Once again, the media picked up the story, prompting superintendent Mary Springs to issue a statement decrying TST as an "outside force" trying to "force their beliefs on our community."[49] One resident, who identified as Pentecostal, stated that Satanists don't protect children, but only sacrifice them. The police department received calls to remove the billboard but explained that no laws were being broken.[50] The deep irony of this campaign is that Satanists have traditionally been accused of abusing children and breaking laws, yet TST effectively baited Christians in these communities into defending the practice of hurting children and illegally vandalizing billboards.

A month after launching the Protect Children Campaign in April 2014, TST attempted to hold a "black mass" at Harvard. This had not been intended as a major campaign, but the outrage the event drew from Boston's Catholic community attracted national news. (The Harvard black mass is described in greater detail in chapter 7.) In June, Greaves discussed plans to hold a same-sex wedding as a Satanic sacrament in Michigan and to sue the state on religious grounds if they did not recognize the marriage.[51] In 2004, Michigan created a constitutional amendment banning same-sex marriage. In March 2014, a district court ruled the ban unconstitutional and this decision was still being appealed. But a year after discussing a possible Satanic wedding case, *Obergefell v. Hodges* rendered such a campaign unnecessary. In July, TST again invoked the third tenet, stating their belief that the body is inviolable, to challenge restrictions on abortion access in the state of Missouri. That campaign is described in chapter 5.

Satanic Holiday Displays

The Baphomet statue had attracted national attention, and people all over the country now wanted to get involved with TST's campaigns. In the summer of 2014, a group of artists in Detroit led by Jex Blackmore became TST's first chapter. That fall, Jarry and Greaves created the nonprofit Reason Alliance as a vehicle for collecting tax-exempt donations to fund TST campaigns. Soon activists across the country were identifying as TST members and organizing their own projects. Blackmore was placed in charge of appointing heads of new chapters.

One of the first public activities local Satanists began doing was creating Satanic "holiday displays" to present alongside Nativity scenes and other Christmas displays as part of "open forums" held on government property. This tactic had already been pioneered by the more established Freedom

From Religion Foundation (FFRF), who offered legal support to several TST groups offering displays.

In 2014, TST-Detroit responded to a Nativity display on the capitol grounds in Lansing, Michigan, with their own "Snaketivity" display. The group met at a bar and designed the display on a napkin, loosely basing it on one member's tattoo.[52] They designed an ornately crafted, three-foot, stuffed, red serpent coiled around a Satanic symbol called a "Leviathan cross." The snake extended a copy of *The Revolt of the Angels* (1914) by Anatole France and held a sign declaring "The Greatest Gift is Knowledge." By 2014, the novel *The Revolt of the Angels* had already become a key text in TST's emerging philosophy. Several state senators heaped scorn on the display calling it a "mockery" of religious freedom.[53] But the chapter continued to display the "Snaketivity" in 2015 and 2016. TST-Detroit eventually disbanded, but in 2018 the newly formed TST-Chicago kept the tradition of "Snaketivity" alive with a new installation at the Illinois capitol. Their sculpture, entitled, "Knowledge Is the Greatest Gift," featured a female arm clutching an apple with a serpent coiled around it, all set on a glowing red pedestal. Several Illinois senators were so upset they introduced a formal resolution condemning the sculpture.[54] Meanwhile, a group called West Michigan Friends of The Satanic Temple erected a Satanic "Star of Reconciliation" display in Lansing.[55]

In Tallahassee, the Florida capitol erected Christmas displays by declaring an open forum. In 2013, TST requested permission for a display, but their proposed display—an angel falling into hell accompanied by a quote from Isaiah 14:12 "How you have fallen from heaven, O day star, son of the Dawn!"—was rejected on the grounds that it was "grossly offensive during the holiday season." But by 2014, TST had grown substantially. They reapplied with help from attorneys from Americans United For the Separation of Church and State and their display was allowed.[56] Film editor Joy Davenport, who had been recruited to film the Rick Scott rally, constructed a Satanic diorama, ironically using skills she had learned as a child in Christian summer camps.[57] Davenport's scene of a falling angel stood alongside other holiday displays until fifty-four-year-old Susan Hemeryck entered the capitol wearing a "Catholic Warrior" T-shirt and attempted to tear it down. She was arrested and charged with criminal mischief although all charges were later dropped.[58] In 2015, a Nativity scene was not displayed in the Florida capitol, and so TST felt no need to make an appearance.

Vandalism has been a common response to Satanic holiday displays. Preston Smith, an atheist who is not affiliated with TST, constructed a Satanic display at an open forum in a park in Boca Raton, Florida, in 2016. Smith, who is also a language arts teacher at a public middle school, constructed a red pentagram from aluminum that stood ten-feet tall and weighed 300 pounds. It featured such slogans as "In Satan we trust" and "May the Children Hail Satan" and was placed next to a Christmas tree and a Nativity scene. After authorities explained that Smith had a permit to express his viewpoint, interfaith groups released statements condemning the display, prayer rallies were held against it, and petitions were signed demanding Smith be fired from his job. Even Mat Staver, founder of the conservative evangelical Liberty Counsel intervened, demanding the school district turn over any of Smith's emails containing the words "Satan," "Christian," or "atheism."[59] Although Smith was not affiliated with TST, Greaves contacted the petition organizers warning that more Satanists would become involved in their school if they continued to engage in religious harassment.

In addition to legal forms of pressure, Smith's display was vandalized a total of eight times. First it was repeatedly spray painted. Smith called the vandalism a hate crime and filed a police report. The FFRF offered a reward for the identity of the vandal. Then someone apparently used a vehicle to run over Smith's display, carving deep tire tracks into the lawn in the process. Smith declared, "This experiment successfully exposed what local religious folks are—paranoid, uber-sensitive cowards afraid of the changing demographics."[60] A few citizens, however, supported Smith's freedom of speech by righting the toppled pentagram. A local welder even repaired it, free of charge. When Smith threatened to bring his pentagram back to the park in December 2017, a local pastor told the news he planned to personally demolish it, even posing for cameras with the sledgehammer he intended to use. Atheist blogger Hemant Mehta expressed shock over the double standard that allowed a Christian pastor to announce his intent to commit a crime on the news and face no consequences for it. In the end, the pentagram did not return due to a technicality with Smith's application.[61]

Even though Satanists have a First Amendment right to erect holiday displays, and the displays never say anything openly hostile toward other religions, some critics have claimed that since Satanists have no major holiday in December, the only purpose of these displays is to upset Christians and that they amount to a "publicity stunt." Mehta retorts that, " 'Publicity stunt' is in the eye of the beholder" and that by erecting holiday displays at government buildings instead of their churches, Christians are likewise engaging in a publicity stunt by signaling their religion's link to the authority of government.[62]

Unveiling Baphomet

While more people continued to become active in TST, the statue of Baphomet was finally completed. A grand unveiling ceremony was scheduled in Detroit for July 25, 2015. TST-Detroit spent several months planning the event. Chapter member Shiva Honey recalled that the energy put into the unveiling left everyone feeling drained and ultimately contributed to the implosion of the chapter.[63] TST had become so controversial that securing a venue proved difficult. A series of threatening messages appeared online including statements such as, "IT IS EVERY CHRISTIAN'S DUTY TO DESTROY THIS IF YOU SEE IT DESTROY THIS STATUE DESTROY THIS STATUE DESTROY THIS STATUE." Another message advised readers to avoid the area near the unveiling lest they receive "a parting gift you didn't even ask for or never wanted."[64] TST felt these threats were being fueled by local Baptist pastor David Bullock. Greaves contacted Bullock and asked him to condemn the threats, but this went unanswered. Bullock did give an interview alongside Jex Blackmore on a local radio show, although Bullock seemed intemperate and the conversation was unproductive.[65]

TST paid Bert's Marketplace $3,000 to rent the venue for the unveiling, but the owner later cancelled the reservation and returned their deposit. Even though the name "Satanic Temple" appeared on the rental contract, the owner claimed he "wasn't aware they were into devil worship." TST postponed the unveiling to July 26 and booked a new venue—the location of which would not be revealed until the date of the event and then only to guests who had purchased tickets and signed a contract pledging their soul to the devil. (The "soul contract" was meant to deter Christian protestors.[66] These contracts are still used when TST holds public events.) Malcolm Jarry recalled being anxious that the venue had only one exit. He also described a flash rainstorm that hit fifteen minutes before the event, leaving four inches of water on some parts of the floor.[67]

On July 25 about one hundred Christian protestors demonstrated in front of Bert's Marketplace—the last known location of the event—where they chanted and blew shofars.[68] Local Catholic churches held a mass and Eucharistic holy hour as an act of "reparation" for the city of Detroit.[69] An online petition asked the Obama administration to "Shut Down the Satanic Temple in Detroit," stating: "These Satanist [sic] are just slowly gaining freedom throughout our nation. Their goals to the achieve [sic] are to cause conflict and more problems upon our nation's [sic] as a whole. If we the people, don't do something about it now, they'll just keep on gaining more and more freedom and powers."[70]

A Catholic group called Church Militant reported that they successfully discovered the event's secret location, which they divulged to the police and local news. They arrived alongside a line of ticket holders in a flatbed truck bearing a six-foot bronze statue of the archangel Michael secured with chains and bungee cords. According to Church Militant's report, the line led to an empty warehouse where several nude performers waited. Ticket holders were then directed to a parking lot fifteen-minutes away, where a woman would examine their tickets and reveal the actual location of the building.

Eventually the Catholic investigators were able to witness the unveiling. They reported a party of about 400 people with bands and a dance floor buttressed between the Baphomet statue at one end and a large, neon inverted cross at the other. Two male TST members ripped off the veil and then kissed in front of the statue while the crowd applauded. Church Militant's reporters were suitably horrified. They drove their truck bearing the St. Michael statue around the venue three times in a sort of ad hoc exorcism. Their report noted that the event fell on the Feast of St. Anne, patron saint of Detroit.[71]

Days later, conservative pundit Glenn Beck was moved nearly to tears describing how upset he was by the statue. In December 2015, the unveiling was featured on an hour-long episode of CNN's "This Is Life with Lisa Ling." Ling presented a very sympathetic portrait of TST and emphasized how they were fighting for religious freedom. However, TST members recalled that Ling's producers instructed her never to be filmed standing in front of the Baphomet statue.[72]

Getting Organized

In only three years, TST had grown bigger and faster than Jarry and Greaves could have imagined. But with growth, its mission had begun to shift. Greaves had initially hoped his provocations would inspire a sort of decentralized movement of Satanic activism. In 2014, TST's website stated that it "facilitates the communication and mobilization of politically aware Satanists, secularists, and advocates for individual liberty."[73] But by the end of 2015, it had organized chapters across the country. These chapters were largely autonomous, but there was also the national brand to consider. On major projects—such as an abortion lawsuit in Missouri—there were disagreements between national leadership and local leaders about things like funding and strategy. With national news outlets paying attention to TST, there was also a growing risk that a local group might do something that impugned the entire organization. Finally, there was a fear that local chapters might threaten lawsuits or other actions that TST would be unable to follow through on. No one would take TST's campaigns seriously if they became known for idle threats.

One issue that threw these problems into relief was a campaign to protect Muslims following a wave of attacks by Muslim terrorists in Paris in November 2015 that killed 130 people. In December there was another terrorist attack in San Bernardino followed by a spike in attacks on American Muslims.[74] The Minneapolis chapter announced on social media that TST members would protect Muslims and encouraged Muslims who felt unsafe or desired an escort to contact them. The San Jose chapter followed suit. No Muslims requested a Satanic escort, and some apparently felt the offer of protection seemed paternalistic.

Jarry and Greaves saw the escort plan as a serious liability. TST was careful to work within the law and having untrained people working as bodyguards threatened to take the organization into a legal gray area: if an actual altercation occurred and the TST escort was not ruled to have acted in self-defense, TST's enemies could cast the entire organization as some sort of gang. Jarry sent an email out to all chapters warning that the entire chapter system might have to be terminated.[75] Greaves decided such measures were not necessary, but, for the first time, he asked local TST chapters to cease a campaign they had initiated. He explained, "The Satanic Temple is not in the personal security business." Some felt the co-founders' veto went against the transgressive spirit of the movement. One journalist opined, "Turns out the Satanic Temple is just as frustrating a bureaucracy as any other."[76] Not long after, TST-Minneapolis dissolved. It later reformed as an independent group called the Minnesota Left Hand Path Community that was less atheistic and more spiritually eclectic.

In January 2016 it was decided that some sort of advisory board was needed to give guidance to local groups using the TST brand. Jarry and Greaves became "the executive ministry," but decisions that concerned specific chapters were made by the National Council (NC). Greg Stevens, who has served on the Council almost since its inception, explained that TST had grown too large for any two people to lead. But the Council also strengthened TST by having a more democratic form of leadership. Stevens reported that Greaves encouraged the NC to set their own agenda for what TST's chapters ought to be doing.[77]

The size of the NC has varied from as high as ten members to as few as four. There is a high rate of turnover due to the demands of the job. All NC members are volunteers and have full-time jobs in addition to their positions within TST. Shiva Honey, who has served on the NC, recalls periods where the Council held three-hour teleconferences every week and members received emails about TST campaigns every fifteen minutes.[78]

The NC has experimented with different procedures for vetting new chapters. Local groups that wish to become official chapters are often asked to conduct an event or campaign to demonstrate their organizational skills. Chapters are assigned to a Council member as their "point of contact" who functions as a line of communication between the local and national levels. When chapters want to take on new campaigns or hold public events, they are expected to run their plans by their point of contact and gain approval from the Council. By 2017, there were more groups wanting to form chapters than there were Council members to serve as points of contact. This situation has required TST to periodically hold moratoriums on creating new chapters. To circumvent this, local groups began forming with names like Friends of TST—San Antonio. Such groups function as unofficial chapters, and many hope to gain official chapter status in the future. There have also been tiny groups around the world, often consisting of little more than a Facebook page, that call themselves a TST chapter but have no actual connection to the organization. There is, however, an official chapter in Ottawa, Canada, and there was one in London until 2018.

Chapters are required to have at least two leaders who are interviewed by the NC and are willing to undergo criminal background checks and sign contracts about how they will represent the TST brand. Vetting two people reduces the likelihood that a local chapter head will become a dictator, engage in self-aggrandizement, or leave the chapter suddenly leaderless. Chapter leaders are known as chapter heads, and most chapters have multiple co-heads. Beyond this, chapters are free to have their own leadership structure. Many have a "media liaison," governing boards, or subcommittees as well as chapter heads. Chapter leadership is a stressful volunteer job, and many of the chapters I met had experienced frequent turnover. Chapters themselves tend to be ephemeral, forming and then either becoming moribund or leaving to form their own Satanic groups. Some cities have had multiple incarnations of TST chapters.

There is no official geographical size that chapters must conform to. For example, there is a "West Florida" chapter for TST members in Pensacola and the surrounding area. One of the largest chapters is TST-Colorado, which concerns itself with an entire state, and one of the smallest was TST-San Marcos. San Marcos, Texas, is only a half-hour's drive from Austin or San Antonio, both of which had their own official and unofficial chapters, respectively. Most chapters have a core of "official members" who attend regular meetings and a larger periphery of affiliates that can be called on for major projects or events. Being a chapter member does not require any sort of dues or tithing, and while chapters may hold fundraisers for national campaigns, they do not send money to the national organization.

I began interviewing members of local TST chapters in 2018. As I did so, it became clear that TST is a very heterodox culture. Each chapter is shaped by local culture, resources, and demographics, and has its own focus. TST-Los Angeles held a "black mass" fundraising event in January 2017 that sold 1,200 tickets. Attendees could see multiple bands and other performances as well as on-site tattooing and a blood-letting ritual.[79] Hofman Turing, who was a chapter head for TST-New York City when I first interviewed him, explained his chapter's focus: "We do what New York is good at and that's fundraising."[80] At that time, the chapter held public events at clubs and other venues to raise money for TST's national campaigns. By contrast, TST-Indiana enjoyed holding picnics in public parks called "Lunch With Lucifer" to which many members brought their children. Chapter co-head Mara Gorgo explained one of the chapter's goals is to "promote a sense of family."[81] Leaders from TST-Dallas were more interested in the religious dimension of Satanism, which entailed designing rituals and other traditions as well as hosting lectures and seminars analyzing Satan as a mythological character. The chapter's membership included a linguist knowledgeable in liturgical Latin, Greek, and Hebrew.[82] Many chapter heads expressed that their current focus was simply "building a community." This often included going to concerts, movies, or doing other social activities together or tabling at such events as LGBTQ pride parades or "Pagan Pride" festivals. By 2016, there were over a dozen chapters, and a Satanic subculture was blossoming in cities across America. In fact, it was developing far faster than the movement's founders could track.

In July 2015, TST began renting a building in Salem, Massachusetts, that came to serve as its national headquarters. It is a Victorian-style house built in 1882 that once served as a funeral home. The headquarters contains a lecture hall, an art gallery, a gift shop, and an exhibit called "The Panic Room" where visitors can watch a video on the history of moral panic. The Panic Room also contains a library of books on Satanism and Satanic Panic as well as historical documents from the Process Church of Final Judgment, a Satanic religion that had its heyday in the late 1960s. Outside is a large shed where visitors can see the bronze statue of Baphomet. It seemed appropriate for TST to set their headquarters in a town associated with witch trials. But in reality, Salem was simply more affordable than Boston. On September 22, 2016, TST was ready to announce their headquarters to the world. They had an open house with tea and cookies and invited their neighbors as well as the mayor of Salem and the City Council.[83] The following day they made an official press release. A few people called the mayor's office with concerns about the headquarters, but TST has generally enjoyed good relations with their neighbors.

Grey Faction

As TST gained momentum, Greaves was able to advance the work he had started as Doug Mesner, reporting on mental health professionals who disseminated conspiracy theories about Satanic cults and repressed memories through the organizations SMART and the International Society for the Study of Trauma and Dissociation (ISSTD). By 2015, atheists and secular groups were inviting Greaves to speak on the dangers of pseudoscience being promoted by mental health professionals.

In early 2016, TST announced a new initiative called "Grey Faction" that worked to expose therapists who promoted conspiracy theories about Satanic abuse and to counter their work. At the time, there had been a plan to assign a color to each of TST's initiatives. "Grey" was chosen because "grey matter" makes up much of the brain. The color scheme was subsequently abandoned, but the name stuck. Several interviewees said Grey Faction was what most

attracted them to TST, especially members interested in psychology or philosophy of mind.

Grey Faction's first major cause involved Gigi Jordan, a woman who murdered her eight-year-old autistic son in 2010. Jordan's son was nonverbal,
but Jordan had come to believe that he was being ritually abused by multiple
people and being forced to drink blood and kill animals. At her trial, Jordan
argued that this had been a "mercy killing" because killing her son was the
only way to stop the ongoing abuse. Grey Faction argued that Jordan had been
encouraged in these delusions after she contacted psychologist Ellen Lacter.
Lacter's website features articles describing forms of ritual abuse and mind
control allegedly perpetrated by cults of witches and Satanists. Grey Faction
launched a petition demanding that the California Board of Psychology in-
vestigate Lacter. Grey Faction also filed a complaint against Neil Brick, the
Massachusetts counselor who founded SMART, noting that Brick described
having recovered memories of committing rape and murder, which he
believes he did while he was the victim of mind control. Grey Faction argued
that whether these crimes really occurred or whether they were a delusion,
Brick should not be a mental health counselor. Despite the case presented by
Grey Faction, the state licensing boards responded that they would not take
any action against Lacter or Brick.

Grey Faction has also drawn attention to national conferences organized
by SMART and ISSTD where ideas of mind control and Satanic ritual abuse
are promoted. They have repeatedly infiltrated these conferences posing as
people who believe they are victims of abuse and reported on the proceed-
ings. (Ironically, by alleging for years that they were being targeted by a conspiracy of Satanists hiding in plain sight, ISSTD created a situation in which
actual Satanists were disguising themselves to monitor their activities). TST
has also drawn attention to these conferences by bringing TST members to
the cities where they meet and holding theatrical performances on sidewalks
outside the conference venues. Grey Faction continues to be one of the
campaigns that Greaves is most passionate about.

After-School Satan

As an organized national network of chapters, TST could now take on larger
projects. In the summer of 2016, TST announced that it would be holding
a Satanic after-school program in public schools across America. Like the

statue of Baphomet, this was a direct response to what TST saw as conservative evangelicals using public resources to advance their privilege over other religions. The events that led to a Satanic after-school program began in 2001, with the Supreme Court case *Good News Club v. Milford Central School*. The Good News Club is a ministry run by Child Evangelism Fellowship (CEF) founded in 1937. When a school in New York barred the Good News Club from holding after-school worship services, the organizers sued, claiming it was discriminatory to allow secular outside programs, such as the Boy Scouts, access to the school but not religious programs. In a 6-3 decision, the Court ruled that after-school programs amounted to a limited public forum and that the Good News Club taught values from a religious "viewpoint"; as such, allowing other groups but not the Good News Club amounted to "viewpoint discrimination." The school could either allow the Good News Club or deny access to all outside after-school groups. Following this decision, CEF began expanding aggressively. By 2011, there were 3,439 Good News Clubs located in more than 5 percent of all public elementary schools.[84]

The Good News Club typically requires parental permission slips for children to attend, which reduces its ability to abuse its access to public schools as a platform for proselytizing. However, critics regard the Good News Club as an intolerant sectarian organization that has effectively strong-armed its way into public schools using threats of lawsuits backed by its ally, the Liberty Counsel.[85] In her highly critical book *The Good News Club*, journalist Katherine Stewart suggests that the aim of these clubs is not to teach values but to convert impressionable children to evangelical Christianity. The clubs meet in public schools even when nearby churches are available because they seek to create the impression that they are part of the school. Children who attended the clubs reportedly said things about their religious training like, "I learned it in school and they don't teach things in school that are not true."[86] In some cases, children are lured to club meetings with candy and other treats. The clubs encourage children to convert their classmates and even their parents and emphasize that nonbelievers will suffer damnation. Some accused the club of traumatizing children with elaborate discussions of death and hellfire. CEF also regards Catholics and mainline Protestants as false Christians in need of conversion. Stewart describes hearing a lecture at a CEF conference that strategized, "How to subvert Catholic teachings and practices so subtly that the Catholic-born students won't alert their parents to the fact that the religion of the Good News Club is at odds with their families' religion."[87] Interestingly, Stewart characterized CEF leaders as taking a "perverse delight" in the controversies they cause—an accusation that is often hurled at TST.[88]

Stewart also found that while the law allowed any religion to enter public schools in this manner, this was rarely true in practice:

> In the rare instances that minority religions seek to flex their muscles in public schools as conservatives do, it becomes clear that our society has a two-tier system of religious freedom—the top tier for Christians and a lower tier for just about everyone else. Minority faiths, as it turns out, are often blocked by the majority from exercising the very freedoms that the majority claims to be defending.[89]

She cited a family in Miami, Oklahoma, that attempted to distribute Qurans at a school where Bibles were distributed: the school prohibited this, and the family received a torrent of hate mail. When two humanists in Albemarle, Virginia, attempted to distribute flyers for a humanist summer camp, teachers rejected the flyers as "offensive" and refused to distribute them. So many concerned Christians emailed the school that its server crashed. This sort of suppression is not the law, but it is politics, and sometimes the mob, in action.

Stewart heard Jeff Kiser, a top CEF leader in Washington state, discuss the implications of what they were doing for minority religions: "One thing I hear from school administrators is, 'If we let you in, the Satanists will come in' . . . But other religious groups are not interested in coming into the public schools. . . . That's because kids don't have money. . . . Other religions don't think children are worth going after."[90] In hindsight, Kiser sounds as if he was challenging TST to intervene. In fact, some parents joined TST or even founded chapters specifically because they were disturbed by attempts to evangelize their children in public schools.

On July 10, 2016, Greaves held a strategy meeting with chapter heads from New York, Boston, Utah, Arizona, Minneapolis, Detroit, San Jose, New Orleans, Pittsburgh, and Florida.[91] By the end of the month, they were ready to announce their new program, the "After School Satan Club" (ASSC), to be offered specifically in public schools that hosted Good News Clubs. In some ways ASSC built on an idea Malcolm Jarry had in 2002 of demanding federal funding for a Satanic youth center. Like so many of TST's campaigns, ASSC was calculated to seem shocking and intolerable to conservative Christians and yet contain nothing objectively offensive or unreasonable. Just as the

Good News Club argued they did not use public schools as a platform for indoctrination but merely promoted values from a religious viewpoint, ASSC planned to offer lessons in critical thinking and social skills, as well as a healthy snack. But a video released for the program was clearly meant to disturb and featured eerie footage of children walking backward. An op-ed in *The National Catholic Register* advised readers to say the Prayer of St. Michael before watching it.[92]

But ASSC was not a prank. Chalice Blythe, chapter head for TST-Utah, was placed in charge of finding volunteers, vetting them, and conducting criminal background checks on them. Blythe designed a curriculum working with Amy Monsky, an executive director for Camp Quest, a program of humanist summer camps.[93] It consisted of eight complete lesson plans (enough to meet once a month for a whole school year) exploring topics from arts and crafts to gender roles to Native American history. For October, there was a lesson on bats where children learn about echolocation.[94] Within twenty-four hours of the announcement, several dozen people reached out to TST to volunteer to lead instructions. These were mostly non-Satanists who opposed proselytizing in public schools.[95] ASSC also produced a volunteer handbook that covered how to propose programs in school districts, how to write press releases, and how to handle protesters. Advice to volunteers included the following:

> Do not allow anybody to frame the debate in any way that contextualizes ASSC as a mere affront to Evangelical after-school clubs, rather than a necessary counterbalance to them. We're providing an alternative after-school club to those which instill children with deranged superstitions. Don't allow oppositional voices to present ASSC as the agenda-driven political statement while pretending that evangelical indoctrination clubs are somehow *more* concerned with children's' education and well-being. Similarly, do not accept the notion that ASSC is somehow less legitimate than Evangelical clubs because of its stated purpose in counter-balancing them.[96]

When I spoke with Jarry about Satanic children's programming, he seemed excited to discuss his philosophy of education. He believed in self-directed education, following theorists such as John Taylor Gatto. He felt teachers should act more like librarians, helping pupils to educate themselves. By contrast, he felt the Good News Clubs "deprive children of free will." Accordingly, the ASSC volunteer handbook contains an appendix of books on self-directed learning. At this point, I asked Jarry why ASSC needed such a detailed philosophy of education if the point was simply to demonstrate why *Good News Club v. Milford Central School* was a bad decision. Jarry answered, "We're not going to throw something out there we don't believe in."[97]

The announcement of ASSC may have been TST's biggest media coup ever. Since beginning my research on TST, I have received a daily news alert for headlines containing the word "Satanic." In the summer of 2016, my inbox began filling with literally hundreds of headlines about ASSC. In her research on claims of Satanic ritual abuse in daycare centers, Mary de Young describes the innocent child and the devil as "master symbols" that stood in proxy for deeper societal strains in the 1980s.[98] Whether it was intentional or not, ASSC triggered these master symbols. Some saw the announcement in literally apocalyptic terms. One person tweeted, "Well, people, do NOT be surprised when nuclear war destroys America. It is coming soon if this is not stopped."[99] A woman in Maryland told local media, "I can't think of anything else that would be the worst thing in the world."[100] Some parents threatened to remove their children from public schools entirely if ASSC were allowed. Evangelist Franklin Graham called on Americans to pray for Lucien Greaves, while Peter Gilmore, high priest of the CoS, released a statement chastising TST for proselytizing to children.[101]

At least some people seemed persuaded by the point TST was trying to make. Some parents did not know their children's school hosted a Good News Club until the ASSC story broke; when the situation was explained to them, they felt that neither group should be allowed. Jay Howard-Brock was the former PTA president of Bradbury Heights Elementary School in Washington, DC, one of the schools where TST sought to introduce ASSC. Howard-Brock had supported the Good News Club, but when asked about ASSC she told *The Miami Herald* that all religious groups should stay out of public schools: "It's going to become a distraction. . . . We should just abolish groups like that from being on school premises, because it just may offend someone. The kids really need to focus on the education piece."[102] Tellingly, in news stories about ASSC, representatives of the Good News Club began declining to tell journalists which schools had a club.[103]

Mat Staver, president of the Liberty Counsel, initially acknowledged that this was the price to pay for allowing religious groups in public schools, telling the *Washington Post*, "I would definitely oppose afterschool Satanic clubs, but they have a First Amendment right to meet."[104] But only a few days later, when it seemed ASSC might be more than just a stunt, Staver reversed course, claiming TST was not a "legitimate" religious group entitled to the same rights as the Good News Club: "The so-called Satanist group has nothing good to offer the students and its entire reason for existence is to be disruptive. Schools do not have to tolerate groups which disrupt the school and target other legitimate clubs."[105] TST attorney Stu de Haan characterized Staver's concerns about "disruption" as a "heckler's veto."[106] Greaves countered that the Good News Club is more disruptive and exists only to counter secular education.[107] He also said that if ASSC were denied access to a school, TST would request legal support from the Liberty Counsel, stating, "I would like to see how far their dedication to religious liberty actually goes. Are they only talking about one particular religious point of view or are they including us?"[108] In fact, The Liberty Counsel offered pro bono legal support to any school seeking to bar ASSC.

On August 1, 2016, TST posted a list of nine schools on their website where they hoped to host ASSC alongside Good News Clubs. The schools were located near the cities of Atlanta, Los Angeles, Pensacola, Portland, Salt Lake City, Seattle, Springfield, Missouri, Tucson, and Washington, DC. The list included the name, location, and phone number of specific elementary schools, causing some people to assume the school administration had already approved Satanic programming for children. At a PTA meeting, the principal of Centennial Elementary in Mount Vernon, Washington, told irate parents, "We didn't invite them to the school, they put our name on a website. . . . We feel like we're pawns in a game—someone else is manipulating us."[109]

Local chapters wrote the schools with formal applications to create After-School Satan Clubs. Some administrators simply ignored these requests. Fred Mephisto of TST-Atlanta sent an application via FedEx to Still Elementary in Powder Springs, Georgia. When there was no reply, he made two phone calls to the superintendent of the Cobb County School District that were never returned. After a month, Mephisto arrived at a board meeting and threatened legal action if there was no response to his application.[110] Christopher Paul of TST-Atlanta recalled their efforts to talk to the school district: "Everyone we reached out to was mysteriously sick, couldn't be reached, didn't answer emails, et cetera."[111]

When chapters did get the attention of school districts, they were usually required to produce paperwork including proof of insurance, background checks on any volunteers, and financial audits of TST. TST members were typically not allowed to use pseudonyms when dealing with the school districts. For most chapters these obstacles proved too difficult. TST-Atlanta was able to get insurance and instructors who passed background checks. They even found families whose children did not attend Still Elementary but said they would be interested in taking their children there to participate. However, Mephisto complained that the school district simply moved the goal posts, demanding more and more specific paperwork. He was told that TST's nonprofit, Reason Alliance, must be registered not only with the IRS but with Georgia's secretary of state.[112] After battling with the Cobb County School District for the entire 2016–2017 school year, TST-Atlanta finally gave up. Paul told me, "To be blunt, they simply called our bluff."[113] The Arizona and Los Angeles ASSCs failed due to similar problems.

Some chapters were more successful. TST-Portland successfully organized clubs at Sacramento Elementary in Portland and Nehalem Elementary School in Nehalem, Oregon. Club meetings were planned to meet one Wednesday a month, during the same time as the Good News Club. (Some elementary schools have "early release" on Wednesdays, making programming like the Good News Club one of few options for working parents). On September 22, ASSC hosted an "open house" in Nehelem, a town of less than 300 people. On November 16, ASSC held another open house at Sacramento Elementary School. Lucien Greaves and Jex Blackmore flew to Portland to mark the occasion. At least one parent showed up in a hoodie that read "Hail Satan Est. 666" and watched her children play with a Satanic coloring book created by TST. America Needs Fatima, a campaign under the auspices of a traditionalist Catholic group called The American Society for the Defense of Tradition, Family, and Property (TFP) mobilized its "anti-blasphemy network" in response. TFP flew several members from Pennsylvania to Portland to lead local Catholics in a rosary rally protest.[114] Despite this auspicious beginning, the Portland ASSCs failed to hold any subsequent meetings.

TST-Seattle initially hoped to bring the ASSC to Centennial Elementary in Mount Vernon, Washington. The Mount Vernon School District responded that all available space at the school was currently being used by district-sponsored after-school activities: as such neither ASSC nor the Good News Club could be accommodated.[115] The chapter moved its campaign to Point Defiance Elementary in Tacoma, Washington, where it obtained permission to meet on the second Wednesday of every month. On December 14, TST-Seattle held an open house while "Return to Order," another campaign associated with TFP, held a protest outside the school. The meeting drew eleven adults and nine children. A parent reportedly asked whether TST sacrifices children.[116] One child—a precocious eleven-year-old girl named Veronica who did not attend Point Defiance—was signed up for ASSC by her parents.[117] The Point Defiance ASSC continued to meet once a month with Veronica through the rest of school year. Veronica told reporters the club was fun.[118] But the Point Defiance ASSC lacked the resources, as well as sufficient volunteer instructors, to continue into the 2017–2018 school year.[119]

TST-Utah launched an ASSC meeting at Vista Elementary in Taylorsville, Utah, in January 2017. At least one child was un-enrolled from the school in response ASSC's presence. The school district sent a letter to parents reminding them that they were legally required to rent space to outside entities and to write their representatives if they had concerns. Chalice Blythe oversaw this program personally and deliberately kept a low media profile so as not to antagonize school officials. The Vista Elementary ASSC also had one student who attended for the rest of the 2016–2017 school year.[120]

Just as the clubs seemed to be making progress, ASSC's insurer declined to renew their policy. A cryptic email from Philadelphia Insurance Companies said only: "U/w has advised Phly not interested in writing this account due to the political activist exposure and PHLY was planning on non-renewing the coverage next year if they had renewed with us."[121] Without liability insurance, ASSC was unable to operate in the 2017–2018 school year. Insurance has remained ASSC's greatest obstacle with some insurers asking up to $7,000 to cover a single school. However, Blythe is continuing to organize ASSC programs for the future as well as monitoring the spread of the Good News Clubs. She commented:

> I am very proud of the efforts that have kept ASSC from dissolving completely and what I always like to remind people is that ASSC is in its infancy. GNC's have been around for decades and have the advantage of time and resources to continue expanding as they have while we are still navigating the process and dealing with the hurdles. Because we are tenacious and believe very strongly in this campaign, I believe ASSC will eventually grow beyond our initial vision and become not just a tool to challenge church/state separation, but a truly exceptional and widely available club for students in need.[122]

Bedlam in Belle Plaine

Months after launching ASSC, TST's next major controversy was already forming. Belle Plaine, Minnesota, is a town of 7,000 people. In 2001 it created Veteran's Memorial Park near highway 169. In August 2016, the Belle Plaine Veteran's Club installed a small monument consisting of a silhouette of a soldier named "Joe" kneeling in front of a cross. In October, an attorney for the Freedom From Religion Foundation (FFRF) sent the city a letter explaining that the cross amounted to an unconstitutional government endorsement of religion. The city's attorney explained that the Veteran's Club had acted unilaterally, and in January 2017 the city ordered Joe to be taken down. This upset some town residents in part because Joe had been sculpted by a Belle Plaine veteran who had died only two months after it was installed. Residents organized a "rotating guard" that occupied the park for a month, brandishing flags and crosses. In February, one hundred demonstrators marched from the local Veterans of Foreign Wars hall to the City Council demanding that the cross stay up. The Council voted 3-2 to make the park a "limited public forum." This would allow the cross to stay up, but also invited other monuments honoring veterans.[123] So the FFRF reached out to TST.

TST commissioned New Mexico artist Chis P. Andres, whose worked earned him a scholarship from Notre Dame, to design a Satanic monument honoring veterans. By the end of February, Andres had designed a three-foot high black steel pedestal with a square base, each side of which is marked with a gold inverted pentagram. Atop it sits an inverted military helmet made of black metal that serves as a "Baphometic bowl of wisdom" into which visitors may leave notes, offerings, or simply thoughts for fallen soldiers.[124] Having declared the park a public forum, Belle Plaine's hands were tied and on March 29 they approved TST's monument. Massachusetts company Pretty Hate Machining was contracted to build the monument, and most of the costs were covered through crowd-funding. The Minnesota Left-Hand Path Community, although not formally connected with TST, was excited to have the first public Satanic monument in history installed in their state and held a bake sale for it that raised $1,000.[125]

The juxtaposition of Satanism and veterans proved nearly as upsetting to the public as Satanism and children. One June 5, Brian Lynch, a Catholic priest from Belle Plaine, gave a five-minute address to the City Council urging them to reject TST's monument. Lynch argued the monument was illegal because it constituted an "offense against decency." Furthermore, he speculated that the monument would attract Satanists, making Belle Plaine, "a place for theistic Satanic ritual activities that victimize our children." Lynch testified that Satanic ritual is "known" to include sex with children. Since the monument was in a public park, Satanists could use it to "groom" children for abuse. After his address, Lynch led some thirty of his parishioners from the City Council to church to pray the monument not be installed.[126] In a blog post, Greaves responded, "It is unnecessary to point out the irony in seeing a representative from the Catholic Church decrying a perceived threat to children posed by religious Satanists."[127] On June 29, TST informed the city that the monument was completed and ready for installation.

On July 15, TFP's "America Needs Fatima" mobilized again, transporting over 200 protestors from five different states for a rally against the monument.[128] Bernard Slobodnik, an organizer for America Needs Fatima commented, "What gives this rosary rally special historic meaning is the fact that on this very day, 918 years ago, the crusaders took Jerusalem from Islam. . . . The crusader saints will be invoked during the rosary rally as our special patrons in the spiritual war against the devil and his followers."[129] About twenty-five members of Minnesota Left-Hand Path Community were also present and held a picnic to show there is a Satanic presence in Minnesota.

The controversy made Belle Plaine infamous. Greaves appeared on Fox News to debate Tucker Carlson. The protests were reported by Christian news sites as far away as Pakistan.[130] Two days after the demonstrations, the City Council voted unanimously to abolish the public forum so that neither Joe nor the Satanic monument could be present in the park. A statement explained that the controversy "portrayed our city in a negative light."[131]

But by the time the public forum was revoked, TST owed $35,000 for constructing and shipping a monument that the City Council had approved. Jarry began a lawsuit to recover those costs. In October, Martin Flax, a Massachusetts attorney representing TST, demanded the city compensate them for the cost of construction. He accused Belle Plaine of religious discrimination, pointing out that Joe was displayed for months, while the Satanic veteran's monument was not displayed for a single day. The city attempted to return TST's $100 application fee but refused any other form of compensation. TST began looking for a Minnesota-based lawyer to sue Belle Plaine. In letter to TST members, Greaves explained the need for a lawsuit:

If we allow this precedent to stand, we create an environment where alternative voices outside the Christian majority are burdened with creating monuments and displays, at great cost, with no actual hope of public placement, before the lie of the "Free Speech Zone"—having long been inhabited by an exclusive religious voice—is revealed. There must be a consequence to opening a Free Speech Zone without the intention of allowing it to be free.[132]

The suit was delayed when one of TST's attorneys dropped out due to health problems but relaunched in April 2019. This time, TST obtained the services of Bruce Fein who served as associate deputy attorney general and as general counsel to the Federal Communications Commission during the Reagan administration. Fein told the City Council, "As you well know, you can't decide to suppress speech just because hecklers didn't like it."[133]

The controversy in Belle Plaine seems like a tempest in a teapot, but it also stands as an important benchmark in TST's growing political significance. When the city declared their space a "public forum" the FFRF—which is far more established, having been founded in 1978—turned to TST. While TST was frustrated with the outcome, the FFRF achieved its goal of getting Joe removed from public property. TST was now a known quantity in the legal calculus concerning these debates. Greaves told the *Star Tribune*, "I think they were maybe taking the gamble that we wouldn't come through on producing our monument, and now I think they're maybe gambling that we won't file a lawsuit. . . . They would be wrong on both counts."[134]

3

Satanic Schisms

Speaking of "religious groups" or "denominations" has the consequence of projecting a false sense of unity. The reality is that instead
of being a single organic being, a religious group or denomination is
a heterogeneous collective of different organizations and individuals
all connected by various networks of social ties.

—Roger Finke and Christopher P. Schietle, "Understanding
Schisms: Theoretical Understandings of their Origins"[1]

The schisms, to me, are the greatest compliment, because they show
it's real.

—David Guinan[2]

On August 7, 2018, the website *Jezebel* ran the headline, "The Satanic Temple
Is Engulfed in a Civil War over a Decision to Hire an Attorney with a Stable
of Alt-Right Clients."[3] What the article dubbed a "civil war" was actually the
defection of two chapters, only one of which specifically cited TST's decision to work with controversial free speech lawyer Marc Randazza among its
reasons for leaving. But discussion of a civil war within TST catalyzed further
arguments and accusations. By the end of the summer, a substantial number
of chapters had either defected, dissolved, or lost the bulk of their membership. In interviews, all parties agreed this had never *really* been about a decision to hire a lawyer, but much deeper fault lines. In only six years, TST
had grown from a small social experiment among friends to an international organization with thousands of members. Some had invested a great
deal into the organization, and a few people had become minor celebrities.
With this explosive growth came divergent ideas of what TST's mission is
and ought to be.

Speak of the Devil. Joseph P. Laycock, Oxford University Press (2020). © Oxford University Press.
DOI: 10.1093/oso/9780190948498.001.0001

TST's civil war began with a tweet on the social media platform Twitter on January 10 at 2:40 a.m., from an account that was subsequently deleted. A woman named "Laurie" wrote:

> I doubt nothing anymore. I have em. In Salem MA. Opened a Satanic Church last year!!! The Witches are evil. And Satanists and Cults are VERY real! W [sic] a church like this Should not exist! Burn it! Blame Hillary I don't care! It's gutta go. If anyone likes this idea they r FKed.[4]

This message was re-tweeted by actor Corey Feldman. Feldman claims that while working as a child actor in the 1980s he was molested by a powerful ring of Hollywood pedophiles. He has also alluded to his belief that this pedophile ring is part of a larger Satanic conspiracy.[5]

TST leadership viewed Feldman's re-tweet as encouragement to his 152,000 followers to commit a religiously motivated hate crime. The TST headquarters is zoned residential, and staff members sometimes live on the second floor. Greaves tweeted "at" Feldman, asking why he was amplifying a call to arson. He also called on his own Twitter followers to report Laurie's tweet as abuse. To Greaves's surprise, he received a message from Twitter informing him that *his* account was being permanently suspended. At the time, Twitter was attempting to purge white nationalists and other extremist voices from its platform.[6] TST regarded Twitter's response as a case of religious discrimination: surely, they argued, if someone was reported for encouraging the arson of a church or a mosque, Twitter would punish the person calling for violence and not the person reporting it.

On January 13 a disturbed man attempted to break into the headquarters. When he was confronted by Lucien Greaves and staff member Ash Astaroth, he brandished what appeared to be a sharpened screwdriver, threatening to stab them and himself. When police arrived, he fled to his home and barricaded himself inside before he was arrested.[7] Greaves wrote, "I have no way, right now, of knowing what directly inspired this man's actions today, but I do know that when threats of violence against us seem to have the sanction of social media mega-giants, delusional would-be heroes against an imaginary Satanic Cult Conspiracy are likely to feel emboldened."[8] On January 15 at 1:15 a.m., Twitter un-suspended Greaves's account and sent him a terse apology.

This was not sufficient for some members of TST. Twitter had still never responded to calls for arson and had not granted a "verified" status to accounts for Greaves and TST. In April, they began preparing to sue Twitter for religious discrimination. Attorney Marc J. Randazza reached out to TST and offered to take their case pro bono. Randazza specializes in free speech cases and often defends controversial clients including several pornography websites as well as "alt-right" figures,[9] such as conspiracy theorist Alex Jones, alt-right media personality Mike Cernovich, and Andrew Anglin, who ran the neo-Nazi website *The Daily Stormer*.[10] TST already owed over $100,000 in legal debt from waging other lawsuits, and the leadership accepted Randazza's offer. In May, TST leadership filed a complaint with the Massachusetts Commission Against Discrimination.

Letters to the National Council

Other TST members were alarmed that the organization was accepting help from a lawyer with connections to dangerous racist demagogues. Some chapter heads also felt that suing Twitter had been a unilateral decision by Greaves. On a Facebook forum for chapter heads, a chapter head for TST-Los Angeles expressed that she was now reconsidering her affiliation with TST. Someone suggested that if the chapter heads had shared concerns, they should write a letter and submit it to the National Council (NC). If nothing else, the complaints would be in writing where they would be harder to misinterpret.

Dex Desjardins of TST-Albany drafted a letter to the NC raising concerns about the structure of the organization. An approved draft was signed by twenty-seven chapter heads representing nineteen chapters and submitted to the NC on June 20, 2018. The tone of the letter was cordial, and it acknowledged that most of the concerns were related to TST's rapid growth. It outlined four areas of concern: (1) Concerns about transparency in the NC's decision-making process and the appointment of new members to the NC. (2) Concerns about the diversity on the NC, which was perceived as predominately white and male. (3) Concerns about the absence of an ordination program. TST had been planning to create a program to train Satanic clergy, but the leadership seemed to be making little progress on this front. The chapter heads offered to take on the task of designing the program. (4) Concerns over fundraising, which they feared often proceeded in an ad hoc way that was impractical and risked breaking rules for charitable donations. They asked for a clearer system for fundraising so that all parties could track where the money went. The NC responded saying they agreed with the concerns. Some of the suggested changes, such as publishing the minutes of NC meetings and letting chapter heads nominate candidates for the NC were implemented almost immediately.

However, the letter never actually mentioned concerns over hiring Randazza. So a smaller, more left-leaning group of chapter heads began composing a second letter. The NC received word that another letter was coming from a more radical faction of chapter heads, and the anticipation of what it might say led to rising tensions. On June 27 a "leaked" draft of the second letter emerged expressing concerns about connections between TST's leadership and the alt-right. In addition to the issue of Randazza, it raised concerns about Greaves's connection to Adam Parfrey. A prominent member of the Church of Satan (CoS), Parfrey founded Feral House publishing, which published books on marginal and controversial subcultures.[11] Greaves befriended Parfrey, and in 2015 Parfrey curated the first exhibit at what would become TST's national headquarters—an exhibition of artwork by William Mortensen, a photographer whose book *The Command to Look* (1937) influenced Anton LaVey. When Parfrey died on May 10, 2018, Greaves tweeted a short message mourning his passing.

Parfrey had been a controversial figure. An obituary for *Motherboard* called Feral House publishing the forerunner to the controversial Internet forums Reddit and 4Chan, noting, "He pushed free speech to its limits and never apologized."[12] Parfrey had also been part of a clique of CoS members in the 1980s who flirted with Nazi and fascist aesthetics, if not ideology. Parfrey participated in the infamous "8-88" rally held on August 8, 1988, at the Strand theater in San Francisco, which featured a screening of the Charles Manson documentary *The Other Side of Madness* and musical performances by Boyd Rice and Nicholas Schreck, both of whom were members of the CoS at the time. The aesthetics of the rally seemed intended to evoke rallies by fascist movements. Afterward, Rice held an interview sitting before a Satanic altar draped in a Nazi swastika where he stated, "We need to bring power back to the powerful. We need the slaves to be enslaved again."[13]

There is debate regarding how seriously these invocations of fascism should be taken (and fomenting such confusion was likely the point). In his book *Modern Satanism: Anatomy of a Radical Subculture*, Chris Matthews takes it quite seriously, calling Satanism "a soft entry point for the doctrines of Nazism and Neofascism."[14] Satanism scholar Jesper Petersen dissents from this view, suggesting that the 8-88 rally was probably intended to offend mainstream sensibilities and not indicative of a serious commitment to an ideology or a political project.[15]

There were actual extremists on the edges of Parfrey's network, notably neo-Nazi James Mason. Mason admired LaVey and quoted him in his neo-Nazi newsletter *Siege*. Parfrey's associate, Michael Moynihan, published the essays from *Siege* as a book. *Siege* has inspired Atomwaffen Division, a neo-Nazi extremist group that the *New York Times* tied to five killings in 2018. Researchers from the Southern Poverty Law Center report that Atomwaffen has been experimenting with Satanism.[16] While the chain of connections from Parfrey to Atomwaffen is quite tenuous, some within TST were concerned that between Greaves speaking well of Parfrey upon his death and the decision to work with a lawyer who defends white supremacists, TST was implicated in this strain of fascist-leaning Satanism. They argued that at best these connections amounted to "bad optics" that reflected poorly on TST; at worst, they were evidence that despite being openly progressive and antiracist, TST was secretly being infiltrated by fascists.

The official draft of the second letter was submitted on July 5 and signed by thirteen chapter heads representing nine chapters. It did not discuss Parfrey, but it raised concerns about Randazza's past, including accusations of bribery and apparent friendships with alt-right figures. It pointed out that many Satanic groups were already associated with the far right and warned that working with Randazza could cause others to put TST in this category as well. Such an image problem, they argued, could damage TST's campaigns and even put its members at risk. Finally, the letter speculated that TST could be subverted by extremists: "As allies leave out the front door, there is an increased likelihood of alt-right and other racists, misogynists, and homophobes sneaking in through the back door."[17] Despite all of this, the letter did not demand that TST sever ties with Randazza, only that the national leadership respond to their concerns.

Global Order of Satan

In the midst of all of this controversy, TST leadership was preoccupied with its plan to hold an interfaith rally for religious freedom in Arkansas, scheduled for August 16, 2018. This was a massive undertaking in terms of logistics and security, requiring cooperation from multiple chapters. If successful, it would also be an important victory demonstrating TST's ability to orchestrate major demonstrations even in the heart of the Bible Belt.

On August 3, TST-UK and London, one of the few official international chapters, announced that they were becoming independent and would henceforth be known as Satanic Temple International (STI). STI planned to work with unofficial international chapters in Europe, Australasia, and the Middle East. Their declaration praised TST's accomplishments but stated the need to address their own circumstances.

Tensions had been building since May 2018 when TST-UK collaborated with artist Darren Cullen to subvert a new law in Bavaria requiring all public buildings to be adorned with a cross (in response to an influx of Muslim immigrants). The chapter mailed out crucifixes with hangers on the bottom so that they could only be hung upside down.[18] However, chapter head Zeke Apollyon, an expat from the United States, explained he was unable to get approval from the NC in time to work with Cullen by June 1, the date the law went into effect. So the chapter decided to go forward without submitting their project for approval.

When TST leadership learned of this, they asked Apollyon to step down as chapter head. Greaves felt they simply could not have chapter heads taking actions without telling the leadership, stating: "That's the one rule! I don't think that's asking too much of *any* organization."[19] Apollyon recalled, "I definitely wasn't happy about it [being removed as chapter head], but I was willing to take a back seat so the chapter could go on." Apollyon was briefly replaced as chapter head by Cain Abaddon, however, there were personality clashes and the NC voted to remove Abaddon as well. TST-UK was told to do nothing until a suitable chapter head could be found. At this point TST-UK had what Apollyon called "a universal vote of no confidence" in the NC and elected to become independent. Apollyon told me, "National Council is absent in their duties and way beyond their capacities."[20] STI created its own leadership, rituals, and tenets (the six pillars) and began networking with TST members in such countries as France, Italy, Belgium, and Switzerland. In February 2019, the group changed its name to the rather ominous sounding Global Order of Satan.

The split with TST-UK may have been inevitable. There are communities all over the world that have expressed interest in TST, and many formed unofficial chapters. However, there have been numerous difficulties in incorporating these groups into the US-based structure. (Apollyon noted the difficultly inherent in simply converting pounds into dollars for purposes of international fundraising). Greaves explained the NC was already overwhelmed by the demand for new chapters in the United States. He also had concerns about extending the TST brand into nations troubled by conflict. He had been contacted by a woman in Peru who wanted to create a chapter but was worried they might be subjected to violence by "Catholic militants." Greaves explained he had no idea whether Catholic militants in Peru were a credible threat but advised the woman to be safe and not start a chapter. Greaves explained he could never endorse, say, TST-Uganda, asking, "How are we gonna feel if they all get fucking gunned down over it?"[21]

TST-Los Angeles

On August 4, the day after TST-UK departed, TST-Los Angeles announced that they were also leaving TST to form a new group that eventually became known as HelLA. In a statement, they specifically cited the Twitter lawsuit, which they viewed as a waste of resources, and the decision to work with Randazza. The statement read, "We believe Randazza is opportunistically using The Satanic Temple as both a shield and a lever as he continues to work on behalf of the alt-right, and we in the Los Angeles chapter want no part of this." It also cited, "the complete lack of racial diversity within leadership."[22]

Some within TST felt this defection had been deliberately timed to take momentum away from their rally in Arkansas, less than two weeks away. However, I spoke with Bel Citoyen, a former chapter head for TST-Los Angeles, who explained the decision happened very organically, stating, "Individual decisions happened to coalesce." He had decided to resign as chapter head and leave TST as had his co-chapter head. On the chapter's Facebook page, no one expressed any interest in replacing them, so the chapter naturally disbanded. Citoyen expressed feeling ignored and condescended to by the NC. He also took issue with the position of "free speech absolutism" advocated by Greaves, arguing, "The right to free speech doesn't mean the right to a platform." Citoyen is also black and found the experience of being a minority in TST increasingly exhausting. He felt TST suffered from institutional racism, noting, "[Satanism has] inherited a bourgeois white guys club, TST can only do so much to diffuse it." Citoyen compared the creation of HelLA to a lobster shedding its shell: "It's exhausting and tiring and potentially deadly to the lobster, but if it succeeds it's more fit to survive."[23]

Accusations

While both the TST-UK and TST-Los Angeles cited frustration with the NC, the reasons for their departures were quite different. The controversy was stoked further when *Jezebel* writer Anna Merlan began interviewing TST members for a story on a Satanic "civil war." Merlan reached out to Jex Blackmore, who had left TST in February. Blackmore had been an incredibly charismatic spokeswoman for TST's reproductive rights campaign, especially with readers of *Jezebel*. Several young women I interviewed cited Blackmore as the reason they became interested in TST (Blackmore's work as a performance artist is discussed further in chapter 6). However, Blackmore had stepped down as head of the Detroit chapter and had little engagement with TST leadership. During this time the NC was established and approval for actions became mandatory. On February 10, Blackmore performed a "Subversive Autonomous Ritual" in Detroit. The *Detroit Metro Times* described it as a "Satanic Temple" performance and documentarians for the film *Hail Satan?* about TST were invited to film it.[24] However, the NC was not informed about it. In keeping with Blackmore's Satanic philosophy, the performance deployed violent imagery such as hog's heads impaled on spikes in order to shock the audience into resisting the forces of theocracy and patriarchy. At one point, Blackmore stated, "We are going to disrupt, distort, destroy. . . . We are going to storm press conferences, kidnap an executive, release snakes in the governor's mansion, execute the president."[25] In an interview, Blackmore explained that she was not calling for literal violence and that "the president" referred to an office of authority, not a person.[26] In a 2019 interview with Merlan, she suggested that the performance was also meant to mirror and call into question the violent rhetoric seen at Trump rallies and other "acceptable" political events.[27] But the NC saw statements like these as a serious liability that could serve as a pretext for bringing the entire organization under federal investigation. Some NC members suggested releasing a public condemnation of the performance. Instead, Blackmore was asked to quietly resign. This suited Blackmore and she agreed.

For six months Blackmore said little about her break with TST. But when Merlan approached her for comment, this seems to have prompted her to tell her side of the story. A day ahead of Merlan's story, Blackmore published an article on the website *Medium* where she wrote:

My departure [from TST] was mutually agreed upon, but it was also business as usual—a small group of individuals with no accountability to the
organization they represent asserting a paternalistic need to put a woman
in her place, gain control, and undermine her autonomous power.

Blackmore wrote that she had tried and failed to combat "a culture of racism
and sexism," stating, "I misrepresented TST as a group that genuinely cares
about the rights and liberties of marginalized groups. They do not."[28] She
reported experiencing harassment and abuse while in TST, implied there
is corruption in TST's fundraising, and echoed a claim made by TST-Los
Angeles that the Twitter lawsuit was about Greaves's ego rather than a response to calls for arson.

Blackmore also raised a new talking point. Her article linked to a discussion of a podcast recorded on September 11, 2002, in which Lucien
Greaves—then known as Doug Mesner—made offensive and seemingly
anti-Semitic remarks. Satanist Shane Bugbee had the idea to create a marathon twenty-four-hour live podcast hosted through Radio Satan to promote
the new edition of *Might Is Right*. As the illustrator, Mesner was invited to
appear on the podcast. The tone of the podcast is sophomoric and intentionally offensive in keeping with Bugbee's philosophy of Satanism. In the
exchange in question, Mesner states, "It's OK to hate Jews" if this hatred is
based in contempt for their supernatural beliefs but that "it's not OK to hate
Jews" if this hatred is based in racism or ideas of eugenics. Bugbee then asks
Mesner, "Do you like Satanic Jews?" Mesner answers, "Satanic Jews are fine."
Bugbee replies, "One drop of Jew blood means you ain't breaking bread with
me, motherfucker." At this, someone on the podcast can be heard laughing.
Mesner starts to respond, at which point Bugbee accuses Mesner of being
Jewish himself. In what may have been an attempt to disarm the situation,
Mesner then replies, "Look at me, I'm an Aryan king." This is met with more
laughter. This exchange is followed by a more serious discussion by Bugbee's
wife, Amy, about how Jews exaggerated the numbers killed in the Holocaust
and have exploited it for political gain, during which Mesner is silent.[29]

It is a disturbing and confusing exchange, and this is partly the point.
Intentionally offensive polemics like this are par for the course within the
milieu of Satanism. Petersen locates Bugbee specifically, along with Adam
Parfrey, within "a genealogy of aesthetic terrorism." He notes that all Satanists
"play" with society's associations of Satan with evil, transgression, and violence,

writing, "It can be very difficult to discern when it is serious and when it is irony, play, stupidity, or plain provocation, especially when moving to the fringes of the margins, so to speak, among one-man groups and nebulous networks."[30] In an interview, Greaves said of the entire podcast, "It was dumb." When I asked about this exchange, he pointed out that he was arguing *against* racist forms of anti-Semitism. He added, "At that time I was much more outraged and vindictive against organized religion. Ironically, I have a greater appreciation of religion now because of having this Satanic community."[31] Jarry and Guinan are both Jewish and rejected the suggestion that Mesner harbors anti-Semitic views. Jarry expressed irritation that those claiming Greaves is an anti-Semite never bothered to ask his opinion about the podcast.[32]

The 2002 podcast was all but forgotten until it was discovered by members of the Stop Mind Control And Ritual Abuse Today (SMART), who were angered by Mesner's reporting on their conferences. They apparently listened to all twenty-four hours of the podcast, searching for instances of Mesner making offensive statements, which they transcribed and posted in on-line forums. Many TST members had known about the podcast for years. But when high-profile figures such as Blackmore left TST citing a culture of racism, these comments suddenly took on new significance. Blackmore wrote of the podcast, "Shamefully, I ignored past expressions of racism and sexism."[33] For some, the decision to work with Randazza, Greaves's friendship with Adam Parfrey, and comments from a sixteen-year-old podcast seemed sufficient to conclude TST was actually a racist organization despite being openly progressive. It should be remembered that these concerns were being raised days before the one-year anniversary of the "Unite the Right" rally in which hundreds of white supremacists, some armed with assault-style rifles, marched through Charlottesville, Virginia, leading to violence and the murder of one counter-protestor.

Blackmore's article was followed by several other *Medium* articles from former members, including chapter heads and even a former NC member, stating their reasons for leaving TST. By August 13, one such author described her article as a "YAQTSTP" for "Yet Another Quitting TST Post."[34] TST-Portland left to become Satanic Portland, announcing this in the middle of the night before TST's rally in Arkansas. Most of the members of TST-NYC left as well, leaving the chapter temporarily moribund.

The *Medium* articles marked the beginning of a long series of accusations and counter-accusations between those who remained in TST and those who left. Several former members compared TST to a "cult," intending all the negative associations this term carries. An anonymous blog was created largely dedicated to proving TST leadership actively supports fascism.[35] Some of the accusations raised in interviews, by both sides, included online harassment and bullying, legal harassment, and ultimatums that could be interpreted as blackmail. There were also allegations of TST mismanaging donations and former chapter heads either losing track of or refusing to turn over proceeds from fundraisers. Such accusations are fairly common in the study of emerging religious movements. The interviewees seemed earnest and legitimately upset, but it is beyond the purview of this book to evaluate these allegations.

Significantly, interviewees on both sides expressed that social media aggravated these problems. Zeke Apollyon commented that Facebook "lends itself to contention and performative cruelty" and that "a lot of our communication has become trash."[36] It was clear that the situation took a toll on everyone involved. Some interviewees who had left TST described feeling "traumatized" by the experience and were now seeking therapy or experimenting with anti-anxiety medications. Greaves also reported feeling symptoms of depression and agoraphobia, noting that he was used to attacks from religious conservatives but not from left-leaning Satanists.[37] There were, however, many cases of individuals who remained supportive of one another despite being on opposite sides of the schism.

Arkansas

In the midst of this turmoil, TST proceeded with its rally in Arkansas. In short order, TST crowd-funded the $20,000 needed for transporting the Baphomet statue to Little Rock and hiring a private security detail. It was able to muster a sizable showing of members in Little Rock from Austin, San Marcos, San Antonio, Houston, Oklahoma, Santa Cruz, Michigan, and elsewhere. As the date of the rally approached, white supremacist leader Billy Roper called for "all white Christians" to join him in a counter-protest. Roper said of TST, "This particular group of Satanists are Anarcho-Communists, and celebrate homosexuality and race mixing."[38] Thomas Robb, David Duke's successor as leader of the Knights of the KKK, pledged his support. To prepare for the rally the capitol police force was reinforced by state police and the Little Rock police department.

On the day of the rally, I watched Thomas Robb and a handful of elderly white men from the KKK arrive and stand behind the crowd brandishing flags. After speeches on the importance of separating church and state by an atheist, a Satanist, a mainline Protestant, and an Evangelical, Greaves took to the podium wearing a bulletproof vest. He began his speech:

> I feel I have to comment on the comic relief of these flabby old men who fashion themselves the master race. They may not be fine physical specimens, but they're not fine intellectual specimens either. Nor were they able to rally a good counter rally. But I'm sure your mommies thought you were handsome little boys.

That night there was an after party at a local bar. As at the "Unveiling" event in Detroit, attendees were required to sign a "soul contract" pledging their soul to Satan. The Arkansas version of the contract added, "I support anarcho-communism, homosexuality, and race-mixing."

TST has long used satire against its political opponents. Greaves has argued that the best way to respond to hate speech is with mockery rather than violence. The fantasies of hate groups often involve a descent into violence in which the social order is destroyed so that they can rebuild it as they see fit. While the Satanists appeared to have a good time in Arkansas, Greaves was truly concerned about his safety and the safety of those close to him. Days before the rally, Roper made a blog post "doxxing" Greaves by posting the names and addresses of his family members. After the rally Roper boasted that his followers had collected photographs of TST members and the license plates of their vehicles. TST's security detail noted suspected neo-Nazis standing across the street from the capitol—where concealed weapons are allowed—communicating on walkie-talkies.[39] Several TST leaders remarked on the irony that Greaves was putting himself in danger from white supremacists in this way even as former members accused him of being a crypto-fascist himself. Amber, a chapter head for TST-Austin, commented, "Who do you know who's willing to die for what they believe in?"[40]

The NDA Controversy

TST leaders often ask those they work closely with to sign non-disclosure agreements (NDAs), in part because they use pseudonyms to protect their identities. At the end of August, following a wave of critical articles from former leaders, the NC issued new NDAs to chapter heads with a non-disparagement clause prohibiting any statements or actions "that disparage the goodwill, name, brand, or reputation" of TST, even after the signer has left TST. They were asked to sign and return the new documents immediately.

For chapter heads who were already unhappy with the NC, this was the last straw. Some saw this move as evidence that TST was now a business rather than a religion. A former chapter head forwarded a copy of the new NDA to atheist blogger Hemant Mehta, calling the disparagement clause "unsatanic" and noting if "the Catholic Church had this same rule in their contract, TST would likely be up in arms over it."[41] Greaves responded that the non-disparagement clause was "boilerplate" language composed by one of their lawyers. He added that the NDAs were "an immediate emergency measure against specific bad actors whom we have since parted ways with."[42]

Some chapter heads asked for more time before signing the NDA or stated they wanted an attorney to look at it first. Certain members of the NC seemed to interpret this as a sign that these chapter heads were planning to do further damage before resigning. The NC scrambled to collect passwords for the Facebook pages and other social media pages from these chapters, which further strained the relationship with these chapter heads. On September 1, Salome DeMeur, chapter head of TST-West Florida received a "notice of termination" from the NC. The following day, TST-Dallas sent a letter of resignation to the NC and quietly disbanded.

Ironically, following this controversy, the language was softened to prohibit only false statements. Because non-disparagement clauses are largely unenforceable, some chapter heads suspected the real reason for requiring them was simply to drive out those chapter heads who were already preparing to defect. Regardless, some chapter heads who left during this period described feeling betrayed and attacked.

Aftermath: Understanding the Schism

One anonymous critic wrote that by working with Randazza, Greaves "has now united the TST with alt-right fascist, pro-Nazi website The Daily Stormer, and on-air conspiracy theorist and Christian Warrior Alex Jones."[43] Of the interviewees who remained in TST, some were ambivalent about the decision to work with Randazza, noting that it may have caused more trouble than it was worth. But all regarded claims that TST had somehow joined with the alt-right as hysterical. Several interviewees noted that these concerns were first framed as something outside observers might conclude erroneously. Amber of TST-Austin remarked, "I'm so tired of hearing concerns about 'bad optics.' We're *Satanists!*"[44] As these concerns evolved, more details were seen as potentially signaling sympathies with the alt-right. NC member Sebastian Simpson stated, "Our chapter heads were doing the work of conspiracy theorists for them."[45] Simpson felt that fears about what outsiders might hypothetically conclude gradually morphed into literal accusations.

Some who remained in TST also suggested these fears correlated with age, noting that many who believed TST had acquired fascist sympathies were in their twenties. Sekhmet Solas of TST-Albany felt a younger cohort was more alarmed by Greaves's connection to Parfrey in part because they "don't know their Satanic history."[46] She recalled how important Adam Parfrey's Feral House publishing had been for the Satanic counterculture before the era of widespread Internet. She added, "I got beat up for being a Satanist," indicating that a younger cohort of Satanists has it easier and should not rush to judgment.

In August, Greaves wrote an essay framing the concerns raised in the wake of the Randazza controversy as a "purity spiral."[47] Sociologists Bradley Campbell and Jason Manning define a purity spiral as a phenomenon in which members of ideological and religious movements "strive to outdo one another in displays of zealotry, condemning and expelling members of their own movement for smaller and smaller deviations from its core virtues. . . . The result is an ever-increasing demand for moral purity, and ever-greater effort to meet the standards of the group."[48] Several interviewees saw the controversy in this way. Dex Desjardins claimed he was called "a neo-con" in a Facebook forum. He stated, "This obsession with purity gets toxic. It's downright scary, and I'm a *Marxist!*"[49] Felix Fortunado, who had been a member of TST-Dallas joked, "For some of these people if you throw a bed sheet over a traffic cone, they're going to see a klansman."[50] Many of TST's critics did frame the issue in terms of purity and contamination. In a debate on Facebook, one critic responded to Greaves's essay on purity spirals, "There's an old saying I like 'If there's a Nazi sitting at the table and 10 other people sitting there talking to him, you got a table with 11 nazis.' " One interviewee described the transference of memes from the alt-right through Randazza to TST.

While much of the discussion over the split within TST focused on Randazza or other specific complaints, from a sociological perspective, it seems inevitable that groups would break away. In their chapter on religious schisms, Roger Finke and Christopher Scheitle compare the causes of schisms to the reasons couples divorce: "As with separations of individuals, we must be careful not to let the manifest drama of a schism distract us from its latent causes."[51] Finke and Scheitle present religious schisms as natural, noting that societies with religious freedom generally see frequent schisms that create new denominations. Instead, they outline factors that *reduce* the likelihood of a religious schism. Significantly, TST possesses none of these factors. Religions are less likely to have schisms when they claim to possess an exclusive truth, tradition, or ecclesiastical office. Such exclusive claims are, of course, anathema to TST's atheistic and egalitarian ethos. Another such factor is a strong tie between religion and ethnic heritage such as the one felt by Swedish Lutherans or Greek Orthodox. TST is too new for such ties and is actively seeking to be more ethnically diverse. A third factor is having professionalized clergy. Clergy that undergo standardized training are naturally more sympathetic to the larger denomination than the local congregation. TST could have professionalized clergy in the future: an ordination program is forthcoming, and there is a committee creating a handbook for chapter heads. But for now its leadership consists entirely of volunteers. Furthermore, the central leadership claims they want local chapters to have as much autonomy as can be accommodated. NC member Greg Stevens commented, "The core of the organization is in the local chapters and the community they provide."[52] All of this suggests that it was likely inevitable that chapters would break away sooner or later, regardless of any specific concerns that may have more immediately provoked their departure.

Less passionate observers of the schism regarded it as a necessary occurrence arising from very different visions about what a progressive Satanic organization ought to be doing. Jack Matirko, who blogs on Satanism, compared it to a market correction.[53] Hofman Turing, who resigned as a chapter head for TST-NYC, compared the situation to a band that keeps gradually shifting its style of music until the members break up.[54] Dex Desjardins described the schism as "an exodus of people who wanted to see TST drastically change in scope and mission," adding, "those who remain understood the mission in the first place."[55]

Much of this divergence was political. TST is "progressive," but this can mean many things. Felix Fortunado recalled members of TST-Dallas suggesting the chapter officially endorse Marxism or the Antifa movement. He stated, "I didn't sign up to support every leftist cause we could think of."[56] Varying political philosophies were especially contentious around freedom of speech. Greaves describes having an enlightenment idea of free speech in which good ideas will ultimately win out over bad ideas. Conversely, he feels strongly that censorship—however well intentioned—will inevitably be used by the majority against the minority.[57] This view was echoed by Amber, who posed the question, "If you suppress free speech, do you really think we're the good guys?"[58]

However, some progressives feel that "free speech absolutism" is a sort of hegemonic camouflage that protects the interests of the powerful and provides them with a platform to spread rhetoric and indoctrination. Although none of my interviewees ever mentioned his name, their critiques of free speech seemed influenced by Herbert Marcuse, "the father of the New Left." In his 1965 essay "Repressive Tolerance," Marcuse argued that what is conventionally called tolerance actually benefits a dangerous majority and that a true "liberating tolerance" "would mean intolerance against movements from the Right and toleration of movements from the Left."[59]

These competing views of free speech were already a source of tension within TST more than a year before the Randazza controversy. In January 2017, the right-wing website *Breitbart* announced that TST was partnering with a group at California Polytechnic State University to host a Satanic "counter-event" against a speech by polemicist Milo Yiannopoulos, who was planning to speak at the campus on January 31 as part of his intentionally offensive "Dangerous Faggot Tour."[60] Days earlier, protestors had forced the cancellation of Yiannopoulos's speech at the University of California at Davis.[61] Nearly everything in the *Breitbart* piece was wrong: the so-called counter-event was a screening of two Satanic horror films scheduled days after Yiannopoulos's visit, and it had no connection to TST. The aim of the article seemed to be to suggest that the protestors the University of California-Davis had some connection to organized Satanism. Jarry reached out to *Brietbart* and was quoted in a follow up piece:

> The Satanic Temple was not in any way involved in this, nor would we be.... The Satanic Temple are firm advocates for free speech and, while we may not agree with the speaker in question on some issues . . . we would never move to have him censored from speaking. We are mortified to have our name falsely attached to this and hope it can be corrected immediately.[62]

However, more radical members of TST felt that Yiannopoulos's provocations were so dangerous that it was necessary to use undemocratic means to cancel his public speaking engagements or "de-platform" him. These differences eventually surfaced. In a *Medium* article, a former chapter head expressed that, unlike Greaves, she was "delighted" that protestors had silenced Yiannopoulos.

In December 2017, Malcolm Jarry published an article called "Guidelines for Effective Protest." Among other things, it emphasized that protestors must respect the free speech of others, should have clear demands and plans for how to achieve them, should base their protests on principles rather than identity politics, and focus on specific issues rather than broad views of other groups or individuals.[63] Those who left described this document as "tone deaf," taking issue less with Jarry's suggestions and more with the way they were worded.[64] In an interview shortly after the schism, Jarry suggested it was good some members took issue with the guidelines because it showed they were finally understanding them.

Needless to say, TST is not the only progressive movement to be divided over how to respond to provocations by the alt-right or figures like Milo Yiannopoulos. College campuses have become increasingly divided between those who advocate traditional ideas of free speech and those who frame certain kinds of speech as not only offensive but actually dangerous to minority groups.[65] In an essay for *Vox*, Tara Isabella Burton opined, "The debate raging in TST, in other words, is ultimately a debate about the nature and limits of activism in the age of President Donald Trump."[66]

Moving Forward

While some of the differences within TST appeared irreconcilable, most members who stayed expressed sadness to see their colleagues leave. The schism also caused TST to focus on issues raised by those who left, especially the problem of diversity and their organizational structure. Current and former members agreed that TST ought to be more diverse, although there were disagreements as to how exactly this problem should be approached. On the one hand, TST may be the most diverse Satanic organization that has ever existed. James R. Lewis conducted a series of online surveys of Satanists between 2000 and 2011. In every survey, he found a sizable majority of Satanists were white, heterosexual males.[67] While such a survey has not been conducted

on TST, there are indications that its membership has much higher rates of racial minorities, women, and LGBTQ people than Lewis's sample. At meetings
of the Austin and San Marcos chapters of TST, I encountered a sizable Latinx
presence, reflecting the demographics of central Texas. Nelcitlaly, a leader
from TST-West Florida, is a Latina who was born in Mexico. When I asked
whether TST has a diversity problem she answered, "I'm really disappointed
that that was a conversation we had to have, because there is no racism,"
adding, "I will be the number one person to call out the white-male-in-power-
bullshit-thing."[68] TST meetings I attended appeared to have a near equal balance of male and female membership and, by some estimates, women account
for more than 50 percent of the leadership.[69] TST draws a large number of
LGBTQ members, in part because of its campaigns defending LGBTQ rights.
Chapter heads from Albany and Chicago estimated that as many of 75 percent
of their membership identifies as LGBTQ.[70] People with disabilities make up
a less studied area of diversity. Donny, chapter head for TST-Springfield, estimated that about a quarter of his chapter has a disability, including a significant number of disabled veterans.[71]

There was also agreement that while it would be good to have more racial
minorities within TST, minority communities—particularly the black and
Latinx communities, were less inclined to be interested in Satanism. Black
and Latinx Satanists I interviewed expressed that Christianity is a central
pillar within their ethnic communities. Several black interviewees pointed
out that the subculture associated with Satanism—especially heavy metal
music—holds little appeal for most black people. Steve Hill is a black comedian, activist, and political candidate as well as a former chapter head for
TST-LA. He commented, "The aesthetic sort of pins you into a hole," but he
felt there would be more black Satanists in the future, adding, "people think
we don't exist."[72] There was also a consensus that TST should not attempt
to increase diversity by evangelizing minority communities as proselytizing
violates the Satanic ideal of self-determination.

Complaints about a diversity problem within TST really meant that the
leadership seemed to be predominately white and male and that, as such, it
could not understand the problems faced by minority members. TST's co-
founders are white, heterosexual males. The NC is more diverse, although
its composition has shifted widely over the years. The NC has never been entirely male and has been as high as two-thirds female, including one member
who is a transgender woman. It has also never been entirely heterosexual,
although at times it has been entirely white.[73]

Solving this problem is more difficult than simply appointing minorities to leadership positions for two reasons. First, such a gesture could amount to "tokenism." A black chapter head who was interviewed for a position on the NC before leaving TST, wrote, "I felt like a straight up token. Like I would've been a counterexample when people brought up how white the Temple is."[74] Second, being a leader within a Satanic organization brings social stigma that may fall harder on those with less social privilege. I discussed this problem with Lex Manticore and Lux Armiger, chapter heads of TST-Chicago. Their chapter does a lengthy survey of its membership, asking members what their goals are for the chapter and whether they are interested in leadership. One member worked in finance and expressed interest in serving as treasurer. This member was also black and a lesbian. The chapter heads wanted to appoint her treasurer, but when they discussed it further, she decided it could damage her career if her name ever appeared on financial documents associated with TST. Arminor, a white gay man, explained, "Everyone can be as high-profile as they are comfortable," but pointed out, "The people who are most insulated from social consequences happen to be male, happen to be white."[75] Manticore, a straight white man, acknowledged that he benefited from "white privilege" and saw being the public face of the chapter as a way of shielding members with less privilege, stating, "if people want to send hate mail, I will happily be the target of that."[76]

At the time of this writing, TST was moving forward to create a diversity committee, an idea that was first raised before the defections of August 2018. Greg Stevens, a gay man and a long-time member of the NC, explained the idea behind the diversity committee, "Everyone has some kind of privilege, which means everyone has blind spots."[77] The committee would create guidelines to make event proposals by chapter heads more inclusive and advise the NC on diversity concerns. Most importantly, it would create a place for minority TST members to go to when they had concerns.

The other major area of concern was TST's organizational structure. Those who left TST felt that the NC had come to stifle the chapters. Belle Phomet, who departed along with much of TST-NYC, explained, "TST had a tight grasp on everything; there wasn't much freedom in what we could do. It felt very unsatanic." Phomet reported that chapter proposals often took a month or more to receive approval from the NC. As an example of why this was a problem, she cited the demonstrations held at JFK Airport in January 2017 to protest an executive order signed by President Trump banning travel from seven Muslim-majority countries. The protests organized rapidly through social media with protestors congregating at airports across the country one day after the order was signed. Phomet said that the chapter would have liked to attend the protests in an official capacity but that this kind of quick response was impossible under the NC rules.

More broadly, those who left felt the NC was simply ignoring their concerns or that when they did respond the answer was "tone deaf," demonstrating little understanding of the issue. Those who remained in TST conceded that the organizational structure had room for improvement but pointed out that the NC was only two years old and consisted of a handful of overworked volunteers. Donny of TST-Springfield said, "I have yet to see a case where the NC just blew off a concern. But sometimes the answer is going to be 'no.'"[78]

Concerns that an organizational structure has become "unsatanic" demonstrate what Jesper Petersen calls the "Satanic Procrustean Bed" of individuality versus the collective.[79] How can a philosophy that celebrates individuality and rebellion against "arbitrary authority" not only form a collective identity but also organize for effective social action? Petersen notes this was already a problem within the CoS, which is a far looser organization and openly disdains political action. Several chapter heads explained that Satanism draws strong personalities and compared leadership within TST to herding cats. (Comedian Steve Hill called it "herding cockroaches.")[80]

Despite lingering animosities and accusations, TST has continued to grow. I spoke with several chapter heads who reported they were receiving new applications for membership every month. Meanwhile new chapters continue to form. When I interviewed Jon Winningham and his partner Laura, they were working on gaining official chapter status for TST-Houston. When I asked Jon about the schism, he answered, "We're new! We voted as a whole that we don't care."[81] NC leaders I spoke with were excited about reviving the ASSC program and creating the long-awaited ordination program.

In October 2018, Warner Brothers released a series for Netflix called *The Chilling Adventures of Sabrina*. The show featured a cult of cannibalistic devil-worshipping witches who supplicate an idol that appeared to be a computer-generated copy of TST's Baphomet statue. TST's statue, called *Baphomet with Children*, is protected by a registered copyright. TST demanded an explanation, and, when they were ignored, sued for $150 million. The lawsuit attracted an incredible amount of media as journalists speculated whether TST had a legitimate claim since their statue was inspired by Eliphaz Levi's 1854 illustration. Other media outlets asked how this would affect a popular show and what this might do to the stock prices of Netflix and Time Warner. Greaves expressed his irritation that the copyright case received vastly more attention than the rally for religious freedom in Little Rock. In the end, Warner Brothers and Netflix apologized and agreed to a settlement. It was not disclosed whether the settlement included financial compensation.

The Diaspora

Significantly, almost no one who left TST ceased their involvement in Satanism or activism. In some cases, their zeal for Satanism only intensified. Hofman Turing referred to those who left TST as "the diaspora."[82] Even before the summer of 2018, numerous new Satanic movements had spun off from TST. Damien Ba'al co-founded TST-St. Louis but resigned in 2015. He created his own religion called United Aspects of Satan. Ba'al liked TST's atheistic approach to Satanism but felt it lacked a complete philosophy. He wrote a series of texts expanding his Satanic philosophy, the first of which, *The Satanic Narratives*, is read by many TST chapters in their book clubs.[83]

Koren Walsh (Jezebel Pride) was media liaison for TST-Minnesota before it dissolved in early 2016. She co-founded the Minnesota Left-hand Path Community, which is open to "left-hand path" practitioners of all stripes. The group is currently applying for 501(c)(3) tax-exempt status. Walsh is also developing a left-hand path program for addiction recovery after she attended a twelve-step program where members pressured her to say the Lord's Prayer. Several Satanists I interviewed have discussed the need for such a program. In Walsh's program, participants are free to name any deity, entity, or even themselves as their higher power without being criticized. They are also not required to approach this higher power from a position of submissiveness.[84]

Nikki Moungo was a member of the NC until she was asked to leave in 2017 following a conflict with other Council members. Moungo created her own group called Ordo Sororitatis Satanicae, an explicitly feminist and "cloistered" Satanic group. In 2017, a former member of TST-Detroit became a founding member of Satanhaus, an esoteric group that pursues gnosis through highly transgressive Satanic rituals that sometimes involve bloodletting.[85] Jex Blackmore has continued her work making social commentary through Satanic performance art.

Those who left TST-New York created a new group called LORE: SCNYC— an acronym for League of Rebel Eve: Satanic Collective of New York City.

Their group is explicitly anti-fascist. It is also interested in reimagining religious Satanism by revisiting how Satan was invoked by the Romantics as well as early anarchists such as Mikhail Bakunin and Johannes Holzmann. Members who left TST-Dallas formed a group called the Crossroads Assembly where they could continue the Satanic community they had built in Dallas on their own terms. Former members of TST-New York, Dallas, Los Angeles, Portland, and other areas are also working on a national coalition tentatively called FAUST: The Satanic Federation. This would be national in scope but far less centralized. As it was explained to me, FAUST sounded something like a Satanic version of the National Council of Churches: an ecumenical entity that can engage in collective action while consisting of distinct denominations. Interviewees also expressed that FAUST would also be less explicitly political than TST, focusing more on community, ritual, art, and aesthetics.

I am unaware of TST making any effort to undermine or disparage these new groups. Malcolm Jarry explained, "We are very open about respecting the rights of others to pursue whatever interpretation they believe in and we do not believe we have a monopoly on Satanism."[86] Jon Winningham of TST-Houston stated, "The more official Satanic organizations out there, the better."[87] Everyone I spoke with agreed that TST had started something important. Turing remarked, "TST brought people out of the woodwork who wouldn't have met each other otherwise."[88] When I interviewed Damien Ba'al in July 2018, he was already predicting that TST was going to splinter along philosophical lines. He also predicted that TST will be remembered as a sort of midwife to a new era of organized Satanism. He told me, "If people are looking at it in the future from a sociological and historical perspective, they'll say, 'Oh, that's the organization from which all these progressive groups branched off.'"[89] When Jarry and Greaves first deployed the name "The Satanic Temple" in Florida in 2013, they imagined it would lead to exactly this sort of decentralized blossoming of socially engaged Satanic organizations. It is a great irony that this came to pass only after they created an organized movement with a central authority structure, which other Satanists subsequently rebelled against.

4

The Satanic Reformation

How The Satanic Temple Is Changing the Way We Talk About Satanism

> The Church of Satan is decidedly uninterested in politics and thinks the Satanic Temple is merely one big PR stunt.
> —Magistra Peggy Nadramia, high priestess of the Church of Satan[1]

> The Satanic Temple . . . was as much the cause of a schism within Modern Satanism as it was the result of one.
> —Lucien Greaves[2]

Anton Szandor LaVey was born Howard Stanton Levey in Chicago in 1930. His parents moved to the San Francisco Bay Area when LaVey was a child. After dropping out of Tamalpais High School in Mill Valley, California, LaVey supported himself through his musical talents by playing the organ and calliope in nightclubs and other venues. The Church of Satan (CoS) began in the 1960s as a group of eccentrics and bohemians that met regularly at LaVey's house in San Francisco. He would entertain his guests with lectures on a variety of occult and shocking topics ranging from vampire lore to cannibalism to ESP. This group came to be known as "The Magic Circle." LaVey's lectures became popular enough that he began to hold them every Friday at midnight and opened them to the public, charging $2.50 to attend.[3] The idea to transform the Magic Circle lecture into a formal church appears to have arisen after a newspaper article on LaVey referred to him as "the priest of the devil." According to Nikolas Schreck, a publicity agent named Edward Webber was a regular at a bar where LaVey worked and suggested that he start "some kind of religion" to capitalize on his new-found celebrity.[4]

LaVey described founding the CoS on April 30, 1966. April 30 was significant because it was "Walpurgisnacht," a day associated with witches in Germanic folklore. LaVey declared 1966 to be "Anno Satanas," the first year

Speak of the Devil. Joseph P. Laycock, Oxford University Press (2020). © Oxford University Press.
DOI: 10.1093/oso/9780190948498.001.0001

of the Satanic Age. He painted his San Francisco home black, and it became known as the "Black House." There, he began holding public black masses meant to shock and titillate. LaVey understood that black masses were essentially invented in the imagination of Christians, so in designing his own black mass he borrowed much of the liturgy from Joris-Karl Huysman's novel *Le Bas* (1891). His partner, Blanche Barton, explained, "In Anton's church all the Satanic fantasies became realities."[5]

Writer Arthur Lyons joined the CoS, and in 1970 he published one of the earliest ethnographic accounts of its meetings. Far from the stereotype of Satanists as troubled teenagers, he described meeting doctors, lawyers, engineers, teachers, ex-FBI men, IBM executives, and policemen, as well as street cleaners. Lyons wrote, "Out of eight persons, there were two Ph.D.s and two Ph.D. candidates, one being a prominent sociology professor at a large eastern university."[6] (This was probably a reference to Edward J. Moody, who was also studying the CoS at this time.)

The following year, 1967, LaVey worked with Webber to organize a series of media events to draw media attention to his new church, including a Satanic wedding for a journalist and a New York socialite (which was not legally binding), a Satanic baptism for his daughter Zeena (which was performed three times so that the press could take pictures), and a public Satanic funeral for a sailor who had joined the church.[7] That was also the year that Ira Levin's novel *Rosemary's Baby* became a bestseller. The novel described seemingly normal people who were actually Satanists, and it demonstrated a market for all things Satanic. The film adaptation was already in the works when Peter Mayer, an editor for Avon Books, approached LaVey about writing a book.[8] LaVey used some short mimeographs that had been circulated within the CoS to form the basis of *The Satanic Bible*. To flesh out the work into a book-length document, he borrowed and adapted from other texts. He added Aleister Crowley's version of "The Enochian Keys," a text originally created by the sixteenth-century English magician John Dee. But LaVey altered them to produce a "Satanic" translation.[9] He also borrowed and adapted material from an obscure social Darwinist tract published in 1896 entitled *Might Makes Right or The Survival of the Fittest*. The tract's author "Ragnar Redbeard" was probably Arthur Desmond of New Zealand.[10] This borrowing went undetected until 1986, when it was discovered by former CoS member Michael Aquino. Aquino, who by then had become disillusioned with LaVey and formed his own group called the Temple of Set, wasted no time in denouncing LaVey as a plagiarist.[11]

The CoS peaked sometime between 1970 and 1975. Initially, LaVey seemed excited about forming new chapters known as "grottos." He told his friend, sociologist Marcello Truzzi, that he hoped to have a grotto founded in every state by the end of 1971.[12] In 1972, LaVey ceased holding weekly rituals at the Black House and announced that services were to be held at the local grottos. The Black House was to serve as the new international headquarters of the CoS. (In 1971, Martin Lamers of Holland read *The Satanic Bible*. The following year he opened a grotto in Holland, making the Church of Satan an international movement.) But by 1973, splinter groups had started to form. In September 1974, LaVey announced that all regional organization should cease and that individual members and grottos should report to the Central Grotto with only minimal contact between each other. LaVey called this move "Phase IV" of his "master plan," although it seems unlikely any such master plan existed when the CoS was founded.[13] In 1975, LaVey disbanded the grotto system completely. This meant that, for most members, participation in the CoS meant receiving a newsletter. That year, the Black House was painted beige to reduce unwanted attention.[14] With this move, the CoS came to resemble an "audience cult" rather than a full religion.[15]

Also in 1975, Michael Aquino left to form the Temple of Set and took a large section of the membership with him. LaVey responded that this was merely Phase V of his master plan and claimed Aquino's departure served to rid his church of schismatics and "clean house." Despite this boast, the CoS went into a long, slow decline until LaVey's death in 1997. The CoS refuses to state how many members it has, but most estimates suggest there were never more than a few thousand members, even during its heyday.[16]

The CoS has been quite open in their contempt for TST. As one CoS member put it, "They plagiarize our published doctrine, call themselves 'Satanists,' and spout our philosophies when they see fit, but then shoehorn in their own collectivist, social justice flavored ideas. I can't overstress how *not* affiliated we are with those guys."[17] Several critiques are condensed here including CoS's claim that TST has "plagiarized" LaVey's ideas and CoS's disdain for TST's progressive politics. But especially interesting is the use of scare quotes to imply that TST are not really "Satanists." Seraphina of TST-NYC described having acquaintances in CoS who stopped speaking to her after she joined TST. She also told an anecdote about a Satanic metal band that was thrown into turmoil when one musician joined TST and her bandmate accused her promoting of "fake Satanism."[18]

Fox News's Tucker Carlson also accused TST of "fake Satanism" when he interviewed Lucien Greaves in July 2017. Carlson asserted that TST are neither real Satanists nor a real religion:

> I think what you're doing is taking a Christian symbol—Satan—and using it against Christians. And that's kinda the point. Because you could've chosen sort of anything to name this group, since it's basically new, and ya didn't. You chose the one thing that Christians hate the most.

To which Greaves responded, "Satanism means something to us. It's not an arbitrary label."[19]

Political allies of TST have made a similar implication from a different angle, asking whether the organization would be more effective if they simply stopped calling themselves Satanists. With allies too, Greaves has struggled to articulate exactly why it is important to identify as a Satanist:

> Sometimes it's difficult to explain our motivation to someone who simply can't embrace the term. But it's important to think about the meaning. Using the name of Satan is powerful. It helps you to deconstruct the culture you've grown up in. Once you fully embrace outsider status, the symbol of the ultimate rebel, you begin to see more clearly the kind of hold that religion has on people. And that is an important message all by itself.[20]

In fact, TST has increasingly taken efforts to screen out members who are not "really Satanists" but merely see TST as a convenient vehicle for upsetting Christians. Most chapters require prospective members to undergo multiple interviews and complete questionnaires with questions like, "What does Satanism mean to you?" I asked Amber, a former co-head for TST-Austin, what it *means* for prospective members to show they are really Satanists. She answered, "I need people to identify as a Satanist. That sounds simplistic, but it's [Satanism] a journey."[21]

Meanwhile, almost every TST chapter I spoke with had received emails from people in developing countries in Africa and South Asia offering to make deals selling their souls for worldly riches. Some sought initiation into the Illuminati and thought TST could help them. Several chapters described receiving such messages about once a week. Malcolm Jarry, who handles much of TST's email, estimates he receives about fifteen such messages a day with Malawi and Rwanda being the most common countries of origin.[22]

Lilith Starr of TST-Seattle provided a rather baffling example of an application she received to join her chapter:

> **City or Seattle Neighborhood:** Indai [India]
>
> **Can you attend our meetings regularly? (2nd and 4th Sundays)** Yes
>
> **What does Satanism mean to you?** I like it
>
> **What skills do you have that could benefit us?** I want to become rice [rich]
>
> **What social/political issues are you most passionate about?** I am a Christian pastor
>
> **Tell us what drew you to the Satanic Temple:** I am a poor I wanna to became rich and famous so I want to join[23]

In fact, Lucien Greaves discovered numerous people online who were impersonating him in an attempt to bilk desperate people like this one for "initiation fees."[24]

We have then, accusations of "fake" Satanism, defenses of the meaning of Satanism, mechanisms for detecting sincere Satanism, desperate hopes that TST wields Satanic power over the world, and literal "fakes Satanists" scamming these people—all without an operational definition of what actually constitutes Satanism or makes someone a Satanist. Satanism, it seems, is everywhere and nowhere. David Frankfurter has compared Satanism to "a cultural meme," asking, "Is it really an '-ism' or simply a transient identity, style, or symbolic assemblage?"[25]

I argue that instead of defining Satanism by any particular belief, practice, or ideology, it is better understood as what Benedict Anderson termed "an imagined community."[26] That is, every self-identifying Satanist holds a mental conception of a Satanic tradition with which they feel a sense of connection. Anderson argues that all communities are actually "imagined" in this way; unless a group is so small that each member regularly sees the others face-to-face, conceptual work is needed to feel part of a larger community. However, in the case of Satanism—a tradition that for centuries existed almost *entirely* in people's imaginations—there is a far wider disparity in how individual Satanists understand this shared identity.

For example, Peter Gilmore, high priest of the CoS, declared the film *Willie Wonka and the Chocolate Factory* (1971) to be a "satanic" film.[27] There is nothing objectively Satanic about this adaptation of a children's story, but Gilmore feels the film depicts the Satanic value of justice. There is a certain logic to this assessment: if Christianity emphasizes forgiveness, then a film where misbehaving children are punished could be "Satanic" (Charlie's redemption after stealing a "Fizzy Lifting Drink" notwithstanding). Satanists render such judgments all the time, branding various media as well as political viewpoints and ideologies with no obvious connection to the idea of Satan as being either "Satanic" or "unSatanic." The underlying criteria of what makes something "Satanic" are often unstated and appear to be either ad hoc or subjective. Asbjørn Dyrendal has analyzed online debates between Satanists about what films and music are Satanic. While broader principles are sometimes debated, there is often an attitude of "I term myself a Satanist, therefore what I like is satanic." Sometimes, Satanists simply assert that something is "Satanic for me."[28] But despite the illusive and subjective nature of "the satanic," when Satanic groups experience schisms or feuding, they will invariably appeal to the authority of the imagined community by arguing why their opponents are being "unSatanic."

This is not to say that "Satanism" is a complete conceptual free-for-all, only that the range of what can potentially be regarded as Satanic is extremely wide and fluid. For Satanists, "Satanic" beliefs, ideas, practices, and attitudes are rooted—however tenuously—in the mythological character of Satan, especially the myth of Satan's rebellion against God as told by Milton. Satan lies at the center of a vast web of cultural material that Satanists may draw from, including legends of witchcraft and black masses from early modern Europe; demonological grimoires; the writings of Romantics such as Blake, Shelley, and Byron; the work of Mark Twain and other literary cynics; and classic horror films. The Bible has surprisingly little influence on this milieu, in part because it contains relatively little description of Satan. In addition, many Satanists incorporate deities from outside the Judeo-Christian tradition that are deemed *similar* to Satan in being frightening, evil, liberated from social restraint, or residing in the underworld, including Tiamat, Pan, Loki, Kali, or the invented entities of horror writer H. P. Lovecraft.

What is interesting is not the range of material Satanists may draw from, but what they elect to do with it. Daniel Walker of the Satanic Bay Area said rather pithily, "Since Satan's not *real*, it all depends on which traditions you're drawing from."[29] Sociologist Ann Swidler famously argued that cultures are like "toolkits." All "real cultures," she notes, "contain diverse, often conflicting symbols, rituals, stories, and guides to action."[30] Like other cultures, Satanic culture does not push Satanists in a particular direction; rather, it provides a repertoire of possible actions and approaches that Satanists may draw from.

Significantly for understanding TST, Swidler notes that people tend to be more deliberate about how they examine this cultural tool kit during "unsettled times" when taken-for-granted modes of action are called into question or no longer seem to be working. She writes, "Bursts of ideological activism occur in periods when competing ways of organizing action are developing or contending for dominance."[31]

In 2014, Greg Stevens, who would go on to become a member of TST's National Council, wrote an article comparing the tension between TST and CoS to the Protestant Reformation, noting that CoS's claim that members of TST are not "real Satanists" echoes Protestant claims that Catholics are not "real Christians."[32] Later Greaves described TST as instigating a "Satanic Reformation."[33] In Swidler's terms, these are unsettled times within the short history of religious Satanism. Long-held assumptions about Satanism are being renegotiated, and now Satanists are vigorously rummaging through their cultural toolkits, forging new possibilities of what Satanism could be.

One likely outcome of this Satanic Reformation is that the taken-for-granted status of a particular mode of Satanism—one heavily influenced by LaVey with strong affinities for social Darwinism, isolationism, and misanthropy—will weaken. In its place, a new mode of Satanism that draws more from Romantic depictions of Satan than LaVey and emphasizes progressive, prosocial values will gain traction, becoming more normative if not the norm. This shift has likely been a long time coming. Consider this assessment of Satanism from Gilmore's essay "Satanism: The Feared Religion":

> Let us instead look at contemporary Satanism for what it really is: a brutal religion of elitism and social Darwinism that seeks to re-establish the reign of the able over the idiotic, of swift justice over injustice, and for a wholesale rejection of egalitarianism as a myth that has crippled the advancement of the human species for the last two thousand years.[34]

When Gilmore first wrote this essay in 1992, LaVey was still alive and no one had much of a platform to challenge this characterization of what Satanism "really is." However, we know that self-described Satanists have never been quite as saturated with these elitist values as Gilmore suggests. In his "Satan Surveys," James R. Lewis found that few Satanists identified as politically conservative. Not only did Satanists tend to lean left on issues of individual liberty, such as abortion and LGBT rights, many Satanists also supported social welfare and expressed that the government should help fund childcare, healthcare, higher education, and unemployment benefits. Lewis concludes, "In sum, this sample consisted mostly of people that conservative American politicians would label 'Socialists' . . . It also stands in sharp contrast with the social Darwinism advocated by LaVey."[35]

As progressive Satanists turn to their cultural toolkits, they have increasingly been looking past LaVey and are rediscovering older sources of Satanic culture more in line with their values. Much as the Protestants invoked scriptural authority to challenge clerical authority, a new wave of progressive Satanists are turning to ideas of Satan from nineteenth-century Romantics, anarchists, and proto-feminists to justify their values as "authentically" Satanic. In some ways the new progressive Satanism is a return to an older mode of appreciation for Satan as a mythic character. Ruben van Luijk suggests that LaVey repositioned Satanic culture to the political right, noting that, "Sympathy for the devil had up to then been predominantly a Left-wing affair."[36]

Reformation and Counter-Reformation

CoS has framed their grievance with TST in legalistic rather than heresiological terms, claiming that TST has engaged in plagiarism and "theft" of everything that LaVey built. A CoS document called "The Satanic Temple Fact Sheet" concedes the alleged plagiarism is not legally actionable, but claims it is nevertheless damaging:

> TST uses imagery and language obviously inspired by well-documented Church of Satan publications and trademarks, that are different enough to avoid legal issue but similar enough to cause public confusion. Indeed, The Satanic Temple is often referenced by the media as the Church of Satan, and there is evidence of people joining The Satanic Temple thinking they have joined the Church of Satan. . . . Occam's razor would suggest this is not unintentional.[37]

TST counters that "The Satanic Temple Fact Sheet" is inaccurate and, more importantly, engages in "doxxing"—a term used to describe the dissemination of private information online as a form of harassment. The fact sheet attempts to identify Malcolm Jarry and Lucien Greaves and contains addresses and other private information.

CoS has also claimed that TST does not understand LaVey's philosophy and is therefore not real Satanism. Their position is that Satanic organizations should not take political stances because this impairs the political freedom of individual Satanists. The CoS supports the separation of church and state, but it regards TST's attempts to erect Baphomet and other Satanic monuments on government property as a violation of this principle rather than an attempt to protect it. Gilmore writes, "So, like LaVey before me, I think that keeping our precious symbols in our own spaces is another aspect of the elitism which plays a role in our philosophy."[38]

At least some of CoS's hostility is owed to the fact that there *has* been public confusion between these groups. Numerous articles have wrongly attributed TST activities and campaigns to CoS. (However, Occam's razor suggests this is sloppy journalism, not an intentional effort by TST to undermine CoS.) Additionally, some observers of this feud have suggested that CoS is jealous of all the publicity that TST has received and anxious to preserve the legacy of Anton LaVey as the founder of "authentic" Satanism. Zach Black, a former member of the CoS and founder of a social media site called the Satanic International Network, told *The Village Voice*, "I do believe the Satanic Temple is going to replace the Church of Satan, and that's why they're acting threatened. The church—they're just getting fat and old."[39]

Like some of TST's other opponents, CoS also takes the position that TST is not a real religion at all but merely a "prank" and points to the 2012 Rick Scott rally to make this argument. (This argument is analyzed further in chapter 5). In some cases, CoS has attempted to undermine TST's free exercise cases by coaching defendants in arguing that TST does not have sincerely held beliefs. In 2017, while TST was engaged in a lawsuit claiming the state of Missouri's restrictions on abortions violated the sincerely held beliefs of Satanists, CoS wrote an article on the lawsuit declaring, "A little bit of research makes it clear that The Satanic Temple is self-acknowledged satire and an activist group, which pretends to be a religion when it suits their ends. . . . The supposedly 'sincerely held beliefs' of TST adherents are scanty, nebulous, and contradictory."[40]

In some cases, CoS formed unlikely alliances with TST's opponents. The CoS official Twitter account "tweeted" at Missouri's attorney general Josh Hawley, a defendant in the lawsuit, to inform him that TST is "fake" and has no sincerely held beliefs. They also sent a link to "The Satanic Temple Fact Sheet." A similar tweet was sent to a reporter from the conservative news site *The Daily*

Caller.[41] In 2018, when TST sued the state of Arkansas over the proposal to erect TST's Baphomet monument at the state capitol, attorneys for Secretary of State Mark Martin submitted documents to the court arguing that TST was a satirical group and "beneath the dignity of the court." State attorneys cited Peter Gilmore and "The Satanic Temple Fact Sheet." Moreover, their case seemed to rely almost exclusively on sources that had been collected by CoS. Their argument was ultimately rejected by the federal district court in Arkansas.

LaVey's Legacy

Even if TST did not "plagiarize" CoS, Van Luijk asserts, "Genealogically speaking, every known Satanist group or organization in the world today derives directly or indirectly from LaVey's 1966 Church of Satan, even if they are dismissive of LaVey or choose to emphasize other real or alleged forerunners of Satanism."[42] If this is true, what exactly is the connection between LaVey and TST? And is TST building on LaVey's vision of Satanism, perverting it, or actively erasing it?

"The Panic Room" at TST's headquarters in Salem, Massachusetts, has a library with several shelves of books on Satanism, Satanic panic, and related subjects. Conspicuously, there is not a single book by LaVey. On one of my visits to the headquarters, I commented out loud on this fact. Felix Fortunado of TST-Dallas, who happened to be with me, responded, "LaVey was a fraud, but without him we wouldn't all be sitting here."[43]

When I asked TST members about LaVey, only a few had never read LaVey's *The Satanic Bible* (1969). Most had read it as a teenager. Since *The Satanic Bible* hit bookstores in January 1970, it is estimated to have sold over 700,000 copies. It has also been translated into Czech, Swedish, and German, and there are known to be illegal editions published in Mexico and Russia.[44] Based on survey data, Lewis concluded that despite criticisms from some Satanists, *The Satanic Bible* remains "the single most important document shaping the contemporary Satanist movement."[45]

Of course, many people who purchased *The Satanic Bible* never read it. Joshua Gunn argues that the book's distinctive cover has become a "fetishized image."[46] It often functioned as a sort of prop, used by adolescents to signal their transgressive status and by evangelicals to signal their knowledge of a dangerous Satanic underworld.

Many TST members found *The Satanic Bible* distasteful. Seraphina described attempting to read *The Satanic Bible* in college and having to stop because she found it "so offensively dumb."[47] As an English major, she objected to LaVey's writing style more than anything else. These interviewees also objected to LaVey's misogyny, his advocacy of social Darwinism and occasionally eugenics, and his sympathies with Ayn Rand. Some TST members also objected that while CoS claims to be atheistic, LaVey still promoted ideas of mysterious forces that can be harnessed through magical rituals.

Other interviewees, however, found at least some of LaVey's writing enjoyable. Some spoke highly of his ideas of ritual as "psychodrama," his fierce individuality, and his courage in publicly proclaiming the values of Satanism in 1966. Jon Winningham, a chapter head for TST-Houston said, "I liked how arrogant LaVey was. Something about his attitude really fired me up." Some interviewees also expressed that while it was fine to disagree with LaVey, TST members with no knowledge of LaVey were probably not serious about Satanism and only interested in political activism. TST-Houston's book club read *The Satanic Bible* along with Romantic literature and works by contemporary Satanists. Winningham said it was important to read LaVey because "people who don't know the roots annoy the shit out of me."[48] However, even TST members who liked LaVey expressed negative attitudes about CoS, often describing them as "fundamentalists" or "arrogant." A few had tried to become involved with CoS but found that there was not much opportunity for involvement other than paying $225 for an official membership card. Greaves has claimed that the CoS now consists largely of a very active Twitter account.[49]

LaVey certainly paved the way for TST by preparing the world for the *idea* of a global, organized Satanic religion, and many who bought *The Satanic Bible* as teenagers, whether they liked it or not, went on to become involved with TST. But the CoS's inability to satisfy the market LaVey created equally contributed to TST's rise. TST grew so rapidly because there was already a sizable population of "unchurched" Satanists, who were sympathetic to Satanism but either could not participate meaningfully in the CoS or disliked its elitism. Many interviewees described feelings of relief upon reading TST's Seven Tenets. Mara Gorgo, co-head of TST-Indiana said, "When I read the tenets it felt right. I'm a *good person* and I want to do good things and I'm still a Satanist."[50]

(Re)Interpreting LaVey

Since TST never claimed to honor the teachings of LaVey, the charge that it has distorted his ideas is somewhat moot. Nevertheless, it is an interesting question for the genealogy of religious Satanism whether LaVey would have approved of TST. Greaves claimed to have met people who knew LaVey and who said that he would have appreciated TST's political activities.[51] In fact, the argument has been made that CoS members are really the ones who betrayed LaVey's legacy. Brian Werner is a Satanist and singer for the heavy metal band Vital Remains. He was briefly a prominent member of TST before he decided the group's politics had become too progressive. In a 2014 interview he declared, "The Church of Satan does nothing. Their complete inactivity has just caused such an overwhelming amount of complacent consent, not only in the masses but within our own freethinking subculture. The inactivity has led to the complete degradation of everything we built for 40 years under LaVey."[52]

So, which is it? Did TST come to destroy LaVey's law or to fulfill it? One reason this question is so hard to answer is that LaVey was not a systemic thinker. Joshua Gunn noted, "LaVey's genius resides in his ability to package and market Satanism, not necessarily in his articulation of Satanic philosophy"[53] LaVey's writings seem riddled with ad hoc assertions and provocations such that "LaVeyan philosophy" is plagued by contradictions. Journalist and honorary CoS priest Gavin Baddeley described CoS as "a bizarre beast, sustained by a web of conflicting values and concepts. It is an anti-spiritual religion; a totalitarian doctrine of freedom; a cynical romanticism; a profoundly honest scam; a love of life garbed in the symbols of death and fear."[54]

LaVey also openly admitted that he liked to deceive people and con "rubes." His writing has a tendency to flatter the reader for being smarter than "the masses."[55] Readers were free to ignore contradictions, find them profound, or congratulate themselves for noticing them. Deciphering them was unimportant until Satanists began debating concrete strategies of action. It should be noted that paradoxes are not necessarily a liability for the success of a religion and can actually function as a resource for believers who either wrestle with or celebrate such contradictions.[56]

It does not seem that LaVey felt Satanic organizations should be apolitical or refrain from collective action. Arthur Lyons describes a mimeographed handout entitled "Preparatory Course for Witches and Warlocks" that predates *The Satanic Bible* in which LaVey wrote, "Only by working side by side with the Establishment can we create any sizable change in our society. Satanism is the only religion in which a person can 'turn on' to the pleasures around him without 'dropping out' of society."[57] Elsewhere, LaVey was quoted, "Not only will we become a major voting block and economic demographic to be catered to, but we've worked ourselves into places where we pull the strings ourselves."[58]

Rather, it seems that LaVey's political vision was countered by his even stronger impulse toward isolationism. He famously converted the basement of his home in San Francisco into his "den of iniquity," which he designed to look like a seedy bar from 1944. A variety of mannequins were on display dressed in period clothes.[59] One is left with the impression that LaVey would have liked for CoS to change society *in theory*, but that in practice he preferred the solitude of his basement.

LaVey's contradictory message on political engagement is evident in his 1988 essay "Pentagonal Revisionism," that featured five goals for CoS. The expressed purpose of these goals was to move away from defending Satanism against accusations of criminal behavior made during the Satanic Panic and instead to "effect significant changes." These goals were:

1) Stratification, defined as a rejection of egalitarianism in favor of meritocracy.
2) The strict taxation of all churches.
3) No tolerance for religious beliefs secularized and incorporated into law and order issues.
4) The development and production of artificial human companions.
5) The opportunity for everyone to live within a "total environment" of his or her choice.[60]

Goal three is key to TST's platform and, for a time, TST shared CoS's attitude that churches should pay taxes (TST's tax-exempt status is discussed further in chapter 5.) Note, however, that the first three of these goals would require substantial political and social engagement to achieve, while the last two advocate finding new ways for Satanists to retreat from society. A "total environment" refers to LaVey's desire for spaces like his den of iniquity in which an individual can screen out the world and pretend to live in a time and place of her preference. The total environment was inspired in part by Disneyland, which LaVey loved. In a 2012 interview, LaVey's estranged daughter Zeena said of her father, "He lived in a dream world where absolutely nothing to do with social issues was of any importance."[61]

Lewis also suggests LaVey was driven by contradictory desires, noting that he "was not up to making the necessary personal sacrifices that being a founding prophet and leader required because his pecuniary and self-aggrandizing motives for forming CoS were so shallow."[62] The CoS leadership resolved this contradiction by claiming that CoS was never intended to be a socially engaged organization but rather an exclusive club for "the alien elite." It is telling that in the early days of the CoS, recruitment posters could be seen around San Francisco that showed LaVey in devil horns before a nude woman serving as an altar with the words "Satan Wants You!," a parody of the army recruitment slogan.[63] Today, CoS no longer actively recruits, and the army slogan has been replaced with that of the marines: "We're looking for a few good men."

Members of TST and allied Satanic groups have begun to pick apart LaVey's contradictions. This is partly a matter of necessity for anyone seeking a coherent philosophy of Satanism, although polemical exchanges with CoS have accelerated this process. In an essay contrasting CoS with TST, Greaves writes, "For having assigned themselves the role of defining and defending Satanism publicly, the Church of Satan seems very unclear regarding what their Satanism actually means."[64]

Of all the paradoxes stemming from LaVey, the one most vexing for TST members is that which Baddeley called "a totalitarian doctrine of freedom." LaVey encouraged emulating Satan by challenging authority, but he also expressed contempt for the idea of egalitarianism in favor of social stratification where the powerful are allowed to rule over their inferiors. In one interview, he stated, "I'm all for a police state; no messing around. There should be an armed guard on every street corner. The Israelis have the right idea: school bus drivers and MacDonald's managers carrying Uzis."[65] Provocations like this served to build LaVey's mystique, but as a practical matter, this paradox must be resolved before there can be any Satanic political agenda: Is the "Satanic" thing to do to resist arbitrary power or to side with it? The answer depends on what is taken from the Satanic toolkit and whether one is emulating Satan as rebel portrayed by Milton or Satan as God's agent of punishment and the temporary ruler of a profaned world.

For progressive Satanists, one must choose a side, and the "Satanic" thing to do is challenge power, not fetishize it. Daniel Walker critiqued CoS's position: " 'We believe might is right, so we emulate the less powerful character in this story.' What the fuck sense does that make? And there's no getting around this; Satan's martial failure and exile is fundamental to his story, in the same way that Jesus' martyrdom is indispensable to his."[66]

There has also been a move to disentangle these paradoxes by interpreting LaVey in light of his historical moment. 1966, the year he founded CoS, was also the year that *Time* magazine ran its famous cover asking, "Is God Dead?" (Theologian Thomas Altizer, whose ideas the cover was based on, was interviewed by Malcolm Jarry for a film project a few years before his death in 2018.)[67] Many Americans in the 1960s had subscribed to the so-called secularization narrative that predicted the imminent demise of religion. In fact, LaVey seemed concerned that blasphemy was becoming irrelevant with no Christian institutions worth rebelling against.[68] He explained that he was moving on from black masses, which were designed to rebel against the medieval church, and adapting them to challenge more contemporary social forces. LaVey stated, "A modern day form [of the black mass] might consist of such things as urinating on marijuana, crushing an LSD sugar cube underfoot, hanging a picture of Timothy Leary or a famous Indian guru upside down, or exposing the parallel between the hippie generation and 'The Emperor's New Clothes.' "[69]

Decades later, during the Satanic Panic of the 1980s, LaVey did direct his wrath toward the Christian establishment. In an essay entitled "To: All Doomsayers, Head-Shakers, Hand Wringers, Worrywarts, Satanophobes, Identity Christers, Survivor Counselors, Academia Nuts, & Assorted Tremblers" LaVey blasted the Christian right as hypocrites and claimed that they were responsible for driving adolescents toward Satanism.[70] Baddeley frames this shift in Freudian terms: "In a perverse way, LaVey's Satanic group was the progeny of the 1960s revolution. In a fit of oedipal fury the Church of Satan was butchering the father it loathed, the hippie movement, before turning to fuck its mother, the conservative establishment."[71] We cannot know what LaVey would have thought of the administrations of George W. Bush and Donald Trump, both backed by a strong evangelical base, but it seems likely he would have had the same contempt for them that Malcolm Jarry and Lucien Greaves do.

LaVey's endorsement of social Darwinism and "law and order" politics—the greatest shibboleth between TST and CoS—may also be a product of his historical moment. LaVey was a contrarian and his misanthropic statements can be read as a reaction to the counterculture of the 1960s. He later wrote of this period:

I considered the 60's and 70's a barren, aesthetically destructive era. America, especially in San Francisco, was a mire of ignorance, stupidity, and egalitarianism. I created my own world—the Church of Satan. That's the only way I could survive. It turned out to be a real cudgel on the head of mainstream society at the time. Without us there would have been no counterculture. All the Ken Keseys and Timothy Learys did was attach great importance to the worthless.[72]

The 1960s was also a period of rising crime rates. Greaves has suggested that LaVey's conservative attitudes on law enforcement and punishment might have been different had he been writing today when crime rates have been steadily falling.[73]

Greaves has suggested that LaVey was primarily using social Darwinism as a prop to appear "sinister" without advocating positions that were illegal or logically indefensible. Furthermore, he suggests that while LaVey presented this position as "rational," its alleged scientific basis has been increasingly debunked by the findings of evolutionary biology, which suggests that human feelings of altruism are adaptive and contribute to our survival as a species. Finally, Greaves argues that an inherent principle in LaVey's writing is that Satanists should follow the best available evidence. Therefore, if modern Satanists have better scientific evidence about the function of altruism, by LaVey's own reasoning, their philosophy should adapt accordingly.[74]

TST's website maintains an annotated bibliography where visitors can find works on Satanism, the history of moral panics, and other topics germane to TST's mission. At the top of the list, a subsection labeled "Primary Reading" contains only two titles: *The Revolt of the Angels* (1914) by Anatole France and *The Better Angels of Our Nature: Why Violence Has Declined* (2011) by cognitive psychologist Steven Pinker. Pinker argues that there is evidence violence is declining worldwide due to Enlightenment values of democracy and tolerance. TST gives Pinker's book the following gloss in its bibliography:

While not a book about Satanism specifically, this book is nonetheless indispensable to understanding the intellectual roots of the Satanic Reformation exemplified by The Satanic Temple, as it outlines the scientific refutations of crass calls to and Police State policies and counter-productive misinterpretations of Darwinism that have plagued Satanic circles through decades of inaction and unfocused ineptitude.[75]

In other words, Pinker's more recent, scientific perspective is a necessary corrective for LaVey's legacy of social Darwinism.

Kinder, Gentler Satanism

Lilith Starr is the chapter head of TST-Seattle and the author of *The Happy Satanist: Finding Self-Empowerment*. In an interview, she stated, "I see Satanism as a whole really changing really quickly. We're based on Romantic ideas instead of LaVey's work. More people are recognizing Satan through that lens."[76] To be sure, there exist forms of Satanism such as the Order of Nine Angles that regard themselves as more extreme than LaVey, advocating criminal behavior and even murder.[77] But the momentum within Satanism as a whole, as Starr points out, is toward a new mode of Satanism that emphasizes egalitarianism rather than social stratification and draws on older sources to justify these positions as Satanic.

At a public black mass hosted by TST-Los Angeles, black comedian and political candidate Steve Hill stated, "To invoke Satan is to invoke the struggle for justice and equal rights for everyone."[78] This is hardly a LaVeyan conception of Satanism. Bel Citoyen, who left TST-Los Angeles in 2018, also felt that Satanism is fundamentally about striving for equality. Having grown up in a black evangelical household, he cited Isaiah 14:13–15 to explain his philosophy of Satanism. This passage ridicules someone called "the morning star" who has fallen from heaven:

> You said in your heart
> "I will ascend to heaven
> I will raise my throne above the stars of God
> I will sit enthroned on the mount of assembly, on the utmost heights of the sacred mountain.
> I will ascend above the tops of the clouds
> I will make myself like the Most High."

Bible scholars generally believe "the morning star" originally referred to a king of Babylon or Assyria or possibly a figure from Canaanite mythology and was later interpreted as referring to Satan.[79] Christian sermons about Satan sometimes describe this passage as "the five 'I wills.'" For Citoyen, however, the five "I wills" represent speaking truth to power and demanding equality; the morning star does not express a desire to overthrow God but to be God's equal and become "like the Most High."[80]

As TST members are aware, these sympathetic readings of the fall of Satan have a long pedigree. English scholar Peter Schock has described how the Enlightenment "killed" Satan, leaving the Romantics free to resurrect him for their own purposes. Skeptics such as Voltaire and Charles Dupuis claimed that Satan was a figure borrowed from Eastern mythology and then folded into Christian tradition. Such arguments threatened to erase the assumed distinction between Christianity and "primitive" religions. In response, some theologians began to jettison Satan from Christian tradition in the hopes of fending off the skeptics. Theologian Joseph Priestley claimed the biblical Satan was merely an allegory for wicked people and that the idea of a literal Satan was only a "priestly imposition."[81]

As theologians deserted Satan, the character became more amenable to new interpretations. Milton's *Paradise Lost* (1667) had already introduced the idea of Satan as a rebel who possessed noble qualities. By the end of the eighteenth century, this more sympathetic reading of Satan had become entangled with anti-clerical and anti-monarchist sentiments. Political philosopher William Godwin built on Milton in *Inquiry Concerning Political Justice* (1793), pointing out that Satan rebelled because he was motivated by reason and justice rather than deference to brute force. That same year William Blake completed *The Marriage of Heaven and Hell*, which reimagined hell as a needed antidote to the sterile authority of heaven.

The Romantic poets of the early nineteenth century perfected the image of Satan as a tragic rebel. In 1821, Shelley argued in "A Defense of Poetry" that Milton's Satan is morally superior to God because Satan perseveres while God, whose victory can never be in doubt, insists on tormenting his defeated adversary further.[82] That same year, Byron published his play *Cain*. Byron's Cain is a Romantic rebel who, after being enlightened by Lucifer, refuses to praise God. Cain argues that a God who would condemn all humans to death for the sins of Adam and Eve is unjust and unworthy of worship. Also in 1821, Shelley's former mentor, poet laureate Robert Southey, took aim at both Shelley and Byron in "A Vision of Judgment," writing, "The School which they have set up may properly be called the Satanic School; for though their productions breathe the spirit of Belial in their lascivious parts, and the spirit of Moloch in those loathsome images of atrocities and horrors which they delight to represent, they are more especially characterized by a Satanic spirit of pride and audacious impiety, which still betrays the wretched feeling of hopelessness wherewith it is allied." Van Luijk calls Southey's passage, "the official birth certificate of the Satanic School of Poetry."[83]

As reformers of Satanism, TST has increasingly made the Romantics a cornerstone of how Satanism should be understood. There were originally plans for the Baphomet statue to tribute the Satanic school of poetry by having quotations from Byron's *Caine* and Blake's *The Marriage of Heaven and Hell* on its base. The annotated bibliography on TST's website contains links to the works of Milton, Byron, Shelley, Baudelaire, and Huysmans. The text that tops the list is *The Revolt of the Angels*. This is a satirical novel about a second war in heaven in which the angels again rebel against God, who is named Ialdabaoth—a reference to Gnostic myth. This time, Satan has the weapons to succeed, but he realizes that if he replaces God, he will become just another corrupt tyrant. On the eve of battle, Satan tells his army:

> No—we will not conquer the heavens. Enough to have the power. War engenders wars, and victory defeat.
>
> God conquered, will become Satan; Satan, conquering, will become God. May the fates spare me this terrible lot.[84]

Instead of open warfare, Satan urges his followers to battle the Ialdabaoth within themselves. In France's version of the Satan myth, the rejection of religious authority is balanced with tolerance and a command to check one's own hubris. Greaves read this novel while visiting Rome, and it has become the closest thing TST has to a sacred text. When I attended a meeting of TST-San Marcos, a copy was passed around and everyone discussed how much of it they had read.

The chapters that became independent from TST in 2018 are continuing this project of re-examining the cultural toolkit of Satanism to produce new paradigms of what Satanic religion could look like. Interviewees from League of Rebel Eve: Satanic Collective of New York City (LORE:SNYC) have expressed their interest in re-assessing the aesthetics of Satanism. While they plan to continue using dark and blasphemous images, they have discussed what it would mean to consider Promethean science-fiction tales such as Mary Shelley's *Frankenstein* or even *Bladerunner*—a film adaptation of Philip K. Dick's *Do Androids Dream of Electric Sheep*—as part of the Satanic tradition. Could lasers and other science-fiction tropes have a place in Satanic aesthetics? They have also noted that Satanic politics should rediscover what Satan meant to early anarchists such as Mikhail Bakunin.[85]

The Crossroads Assembly, led by former members of TST-Dallas, continues to experiment with Satanic ritual and liturgy. They have incorporated holidays such as the Wiccan "wheel of the year," which celebrates the solstices and equinoxes, and Mardi Gras into their Satanic celebrations. They have also looked at bringing mythologies and characters from beyond the Judeo-Christian tradition into their traditions. Much as the Protestant Reformation led to an explosion of new doctrines and denominations, the emergence of TST has created "unsettled times" for Satanism, and this reassessment of the tradition has brought efflorescence of new Satanic cultural forms.

Meanwhile, the public is gradually being introduced to the idea of socially engaged Satanists who take on charitable projects and preach compassion in the name of Satan. For some Satanists, this move threatens to ruin Satanism by depriving it of the sinister and transgressive elements that made it appealing in the first place. When Brian Werner departed TST in 2014, he posted a resignation speech on YouTube.com in which he declared with disgust, "It's [TST] become a very liberal, compassionate, borderline hippie-like outlook on politics and societal issues."[86] However, for TST's conservative Christian opponents, this re-imagining of what Satanism means is actually the most dangerous aspect of the movement because it threatens to disrupt their entire moral cosmos. In an interview with *The Daily Caller* about TST, Robert Ritchie, director of America Needs Fatima, stated, "The best way that Satan can accomplish his mission of luring souls into damnation is to erode the horror, the natural horror, that men have of the devil."[87] At least from Ritchie's perspective, the Satanic reformers are furthering the devil's work better than LaVey ever did.

5

Religion or Trolls?

How The Satanic Temple Is Changing the Way We Talk About Religion

> When you talk about religion—believe in it, promote it, explain it, condemn it, historicize it—you are making religion up. You are giving weight and shape to it in the world. But religion is also making you up. For whatever *it* is, the questions that made *it* manifest in the world have already contributed to *your* making.
>
> —John Lardas Modern[1]

> The more ritual we do, the more legitimacy we have.
>
> —Stu de Haan, TST attorney and National Council member[2]

When Anton LaVey formed the CoS in 1966, many questioned the morality of Satanism, but almost everyone took for granted that it was a religion.[3] TST is also a non-theistic Satanic group, but its claim to be a religion has been met with intense scrutiny. The reason for this discrepancy seems obvious: whereas CoS does not seek the tax-exempt status entitled to churches, TST has publicly demanded some of the same freedoms, protections, and legal exemptions afforded to other religions, especially Christianity. In response, their opponents have presented various arguments asserting that TST is not a religion, but *something else* that simply camouflages itself as religion. The most common such accusation is that TST are actually "trolls." "Troll" is a rhetorical label derived from Internet communication, referring to people who enter a discussion with the goal of deliberately upsetting people or creating fruitless argument rather than expressing a valid viewpoint.[4] Implicit in the argument that TST are "trolls, not a religion" is a claim about the nature of "religion" as a discrete discourse that is hermetically sealed from both politics and satire.

Speak of the Devil. Joseph P. Laycock, Oxford University Press (2020). © Oxford University Press.
DOI: 10.1093/oso/9780190948498.001.0001

Discourse about "religion," and its distinction from adjacent concepts such as "philosophy," "cult," or "troll," is always an exercise in power. Paraphrasing Foucault, religion scholar Russell McCutcheon notes, "Practical interests motivate the act of distinguishing a 'this' from a 'that.'"[5] The First Amendment incentivizes inventive distinctions between religion and not-religion. The establishment clause incentivizes groups to label their opponents' worldviews as religion in order to banish them from government institutions. For example, some evangelicals have claimed it is unconstitutional to allow Harry Potter books in public school libraries because the novels are a religious text. Conversely, the establishment clause incentivizes framing one's own tradition as something *other* than religion, for example, by claiming a Ten Commandments monument commemorates history. In different contexts, the free exercise clause creates an incentive to frame one's own views as religious, and hence, constitutionally protected, while claiming that opposing traditions are in fact not religions. For example, some evangelicals who claim Harry Potter *is* a religion also claim that Islam is *not* a religion and therefore that Muslims are not entitled to religious freedom.

McCutcheon suggests that these sorts of power plays are not an accident but actually a feature of the category of "religion," writing, "it's [religion's] utility is linked to its inability to be defined."[6] From this perspective, the function of the religion label is to present things sometimes as one thing and sometimes as another, all while making this distinction seem uniquely real. Furthermore, the political utility of granting or denying something's status as "religious" is commensurate with the public's inability to notice how these dynamics operate.

This dynamic is exactly why I find TST's various campaigns and provocations to be significant. Most Americans have never thought about the problem of defining religion or the constitutional consequences such a definition might have. When Stephen Prothero quizzed undergraduates at Boston University, only one in six knew both religion clauses of the First Amendment.[7] By demanding religious rights for non-theistic Satanists—and doing so in court where their arguments must be taken more seriously—TST forces us to consider what "religion" means for a country that promises religious freedom.

Probably the last new religious movement that elicited this level of public debate about these questions was the Church of Scientology, with popular books, documentaries, and even a television series questioning the organization's religious status. Even though Scientologists hold supernatural beliefs, including the existence of immortal spirits called *thetans*, opponents have accused this group of being "a simulacrum of a religion," meaning that it consciously mimics the outward trappings of a religion to obtain legal benefits and protections.[8] By contrast, TST has drawn controversy not because they have conformed to popular criteria about what a religion *ought* to look like, but rather because they have openly challenged these criteria— especially the idea that religion is fundamentally about supernaturalism. When I first asked Lucien Greaves about his sincerity in 2014, he answered, "If I were a fake, I would just claim a theistic belief in Satan."[9]

By admitting that their beliefs are not supernatural, yet claiming they are still worthy of constitutional protection, TST is really demanding a much larger conversation: *Why* do we claim to believe in religious freedom? Why are *some* traditions and viewpoints so precious that they need special legal protection, while other traditions and viewpoints do not? And by what criteria do we make these distinctions? Furthermore, the attitudes and identities of TST members have been shaped by raising these questions. The process of challenging popular assumptions about religion and religious freedom has directly contributed to TST's development and understanding of itself as a religious movement.

"Satanists Troll *Hobby Lobby*"

The best example of TST inserting itself into the discourse of religious freedom is a series of lawsuits they filed against the governor and attorney general of Missouri. In April 2015, "Mary Doe," a twenty-two-year-old from Greene County in southwest Missouri, was seeking an abortion. Missouri had only one abortion provider, a Planned Parenthood center located hundreds of miles away from Mary in St. Louis. Missouri law requires that women review an "informed consent booklet" from the department of health, be given the opportunity to view an ultrasound image of their fetus, listen to the fetus's heartbeat if it has one, and then undergo a 72-hour waiting period before returning to receive an abortion. Mary was already a single mother. She worked part time assisting a mechanic and could not afford to make two separate trips to St. Louis. A friend put her in touch with TST-St. Louis, and Damien Ba'al, who was serving as chapter head, created a crowd-funding page that raised the $800 needed for her travel and lodging. Local chapter members met Doe at the bus station and drove her to a hotel. Satanists babysat her child while she visited Planned Parenthood and escorted her in case there were aggressive protestors.[10] As it turned out, TST's national leaders had been waiting for a case like Mary's since 2014.

Malcolm Jarry had been speaking with attorney James MacNaughton about the Protect Children Project, which involved a religious exemption to corporal punishment, when the conversation turned to abortion. Many states have "informed consent" laws that require women seeking abortions to review state-issued brochures. Critics of this material say the brochures often contain inaccurate information, such as claiming there is a proven link between abortions and breast cancer, and that they attempt to manipulate the principle of informed consent.[11] Could a letter also demand a religious exemption from informed consent laws that restrict access to abortion? MacNaughton, who is a Presbyterian elder, was intrigued by this idea. Although *Roe v. Wade* was framed as a case about a woman's right to privacy, he had long regarded it as a religious freedom case because he viewed the question of when human life begins as a fundamentally religious one. As such, he was offended that the government presumed to determine this question for other people. He pointed out that in Talmudic law, a fetus becomes a person (*nefesh*) after "the greater part" of its body has been born.[12] Thomas Aquinas, drawing on Aristotle's observations about quickening, concluded that a male fetus gains a rational soul forty days after conception and a female soul ninety days after conception.[13] To determine when human life begins, we must answer what exactly distinguishes a *person*. "The answer," Naughton explained, "rests in the hearts and minds of the people involved in the process."[14]

On June 30, 2014, the Supreme Court decided *Burwell v. Hobby Lobby*, which ruled that closely held corporations may claim a religious exemption from laws that burden the owner's religious beliefs. The Greens, an evangelical Christian family that owns Hobby Lobby, claimed that their religious freedom was burdened by the employer mandate of the Affordable Care Act, which required them to provide employees with healthcare that includes access to FDA-approved forms of contraception. Specifically, the Greens asserted a religious belief that life begins at conception and therefore that certain emergency contraception drugs and intrauterine devices, which they believed prevent fertilized eggs from attaching to the uterine wall, are abortifacients. In essence, they argued the government was forcing them either to facilitate abortions or pay a fine.[15] In a 5-4 decision, the Supreme Court ruled that the employer mandate violated the federal Religious

Freedom Restoration Act and that Hobby Lobby could be accommodated by having their employees receive coverage through a separate fund for certain the forms of contraception that the Greens objected to.

Hobby Lobby was based on the Religious Freedom Restoration Act (RFRA) of 1993, which specifies that the government cannot burden the free exercise of religion without a compelling interest, and that even then, the state's interest must be achieved in the least restrictive way possible. In 1997, the Supreme Court ruled that RFRA is applicable only to the federal laws. In response, many states, including Missouri, created their own RFRA laws.

TST members were alarmed by the *Hobby Lobby* decision, which they saw not as a victory for religious freedom but as a case of conservative Christians restricting other people's access to healthcare. They were especially upset by how the Court treated the Greens' belief that certain forms of birth control are abortifacients. An amicus brief filed by the American College of Obstetricians and Gynecologists, Physicians for Reproductive Health, the American Academy of Pediatrics, and the American Nurses Association wrote that none of the FDA-approved forms of contraception cause abortion.[16] However, in the majority opinion, Samuel Alito wrote, "It is not for the Court to say that the religious beliefs of the plaintiffs are mistaken or unreasonable" only that they are "an honest conviction."[17] TST felt the Court had privileged subjective religious beliefs about medicine over objective scientific facts. For Jarry and MacNaughton, however, this was exactly what made the *Hobby Lobby* case interesting: by acknowledging that claims about when life begins are religious convictions, it framed reproductive rights in the context of religious liberty.

That summer TST began working on a plan that would invoke RFRA laws to leverage their side of the reproductive rights debate. In March 2015, Jarry had MacNaughton draft a letter that Satanic women could present to abortion providers demanding a religious exemption to informed consent laws. The letter explained that being forced to consider inaccurate information burdened tenet five, "Beliefs should conform to our best scientific understanding of the world. We should take care never to distort scientific facts to fit our beliefs." Informed consent laws also burdened tenet three, "One's body is inviolable, subject to one's own will alone," because the material was intended to undermine a decision that women had already made prior to arriving at an abortion provider. The letter was put up on the TST website. MacNaughton recalled, "The letter went up on the website at 9 a.m., and by 4 p.m. I was taking calls from ABC news."[18]

After Mary Doe approached TST, Jarry began looking for a lawyer in Missouri who would take their case. He called nearly twenty firms, most of whom could not even comprehend the argument he was proposing. The Missouri director of the ACLU seemed optimistic at first but never returned Jarry's calls or emails. In the end, Jarry had to continue relying on McNaughton.[19] McNaughton provided Doe with a modified version of the letter that also addressed Missouri's waiting period. In 2014, the Missouri legislature overrode a governor's veto to pass new legislation becoming one of only three states to have a 72-hour waiting period, with no exception for rape or incest.[20] On May 8, 2015, Mary became the first Satanist to present this letter to her abortion provider. It read, in part, "I regard a waiting period as a state sanctioned attempt to discourage abortion by instilling an unnecessary burden as part of the process to obtain this legal medical procedure. The waiting period interferes with the inviolability of my body and thereby imposes an unwanted and substantial burden on my sincerely held religious beliefs." The letter requested that copies be kept with any paperwork on her procedure.[21]

The Lawsuits

Unsurprisingly, Planned Parenthood could not wave the state-mandated requirements and TST decided to sue the state of Missouri. The consensus among reproductive rights advocates was that Missouri was a very bad choice for such a test case. It is a conservative state, and the governor's appointees to the Supreme Court must run in "retention elections" to remain judges. A ruling in favor of TST, regardless of the legal arguments presented, was not likely to get a judge re-elected. MacNaughton explained, "They'll take any opportunity they get to throw this out on procedural grounds rather than side with a bunch of Satanists."[22]

But MacNaughton felt that in another way Missouri was a good place to make this case. In 1986, Missouri passed H.B. 1596 that declared: "The life of each human being begins at conception."[23] This law was struck down as unconstitutional by the Eighth Circuit Court of Appeals but this ruling was overturned by the US Supreme Court in *Webster v. Reproductive Health Services* (1989). MacNaughton said, "This really cuts to the bone of a lot of what I believe." He explained that he believes the Nicene Creed and has taught Sunday school to middle schoolers. But he also believes that religious beliefs must be chosen freely and are meaningless if they are imposed by others. He said of H.B. 1596, "The state can no more say that life begins at conception than that Jesus Christ rose from the dead." When TST asked MacNaughton to represent them, he had a conversation with his pastor and asked, "Am I doing the work of Satan here?" MacNaughton concluded, "I don't believe in a Satan. Evil finds its genesis in the execution of free will."[24]

In June 2015, TST filed a lawsuit in Missouri circuit court against the governor and attorney general of Missouri, citing the state's own RFRA law and claiming that Mary had been irreparably injured by the violation of her religious freedom. Days later, they also filed a federal suit, claiming that Missouri law violated both religion clauses of the First Amendment. The informed consent booklet, they argued, violates the establishment clause because it is a state endorsement of a religious viewpoint. The first page of the booklet states in bold letters, **"The life of each human being begins at conception. Abortion will terminate the life of a separate, unique, living human being."**[25] TST argued that this is not a scientific fact but a religious claim. To emphasize this point, MacNaughton decided to refer to this claim about human life as "the Missouri tenet" and the informed consent booklet as "the Missouri lectionary." While the booklet does not explicitly state that the choice to have an abortion is immoral, this is heavily implied. In fact, the 2010 law requiring the brochure and the 2014 law requiring a 72-hour waiting period were advanced by the Missouri Family Policy Council, a Christian group that asserts that God's word is the cornerstone of government.[26] MacNaughton argued that the law "effectively deputizes doctors to preach the gospel according to the state of Missouri."[27] Its purpose was not, in fact, to provide women with accurate information about a medical procedure but rather to convert them to a different worldview. MacNaughton explained, "They want to change her mind, they want to change her heart, they want to change the way she sees herself in the cosmos."[28] The suit also claimed Missouri law violated the establishment clause because Mary's religious beliefs required her to have access to abortion on demand without being presented with unscientific claims designed to shame her and undermine her decision.

TST's argument was not unprecedented. *Harris v. McRae* (1980) tested whether the Hyde Amendment, which limited the use of federal funds to reimburse the cost of abortions, amounted to a state endorsement of a religious opposition to abortion. The Court ruled that it did not. When RFRA was first proposed, the US Conference of Catholic Bishops and the National Right to Life Committee both raised concerns that someone might claim a religious right to abortion. These concerns were rendered moot following *Planned Parenthood v. Casey* (1992), which affirmed the right to abortion for everyone.

In December 2015, TST's state lawsuit was dismissed by Judge Joe Beteem who ruled that the plaintiff had not sufficiently shown why relief was required under the state RFRA law.[29] TST appealed, and in October 2017 an appeals court sent their case to the Missouri Supreme Court. The court's unanimous decision noted that TST's case "raises real and substantial constitutional claims" and that neither the US Supreme Court nor the Missouri Supreme Court had considered whether informed consent laws violated the First Amendment.[30] In January 2018, TST had a hearing before the Missouri Supreme Court in which the state's solicitor general argued Mary's religious rights had not been burdened because Missouri law did not actually require her to read the brochure or even view an ultrasound, only that these be made available. This seemingly ad hoc interpretation of the law had apparently never been made explicit to Planned Parenthood. TST regarded the solicitor general's clarification as a victory in itself. In a press release, TST reproductive rights spokesperson Jex Blackmore was quoted, "Women will no longer be forced to decide whether or not they want to listen to the fetal heartbeat while naked, with their feet in stirrups, and a transvaginal ultrasound wand inside of them."[31]

In August 2016, the federal lawsuit was dismissed. US district judge Henry Edward Autrey did not even address TST's First Amendment claims. Invoking *Roe v. Wade* he regarded this as a privacy issue and ruled that since Mary was no longer pregnant her privacy was no longer as stake. TST found this decision infuriating, noting that Autrey took over a year to respond to their suit; his delay had essentially created the justification for his own dismissal. McNaughton explained Mary still had standing because this was a case about religious freedom and not privacy, "The guilt is not alleviated by having an abortion."[32] Marci Hamilton, a legal scholar known for her criticism of RFRA laws, called Autrey's ruling a "non-sequitur" and wrote that the constitutional violation at stake in the case remained "capable of repetition, yet evading review."[33] TST appealed, and this case is currently before the Eighth Circuit Court of Appeals. In February 2018, a second federal case was filed on behalf of Judy Doe. Doe was still pregnant when her case went before Judge Autrey.

On February 13, 2019, the Supreme Court of Missouri ruled unanimously against Mary Doe in favor of the state. Regarding the argument that the Missouri RFRA law had been violated, the court emphasized again that Doe was not required to read the informed consent booklet or receive an ultrasound, only that these must be made available. As for the argument that Missouri's decree that "the life of each human being begins at conception," violates the establishment clause, the court ruled that this claim merely "happens to coincide" with a religious tenet.[34] Jarry and Greaves described the ruling as "cowardly and fundamentally corrupt."[35] Adding insult to injury, James McNaughton began receiving emails from someone purporting to be Mary Doe, demanding to be withdrawn from the case as plaintiff. The current whereabouts of Mary Doe remain unknown, making further appeal impossible.[36] Then, one week later, Judy Doe's case was dismissed. Despite these overwhelming set backs, Jarry announced plans for a new reproductive rights campaign that would be even greater in scale.[37] Judy's Doe's case has also been appealed to the Eighth Circuit.

The culture wars over reproductive rights intensified further in 2019 following the appointment of conservative Brett Kavanaugh to the Supreme Court. Several states passed tough anti-abortion laws with the stated purpose of triggering a Supreme Court case that might overturn *Roe v. Wade*. Alabama's HB 314 criminalizes abortion at any stage with no exception for rape or incest. Doctors performing abortions can be penalized with up to life in prison. Abortion is only legal in Alabma if the life of the mother is at stake. In May, Missouri's sole abortion provider was nearly forced to shut down following a dispute with the state department of health. On May 28, the Supreme Court overturned a ruling by the Seventh Circuit Court of Appeals striking down Indiana's "fetal burial law" as unconstitutional. The law, passed in 2016 by then-governor Mike Pence, requires that aborted fetuses be either buried or cremated. TST responded immediately with a press release claiming that they were exempt from Indiana's fetal burial law under RFRA.[38] (Pence also passed a state RFRA law in Indiana in 2015 that, ironically, could help TST in a hypothetical lawsuit.)

The Conversation

In 2018, Missouri governor Eric Greitens was indicted on felony invasion of privacy charges after his hairdresser alleged Greitens took photos of her bound and naked to ensure her silence over an affair. As Greitens resisted calls to resign, TST's lawsuit seemed like an asset rather than a liability. He aired radio ads announcing, "Even Satan's own lawyers from the Satanic Temple are suing Greitens."[39] MacNaughton initially advised Jarry to describe the religious organization he was building as secular humanists instead of Satanists. But Jarry refused, and MacNaughton acknowledged that openly identifying as Satanists gives them the cultural impact that they seek. "They're stirring the pot," he said. "They have a unique place in our cultural dialogue because no one on the extreme left is a taking a religious stand, only the extreme right."[40] TST's lawsuit against Missouri generated countless news articles, which continued in spurts for years as each new development emerged. Saturating this reportage were competing and sometimes contradictory claims about the definition of religion. Could the claims in Missouri's informed consent booklet really be regarded as a religious viewpoint? Could a non-theistic Satanic group claim a religious exemption to a state law? While coverage of these questions was generally shallow, unstated assumptions about religion had become unsettled.

TST's pro-life opponents argued that the question of when life begins is *not* a religious matter but a scientific one. *The Catholic Register* stated, "At the moment of conception, the unborn child has a unique DNA. That's science."[41] The Thomas More Society, a pro-life law firm, filed an amicus brief arguing that the informed consent booklet's statements about when human life begins are scientific fact supported by genetics and that TST's claims were therefore "fundamentally confused."[42] This response—that TST was trying to frame scientific facts as religious ones—weirdly mirrored TST's complaint that the *Hobby Lobby* decision wrongly treated the Green's religious beliefs about abortifacients as if they were scientific facts.

Of course, Missouri's informed consent booklet does not make claims about unique DNA but rather when "the life of a human being" begins. This is a nebulous term more akin to the Talmudic *nefesh* or Aquinas's "rational soul." Significantly, arguments that "the Missouri tenet" is a scientific fact do not provide any critical framework for distinguishing a scientific claim from a religious one. The Missouri Supreme Court implied this statement is both a scientific fact and a religious belief, but that this is merely a coincidence.

Significantly, although the courts never questioned whether TST is a "real" religion, numerous media critics opined that TST are "trolls" and as such do not have sincerely held religious beliefs. In fact, when TST first announced their lawsuit, *The Atlantic* ran the headline "Satanists Troll *Hobby Lobby*."[43]

Lifesite news, a pro-life site that has reported extensively on TST, wrote that TST is actually "an anti-religious movement, founded only three years ago, which makes up its own 'beliefs' and then seeks to use those 'beliefs' as the free exercise of established religion."[44] Much of the pro-life reportage on the case put scare quotes around words like "religion" and "religious freedom" in reference to TST. But these insinuations were contradicted by other Lifesite articles about the lawsuit. One stated—incorrectly—that TST was claiming abortion as "an essential religious duty for Satanists."[45] Another opined, "We know satanists believe abortion is sacred as we have documented several times."[46] Presumably, if Satanists are well known to have beliefs about abortion, then their beliefs could not have been "made up" arbitrarily in the last three years. Church Militant pushed this paradox even further in their coverage of the lawsuit, calling TST "an occult and secular activist group."[47] The strategy behind this odd choice of words appears to be to imply that TST is somehow simultaneously "secular"—and therefore unworthy of constitutional protection—and also "occult" meaning its members consciously manipulate evil supernatural forces.

Even news outlets that were friendly toward TST often assumed out of hand that its members were not serious about their religious beliefs. An article for *Jezebel* praised TST's lawsuit, proclaiming, "God bless those Satanists" but it also called them "the nation's best and foremost trolls."[48] An article for *Slate* opined, "As a public act of trolling, this stunt gets an A-plus. It exposes the double standards of those who claim to stand for 'religious freedom,' and it highlights how waiting periods and other restrictions are actually an attempt to impose religious dogma about abortion on those who don't agree with it."[49] These articles frame TST's lawsuit as "trolling" and a "stunt" but not a serious demand for religious freedom.

While many of these critics pointed to how recently TST was created, its relatively small membership, and the parodic elements of its origins, it was TST's rejection of supernaturalism that caused most observers to question whether it was a religion. Emma Green, writing for *The Atlantic*, speculated that TST's suit would be rejected because they do not worship a literal supernatural Satan. She opined, "In short, if the Satanic Temple took this to court, it would probably have a hard time showing that informed-consent laws are a violation of its sincerely held religious beliefs, rather than a group of people's political views."[50] For Green, worshipping the devil is the arbitrary line where politics become religion. Cole Durham, a law professor at Brigham Young University, stated, "It is not altogether clear to me that even if sincere, their

[TST's] beliefs are in fact religious, as opposed to merely philosophical."[51] To which Lucien Greaves responded, "The comment wouldn't be so bad if he had bothered to qualify his delineation between the two (and demonstrated any understanding of our own beliefs and positions)."[52]

All of this discussion begs the question—what *is* religion? What, exactly makes a religious viewpoint different from a scientific claim, a political viewpoint, or a philosophy? And if this issue is so important, why have none of these commentators wagered an operational definition of religion? J. Z. Smith wrote, "The disciplined study of any subject is, among other things, an assault on self-evidence, on matters taken for granted, nowhere more so than in the study of religion."[53] TST challenges the public to "assault self-evidence" and make a more disciplined study of religion. Most importantly, it calls attention to the power dynamics underlying claims about the nature of religion and religious freedom.

TST as Serious Parody

Are TST members trolls? And would being trolls disqualify them from being a real religion? While TST certainly upsets some people, I argue that most of their actions cannot be meaningfully described as "trolling" because "trolling" implies that upsetting people is an end unto itself. In fact, their provocations are usually calculated to achieve specific goals that are clearly stated in their literature. Furthermore, under normal circumstances, being provocative and confrontational does not disqualify a group from being a religion. The Westboro Baptist Church has gone to incredible lengths to upset people, but unlike TST their outrageous behavior is seen as evidence of how sincere they are in their convictions. While this group may be reviled, no one suggests they lack religious beliefs.

A seemingly stronger claim is that TST is not a "real religion" because they have incorporated elements of play, satire, and irony. This is the argument put forward by CoS in the "The Satanic Temple Fact Sheet."[54] In July 2013, *Vice* ran an article called "Unmasking Lucien Greaves," in which Shane Bugbee, then a TST supporter, interviewed Greaves. Bugbee asked, "Is the Satanic Temple a satanic, or a satirical group?" to which Greaves replied, "Why can't it be both?"[55] I argue that TST's use of satire does not disqualify it from being a religion. Like offense, TST uses satire as a means to an end rather than an end unto itself. Melissa Wilcox has written on "serious parody" as an activist strategy that "simultaneously critiques and reclaims cultural traditions."[56] TST enacts serious parody in that they seriously identify as Satanists while simultaneously parodying the fears and rumors associated with Satanic Panic.

TST's satirical elements are also rendered more sensible when it is understood as an "invented religion." While all religions were presumably "invented," this term is used as shorthand for religions that are "self-invented."[57] That is, where other religions may legitimate themselves by appealing to revelation or ancient tradition, invented religions are transparent about the fact that they have been invented by modern people. Carole Cusack, who has written extensively on this phenomenon, notes that invented religions typically invoke elements of play. She points to theorists such as Johan Huizinga and Robert Bellah who suggest that, in a very real way, religion evolved out of play. As a kind of alternate reality where new rituals, norms, and attitudes can develop spontaneously, the playworld is the antecedent to ritual and, ultimately, religion. It was later that religion came to be understood as something "serious" existing in opposition to play.[58] Cusack argues that in the twenty-first century, invented religions have become, in a sense, normative, writing, "Invented religions, as sites of meaning-making in which play and seriousness are united, are the authentic religious manifestation of the age."[59]

Satanism as a whole has been described as an "invented" tradition.[60] In *The Satanic Rituals*, LaVey wrote, "Satanists can easily invent fairy tales to match anything contained in holy writ."[61] LaVey was generally transparent that he was inventing a religion by creatively repurposing tropes about Satanism, most of which came from fiction. His black mass liturgy was openly cribbed from J. K. Huysman's novel *Le-Bas*.[62] His partner, Blanche Barton even wrote that "a complete education in Satanic philosophy is available at your local video store."[63] There is more than a little irony in CoS accusing TST of being insincere because of their origins in play and satire. Satanism scholar Per Faxneld noted, "Irony and playfulness are significant traits of LaVey's texts which are often ignored."[64] Like LaVey before them, TST members are quite transparent that they have invented their rituals and tenets for their own purposes using their own reason and creativity.

It should also be noted that even when invented religions are deliberately absurd, the absurdity is rarely an end to itself. More often, it is a way of calling attention to the way we talk about "religion" as a special category of beliefs and practices, as well as the practical interests at stake in defining "religion." Pastafarianism has been described as a "parody religion," but the original intent of its founder, Bobby Henderson, was to call attention to the Kansas School Board's decision to incorporate "intelligent design" into the high school biology curriculum as an alternative theory to organic evolution. Henderson's absurd "religious" belief that the world was created by "a flying spaghetti monster" was meant to reflect the absurdity of claiming that "intelligent design" is a scientific theory rather than a religious claim.[65]

TST is not a parody religion like Pastafarianism. TST members do sometimes demonstrate an impish delight at the incongruity of Satanists praising conservative Christian politicians or lobbying to open after-school programs. But revealing this incongruity is the purpose; the humor is the side effect. Greaves wrote of TST's mission, "In true Satanic fashion, we turn the whole narrative backward, but in doing so we make obvious that the world had already been operating in reverse."[66] For TST, much about the prevailing political and religious discourse is already absurd and disingenuous. Satire is a strategy for directing the public's attention toward unquestioned assumptions so that they may be reassessed.

Ultimately, the claim that TST is a satire rather than a religion seems to be a fallacy of genesis. It goes almost without saying that as a movement evolves, its beliefs and rituals take on greater levels of meaning and importance. In 2018 Sadie Satanas, a transgender woman and TST National Council member, summarized the absurdity of insisting TST, in its current incarnation, are "just trolls":

> Satanic groups who raise money for reproductive rights, actively combat Christian privilege in social spaces and challenge unjust theocratic laws, clean highways and beaches, hold blood drives, support LGBTQ rights, give blankets and socks to the homeless, perform public Satanic rituals, build monuments, host events, and have thriving communities both online and in the real world are really just trolling.[67]

Another telling bit of evidence comes from Shane Bugbee, who was briefly hired by TST in 2013 to assist with media promotion. He left after a falling out over money and published a blog article condemning Greaves and TST. Bugbee did not claim that TST members were satirists posing as Satanists, but rather the opposite—that he had joined TST to participate in a practical joke, but that the joke had turned into a religion and was now becoming "a cult."[68] Cusack, however, might suggest that this is a relatively normal way for a religion to begin. Indeed, Cusack argues invented religions are worth studying because they "render transparent the process of the origin and formation of religions from play and narrative."[69]

The Case for TST as a Religion

Writing for the conservative blog PJ Media, Debra Heine called TST "tiresome provocateurs who pose as 'scientific rationalists' one day, and a 'very serious religion' the next."[70] Whereas critics from CoS claimed TST is a satirical group and not a religion, Heine implies that they cannot be a religion because their worldview is based on science rather than supernaturalism. In Heine's unstated definition, religion is synonymous with supernaturalism. This assumption dates back at least to the anthropologist E. B. Tylor, who explicitly defined religion as "the belief in Spiritual Beings" in his 1871 work *Primitive Religion*.[71]

Of course, this is not the only way to define religion. In *Torcaso v. Watkins* (1961) the Supreme Court ruled that state and federal governments cannot require citizens to affirm their belief in God to hold public office. In his decision, Justice Hugo Black affirmed that state and federal governments may not "aid those religions based on a belief in the existence of God as against those religions founded on different beliefs." In a footnote, he added, "Among religions in this country which do not teach what would generally be considered a belief in the existence of God are Buddhism, Taoism, Ethical Culture, Secular Humanism and others."[72] In *United States v. Seeger* (1965), which concerned whether someone who did not profess belief in a Supreme Being could conscientiously object to the military draft, Justice Tom Clark ruled, "We believe that under this construction, the test of belief 'in a Supreme Being' is whether a given belief that is sincere and meaningful occupies a place in the life of its possessor parallel to that filled by the orthodox belief in God of one who clearly qualifies for the exemption."[73]

Similar to these rulings, TST leaders argue that belief in God or other supernatural concepts is a poor criterion for classifying something as a religion. Greaves has argued, "Religions enjoy certain privileges and exemptions that would be reprehensible . . . to reserve for supernaturalists alone. While we reject superstition, our values are no less sincerely held. And while we view Satanism in metaphorical terms, our tenets and symbolism are far from arbitrary."[74] Daniel Walker of Satanic Bay Area, a group allied with TST, explained, "We have this assumption that religion and theism are synonyms.

If you can just get [the public] to understand that distinction that's sort of the Rosetta stone."[75]

Chris, a chapter head from TST-Atlanta, added that critics who claim supernaturalism as the sin qua non of religion are intellectually dishonest. He pointed out that while Zeus clearly qualifies as a supernatural entity, most Americans would not respect a Zeus worshipper, and, even if they did, it would not be *because* there is no scientific evidence for Zeus's existence. Furthermore, he argued, when Christians make legal arguments about their sincerely held religious beliefs, they rarely invoke their *supernatural* beliefs but rather their beliefs about values and social norms.[76] I share Chris's suspicion that arguments about supernaturalism are actually camouflaging a different set of assumptions about what religion ought to look like.

Cases such as *United States v. Seeger* expanded the types of things that the Supreme Court might regard as religions, but they provided no definition of religion. Instead, they vaguely framed religion as something analogous to more familiar religions. In his essay "God Save this Honorable Court," J. Z. Smith suggests that in the absence of a formal definition of religion, the Supreme Court operates on an implicit "prototype" of what religion is—and that this prototype is Protestant Christianity. A comparison is made between traditions and Christianity and if significant similarities can be discovered, the tradition is deemed to be a religion.[77] Needless to say, this situation stacks the deck against non-theistic Satanists, partly because Satanism was first imagined as an inverted form of Christianity, but more so because Christianity, especially Protestantism, heavily emphasizes the importance of creeds and faith over law codes and ritual.[78]

While one could argue that TST's moral *beliefs* qualify it as a religion, this would be capitulating to an assumption inherited from Protestantism that religions are reducible to a set of intellectual propositions. This move ignores the richness of what religious cultures are and do. Religion scholars acknowledge that there are many operational definitions of religion and that some are more useful than others, depending on what the scholar is trying to accomplish.[79] One approach that helps highlight the multiple religious dimensions of TST is Catherine Albanese's framework of the "four 'c's." Albanese suggests that a religious system can be understood as the product of four interrelated components: creed, or explanations about the meaning of human life; code, rules that govern human behavior; cultus, rituals that perform the creed and codes; and communities that are bound together by the other three elements.[80] So far, public conversation about TST's religious status has only considered its code, while ignoring the other three elements. This is partly because media encounters with TST occur almost exclusively when TST has entered the political and legal arenas to defend its code. But this lack of data makes it difficult to assess claims about TST's "sincerity," let alone its status as a religion.

Creed

While I was observing a meeting of TST-San Marcos, a heavily tattooed biker arrived with his equally tattooed wife. The biker explained that he had rejected the Catholicism he was raised with and was interested in Satanism. Lanzifer Longinus, a chapter co-head, explained, "Satanism isn't defined by a belief system but by a set of values."[81] For Albanese, creed includes not only such beliefs as God, the soul, or the afterlife, but all questions of ultimate meaning, including how we understand our place in the world and the values we live by. Of TST's seven tenets, I classify the following as being "creed":

1. One should strive to act with compassion and empathy towards all creatures in accordance with reason.
2. The struggle for justice is an ongoing and necessary pursuit that should prevail over laws and institutions.
5. Beliefs should conform to our best scientific understanding of the world. We should take care never to distort scientific facts to fit our beliefs.

These tenets do not prescribe specific courses of action but rather core values that actions should comport with. The tenets do not provide a logical argument as to *why* compassion, justice, and the authority of science should be guiding principles. Rather TST members take the importance of these values as self-evident. Malcolm Jarry, who took the lead in writing the tenets, stated that "justice" is the closest thing in TST's philosophy to a metaphysical belief. "Justice exists only as an ideal," he explained, "Laws bring us closer to justice, but it can never be fully attained."[82] In a subsequent conversation, he went further and described the pursuit of justice as a search for transcendence that—like all quests for the transcendent—leads ultimately to the destruction of the ego.[83]

Unlike theistic religions, TST's creed focuses exclusively on values and does not address specific supernatural ideas. While many TST members do not believe in God, atheism is not a requirement for membership. Chris Turvey, a chapter head from Colorado suggested that TST may be an example of "poly-doxy" or a tradition in which a range of beliefs can coexist.[84] Belle Phomet, a former member of TST-NYC, described herself as a "cold deist," indicating belief in a deity who is detached from the universe.[85] Hofman Turing, also formerly of TST-NYC, described himself as a "Jew-Bu-Satanist" because his affiliation with TST does not preclude his identity as a Jew and a Buddhist.[86] Several members suggested that—at least in theory—a Christian could be a member of TST so long as they were a moral person and shared their values. Co-founder Malcolm Jarry described receiving at least a dozen emails from Christians asking if they can be members. Jarry felt that actions are more important than beliefs and, as such, believing in the supernatural should not disqualify someone from membership who otherwise subscribes to the tenets. Furthermore, Jarry expressed that there was not and should not be a way to police who chooses to affiliate with TST.[87]

Code

I classify the remaining tenets as "code" because they provide more structured rules about how to treat one's self and others:

3. One's body is inviolable, subject to one's own will alone.
4. The freedoms of others should be respected, including the freedom to offend. To willfully and unjustly encroach upon the freedoms of another is to forgo your own.
6. People are fallible. If we make a mistake, we should do our best to rectify it and resolve any harm that may have been caused.
7. Every tenet is a guiding principle designed to inspire nobility in action and thought. The spirit of compassion, wisdom, and justice should always prevail over the written or spoken word.

Tenet seven is actually a sort of "meta code" because it offers instruction for interpreting the other tenets.

Claims that TST is merely satirical or otherwise a "simulacrum" of a religion imply that the tenets are merely "window dressing" meant to disguise

TST as a bona fide religion. But in my interviews with TST members across the country, I found that TST chapters spent a lot of time interpreting and debating the tenets. TST-Colorado has a philosophy club called "The Hellfire Club" that has met to do "deep dives" into the meaning of each of the tenets.[88] In chapter meetings, it is not uncommon for a member to reject a proposed course of action by invoking one of the tenets only to have a different member defend it by invoking a different tenet. For example, how should "the right to offend" be weighed against the ideal of "compassion and empathy for all creatures?" Chapters debated what an integrated understanding of all seven tenets might look like. Adjudicating and finding balance between competing rules and principals is necessary with all codes of law, at least if the code is being used.

Significantly, during the schism of 2018, many of those who left TST continued to cite the tenets even as they accused the authors of the tenets—Malcolm Jarry and Lucien Greaves—of failing to live up to them. This was partly an accusation of hypocrisy, but it also demonstrated that the tenets had acquired a significance that was independent of TST's political actions or organization structure: the tenets had become an end, rather than a means.

Cultus

While TST has little interest in supernatural beliefs, it places great value in ritual. Rose Vespira, formerly of TST-Dallas and now the Crossroads Assembly, said, "We know it's just brain chemistry, but it's meaningful for us."[89] TST has performed Satanic rituals in public as a way of challenging the monopoly of Christianity on the religious landscape. Many chapters have also used rituals as fundraisers by renting a venue and charging admission to witness a black mass, "unbaptism," or similar ritual. These performances may be followed by musical performances or other entertainment, and the proceeds typically go toward legal funds. These events typically contain blasphemy or other shocking elements, and they are visually striking to watch. They often receive heavy, but shallow, reportage in the media with plenty of pictures of black robed or quasi-nude Satanists on stages. This coverage has lent itself to the idea that TST only performs rituals for purposes of shock value or publicity. But TST chapters also hold numerous private rituals to which the media is not invited. These private rituals provide some of the best evidence that TST functions as a religion.

There is not a set canon of TST rituals, and chapters have autonomy to design rituals for their own purposes. Christopher Paul of TST-Atlanta said, "We're talking about building a religion from scratch. If nothing else, it's very interesting."[90] Several chapters have members who specialize in Satanic liturgy, typically with a background in performance art, theology, or even classical languages. Rituals may be used to mark the changing of the seasons, to communally celebrate rebellion against arbitrary authority, or to mark major life events. Marius, formerly of TST-Dallas and now the Crossroads Assembly, is ordained through the universal life church and officiated over a Satanic wedding for his fellow co-head. Marius's will specifies his request for a Satanic funeral.[91] TST-Colorado is exploring a "sexual identity confirmation ritual" that would provide an opportunity for LGBTQ members to publicly declare their sexual orientation or gender identity and have it affirmed by the community.[92] TST-Austin, in conjunction with other Texas chapters, is designing an "impurity ball." This would be an inversion of evangelical "purity balls" in which young girls attend formal dances with their fathers and pledge to remain abstinent until marriage. The impurity ball will have similar features such as dancing and special dresses, but participants will pledge to honor their own bodily autonomy.

One of the more established TST rituals is the "unbaptism," meant to undo the psycho-social effects of a Christian baptism. Some TST members feel that babies cannot consent to being baptized and that unbaptism ritually restores and affirms their spiritual autonomy. TST-Detroit has been credited with holding TST's "first unbaptism" on October 30, 2015—a night known in Detroit as "devil's night."[93] The event was held at the Leland City Club and featured a ritual retelling of the Fall of Man myth from Genesis 3, featuring live snakes. A performer accepted an apple representing fruit of the tree of knowledge, bit into it, and then spat it onto crowd. Instead of falling from grace, biting the apple resulted in freedom represented by removing chains from the performers.[94]

Local variations of the unbaptism ritual have also featured participants being ritually freed from chains or blindfolds, as well as spectacular or blasphemous elements, including sprinkling the subject with ash from burnt Bibles or smudging an inverted cross on their forehead, marks simulating blood, or even a "baptism of fire" involving stagecraft to safely cause a wreath of flames to come off the participant's body. Unbaptisms may be private ceremonies or open to the public. The Austin chapter performed a mass unbaptism in August 2017 at a music venue, which they combined with a charity fundraiser. Anyone who wanted to witness the ceremony, which was followed by a heavy metal performance, was asked to donate either a case of bottled water or five dollars to purchase bottled water. The chapter collected a pallet and a half of bottled water, which was donated to the local homeless shelter.

Unlike Christian baptism, no one is expected to undergo an unbaptism, and it holds no soteriological or supernatural significance. However, the ritual is still a powerful experience for recipients. Alex, co-head for TST-Austin, recalled, "It had a bigger impact than I thought it would. There were folks who were obviously relieved by being freed of something that they didn't believe but still felt tied to."[95] Members of TST-Dallas, which did not allow the public to attend their unbaptisms, reported similar results. Rose Vespira related that some people wept with relief after undergoing this ceremony.

It may surprise some that a community that rejects supernaturalism finds such meaning in ritual. However, theorists of ritual suggest that, in a serious way, communal ritual creates our reality and identity. We might assume that for a former Christian, being baptized or unbaptized is a purely intellectual proposition, contingent only on the individual's metaphysical beliefs. But ontological shifts in status often do not seem "really real" unless they are somehow enacted within a communal context. Adam Seligman et al. write, "What you *are* is what you *are in the doing*, which is of course an external act."[96] There is a demand for TST's rituals because they lend the epistemological weight of a religious community to individuals whose understanding of themselves has become at odds with their religious upbringing.

Seligman et al. describe ritual as creating a "mutual illusion" to which the participants assent to live, but unlike a lie, ritual creates an illusion "with no attempt to deceive."[97] The participants live "as if" the declarations of the ritual are reality. Greaves reached a similar conclusion in an essay for a limited edition print of Clive Barker's horror novella *The Last Illusion*. The novella tells the story of a man who becomes a magician through a Faustian covenant with demons, only to realize that his supernatural power can do nothing to help the world. In revenge, he performs actual miracles but tells the audience they are only illusions to slander the power of the demons. Greaves interpreted this story as a parable for a non-theistic approach to ritual: to claim the power of ritual is actually evidence of the supernatural is harmful, but admitting it is an illusion that the community elects to participate in is empowering:

In this way, Satanism is like the "honest" magician, inviting the audience to enjoy the experience of a religion without asking them to compromise or insult their intelligence. The "performance" is *for* the audience. It empowers them. It is not a bludgeon by which they are imbued with fear of the unknown, and coerced into fearful subservience.[98]

For those who insist religion demands supernaturalism, this is not a "religious" theory of ritual. However, I argue that this culture of ritual and the sophisticated theoretical framework underpinning it dispels the canard that TST are "trolls" engaging in blasphemy purely for shock value.

Community

In addition to expounding on the tenets and performing rituals, TST chapters spend a great deal of time going to happy hours, films, and concerts together, having picnics and barbecues, and other activities that Christian churches generally term "fellowship." I attended a cookout held in a park by TST-Austin where I counted about twenty adults plus five children and a corgi.[99] They prepared hamburgers and tacos on a grill and played kickball. Only a preponderance of black T-shirts hinted that this was an outing of Satanists.

Mara Gorgo of TST-Indiana expressed that events like picnics where she could bring her children were a priority for the chapter, "Indiana is very community and family based. One of the goals of the chapter is to promote a feeling of family."[100] Seraphina of TST-New York said that she joined TST because it provided a sense of community she had not found in her Unitarian Universalist church.[101] Amber of TST-Austin told a story about how she sprained her ankle while jogging on the Austin greenbelt. Not unlike in the parable of the Good Samaritan, two walkers saw her fall but kept going without checking to see if she was all right. She was injured, and her car was still half a mile away. When she couldn't reach her husband on her cellphone, she began calling her fellow Satanists. Within about fifteen minutes, members of TST-Austin responded that they were leaving work and coming to rescue her.[102] Throughout my research it seemed that while many joined TST to participate in a culture war, those that stayed came to appreciate being in a community with like-minded people. Greaves speculated, "The political battles we fight aren't all there is to it. And I feel that, even if we didn't have these fights to fight, most of us would still be here, and we'd still have this sense of community, and we'd still be who we are."[103]

For Albanese, all the "four 'c's" build on each other to create a "religious system." TST members also point to these interconnections when asked why TST should qualify as a religion. Amber explained, "We have sincerely held religious beliefs and our rituals are an expression of those beliefs." Greaves stated, "We have a sense of culture and ethics and a narrative structure that really binds us together."[104] These comments imply a definition of religion that is nuanced and in many ways richer than one that hangs exclusively on supernatural or otherwise "sincerely held" beliefs.

"Religious Freedom Talk" and the Making of Religion

Regarding these battles over how to define religion, Russell McCutcheon writes, "The interesting thing to study, then, is not what religion is or is not, but the 'the making of it' process itself—whether that manufacturing activity takes place in a courtroom or is a claim made by a group about their own behaviors and institutions."[105] While I have defended the position that TST is a "real religion"—and arguably becoming more "real" with each ritual and chapter meeting—it would be a mistake to ignore that there is a provocation built into their claim to be a religion. TST *became* a religion as they attempted to participate in a larger conversation about religious freedom.

Like "religion," the idea of "religious freedom" is a highly loaded and malleable term that has meant different things throughout history. Tisa Wenger uses the term "religious freedom talk" to describe this shifting discourse.[106] While most Americans regard the idea of religious freedom as something universally positive, several scholars have argued that it has been a force for intolerance in the past and may continue to be in the future.[107] Like TST, many scholarly observers were troubled by the *Hobby Lobby* decision and its implications for what religious freedom might mean in a democratic society. Finbarr Curtis frames *Hobby Lobby* essentially as a petty attempt by the Green family to exert control over others: "Failing to persuade its employees of the immorality of their sexual practices, Hobby Lobby attempts to inflict punitive financial harm. Failing to inflict harm, the corporation barricades itself against threats to its property."[108] The religious freedom talk employed in the *Hobby Lobby* case, Curtis argues, is especially insidious because it attempts to exert control not through moral persuasion but by invoking the sanctity of "sincerely held beliefs" defined as ideas that cannot and should not be investigated or discussed. He regards sincerely held beliefs as a sort of trump card that overrides the ordinary processes of democratic governance.[109]

TST's lawsuit against the state of Missouri was not only about reproductive rights, it was their attempt to insert themselves into our religious freedom talk. TST challenges the public to reassess their assumptions: Do we want a model of religious freedom where sincerely held religious beliefs should be given precedence over policies reached through rational persuasion and democratic means? Do we truly believe that religious freedom is an end unto itself? Or is this just camouflage to claim power for specific interests?

Provocations by TST, as well as other Satanic or pseudo-Satanic actors, have elicited new forms of religious freedom talk. In 2014, Preston Smith was allowed to give a prayer invocation before a meeting of the Lake Worth, Florida, City Commission, in which he invoked Satan. In response, a local pastor told the news reporters that the First Amendment only applies to "traditional, accepted religions" and not "malevolent and evil" faiths like Satanism.[110] In response to a TST member giving a prayer invocation in Kenai, Alaska, in 2016, attorney Robert Coleman proposed that a "reasonable" interpretation of the establishment clause meant a form of majority rule in which a religious majority could elect to place religious symbols on public property while a religious minority could not.[111]

Some of TST's Catholic critics have renounced religious freedom entirely. In an op-ed entitled "Liberty of Perdition," Christine Niles, writing for ChurchMilitant.com, wrote:

> The argument goes that if the courts determine satanism is a bona fide religion, having all the hallmarks of a genuine belief system, then it deserves as much constitutional protection under the First Amendment as Christianity or Judaism or Islam, or any other "religion."
>
> Constitutionally speaking, the argument is unassailable. The satanists are correct. But according to the teachings of the Catholic Church, they would receive no protection of the laws.[112]

The op-ed's title was a reference to the 1864 encyclical "Quanta Cura" in which Pope Pius IX condemned the idea of an individual right to conscience and worship as "insanity." In an article for *The Catholic Herald* about the 2014

Harvard black mass, a Catholic Harvard student wrote, "If religious freedom means allowing people to practice and preach whatever evil things they will, it is no ideal to be defended." This is an ironic position for American Catholics to take, considering that, in the nineteenth century, Catholics invoked religious liberty to resist the bigotry of the Protestant majority.

This discourse suggests that many people do not truly value religious freedom as a human right. Instead, they value their own cultural dominance, and when religious freedom is no longer in alignment with that goal, it is either discarded or else utterly reimagined. In his book *Masking Hegemony*, Craig Martin suggests that the ideas of religion and religious freedom will always be used to conceal and distort particular interests, in other words to mask hegemony. He adds that if the paradoxes and contradictions that mask this hegemony are ever broken down (which he has little hope of) that "it will be the result of the diligence of those who tirelessly pick at the almost invisible seams of dominant discourses."[113] In the final analysis, I see TST as an invented religion that is not so much "trolling" as picking at these invisible seams. While the seams are far from unraveled, they have perhaps shown some signs of wiggling.

As TST has inserted itself into our religious freedom talk, it has also become a product of this discourse. Several scholars have noted that the act of treating religion as special produces the very differences it seeks to protect.[114] Many TST members described how their attitudes about religion have shifted, and they have come to think of themselves as religious people. Malcolm Jarry described composing the seven tenets: "Raised in an atheist household, religion was always something fundamentally dishonest. . . . It never occurred to me that religion could be wholly constructive. What was fascinating was to be able to sit down and compose tenets that I wholeheartedly agreed with. For me, that was a radical notion."[115] Jill, a chapter head from TST-Boston described how people would introduce their friends to her and try to assure her by saying, "Don't worry, they're not very religious." This bothered Jill. She said her response was to think, "We'll I'm *very* religious!"[116] At stake in this exchange is an assumption that TST is "against religion." For Jill, TST is not against religion but rather against theocracy and religious monopoly. The examples above suggest that by engaging vigorously in religious freedom talk, many TST members have arrived at new perspectives not only of what religion is but also its potential value to individuals and society. This suggests that not only is TST "really" religious, but it also is a striking example of how the process of "making" religion also "makes" us.

Becoming "Official"

While I was researching this book, TST began achieving small victories toward receiving official recognition as a religion. Donny of TST-Springfield described an incident where a chapter member had failed to keep up with electricity bills and their power had been cut off. Some power companies will reactivate accounts if the client can submit a letter from their church pledging to support the delinquent account. TST-Springfield asked the National Council for a pledge letter and received one in only a few hours. Significantly, the power company felt TST qualified as a "church" and turned the power back on.[117]

Another interesting case occurred in 2018 when a mental patient suffering from schizophrenia at Bridgewater State Hospital in Massachusetts refused to take antipsychotic medication, claiming that they were a member of TST and that this would violate their religious beliefs. Because the patient was considered legally incompetent, the court attempted to assess whether they would still have refused antipsychotics *if they were competent*. Lucien Greaves was brought in as an expert witness. He explained that while TST has no stance on psychiatric medication, the third tenet—that the body is inviolable and subject to one's will alone—naturally includes the choice of what medications to take. On December 17, 2018, Brockton District Court sided with the patient. The opinion stated:

> The court's decision is based on the following subsidiary findings, not necessarily in the order of their significance:

1. The respondent holds a sincerely-held belief in Satanism;
2. One of the core tenants [*sic*] of Satanism is that one's body is inviolable.
3. While Satanism does not prohibit the use of antipsychotic medications, their use is left to the sole discretion of its members
4. Satanists are free to refuse antipsychotic medications, provided refusing such medications will not pose a danger to others;
5. There is no evidence before the court that the respondent is violent or that his refusal to take antipsychotic medications poses a risk of harm to other patients or staff at BSH;
6. The respondent has clearly expressed his preference not to take antipsychotic medications to his doctors at BSH; and

7. None of the other factors override the respondent's expressed preference or his religious convictions.[118]

Admittedly, it was a minor case and, from a public relations standpoint, a
hospitalized schizophrenic—even a non-dangerous one—is not an ideal
member for a marginalized religion to boast about. Still, for a court to rule
that TST members have a sincerely held religious belief and also make an important accommodation to honor the third tenet set a major legal precedent
for a six-year-old religion.

In February of 2019, TST received a letter from the IRS granting them tax-
exempt status as a church, without conditions. This development, which was
owed largely to the work of Malcolm Jarry, made TST one of the first Satanic
religions to receive such status.[119] Initially, TST had claimed they were un-
interested in tax-exempt status in keeping with their view that churches
should be taxed. They softened this position in early 2017 after President
Trump announced at a National Prayer Breakfast that he planned to "totally
destroy" the Johnson Amendment, which prohibits tax-exempt organizations from endorsing political candidates. On May 4, 2017, Trump signed
the "Presidential Executive Order Promoting Free Speech and Religious
Liberty." The order did not actually repeal the Johnson Amendment, but in
July 2018 the House passed legislation making the Johnson Amendment
procedurally more difficult to enforce. In response to these changes, TST
announced that they were re-evaluating their refusal to accept religious tax
exemption. Greaves described the need to be on the same footing as his theocratic opponents in what he called "a frighteningly asymmetrical battle."[120]

In April 2019 TST announced their tax-exempt status, which horrified
their religious opponents. LifeSiteNews immediately launched a petition
demanding that the IRS reverse this "horrible decision" that "runs counter
to everything America stands for."[121] On the Eternal World Television
Network, Robert Warren of the Catholic University of America argued the
IRS made the wrong decision because TST does not believe in God or a literal Satan.[122] But supernatural belief is not among the characteristics that
the IRS associates with a church. Of the fourteen characteristics the IRS does
list, TST meets nearly all of them. Even the attribute of "Sunday schools for
the religious instruction of the young" is arguably met by TST's After-School
Satan Club.

These groups were not upset because TST may now gain more revenue
from donations or its modest sales of T-shirts and other merchandise.

Rather, they understood that this move signaled that the US government was placing TST on the same level as Christianity. J. Z. Smith wrote, "The Internal Revenue Service is, both de facto and de jure, America's primary definer and classifier of religion. It reproduces the imperial Roman government's efforts at distinguishing licit and illicit religions as subtypes of a wider legal concern for distinctions between licit and illicit associations."[123] Legally speaking, tax-exempt status is the best possible evidence that TST is a "real" religion and not a prank or a purely political movement. There are, of course, groups such as the Church of Scientology who have tax-exempt status and are still seen by large segments of the public as illegitimate simulacrums of religion. However, the long-term effect of a tax-exempt Satanic Temple is likely to be that the public will think a bit harder about the issues of religious liberty raised by TST's provocations now that the dodge of framing TST as something other than a religion has been hobbled.

6

Satanic Bake Sales

How The Satanic Temple Is Changing the Way We Talk About Evil

People have this perception that one side does the good stuff and the other side does all the bad stuff. . . . We are showing [Satanists] do have a sense of community, and they want to get involved.

—Stu de Haan, The Satanic Temple, Arizona[1]

This explains the new Satanic offensive. The target is the moral order, especially as upheld by Christian civilization.

—John Horvat II, vice president for the American Society for the Defense of Tradition, Family, and Property[2]

Culture jamming, on its most profound level, is about remaking reality.

—Mark Dery[3]

In 1692 in Jurgensburg, Livonia (modern Latvia), an octogenarian man known simply as "Old Thiess" was put on trial for heresy. Thiess, who had initially been brought to court as a witness to a crime, confessed that he was a werewolf (*wahrwolff*). In the seventeenth century, werewolf trials were common in northern Germany and the Baltic states. Much like witches, werewolves were believed to be people who had gained magical powers by making a compact with the devil. Those who confessed to being werewolves were frequently executed. But to the court's surprise, Thiess insisted that werewolves hated the devil and were in fact "the hounds of God." Several times a year, he explained, the werewolves descend into hell to do battle with Satan's forces. They do this to return the bounty of the earth that is stolen by the witches, who are the true servants of Satan. When the werewolves succeed

Speak of the Devil. Joseph P. Laycock, Oxford University Press (2020). © Oxford University Press.
DOI: 10.1093/oso/9780190948498.001.0001

in this mission there is a good harvest, and when they fail there is famine. The court was bewildered by Thiess's testimony. The pastor was brought in who pointed out that werewolves defy God by taking a different shape than the one their creator gave them. Thiess insisted his deeds were neither diabolical nor evil. In fact, God would soon welcome him to heaven for his years of service. Furthermore, he understood all these issues better than the pastor who was "just a young fellow." The prosecution was flummoxed: there was no evidence that Thiess had consorted with the devil, and he had not confessed to doing so. The case was referred to the royal high court who sentenced Thiess to ten lashes for superstition and idolatry.[4]

Historian Carlo Ginzburg found similarities between Thiess's account of werewolves traveling to hell to restore the fertility of the earth and the *benandanti*, a tradition of "good witches" from northern Italy. Under interrogation during the Inquisition, the *benandanti* claimed to leave their bodies at night to battle evil witches. Ginzburg concluded that both confessions showed traces of an ancient shamanic tradition that had influenced numerous European cultures. But Bruce Lincoln proposes a different interpretation of this pattern. Lincoln noted that seventeenth-century Livonia consisted of a Slavic population under the rule of ethnic Germans. The Germans asserted that the Slavs were not truly Christian and were prone to idolatry, superstition, and entering pacts with the devil. This claim legitimated German rule by framing an ethnic difference as a moral and religious one. Lincoln notes that in all the werewolf trials for which we have records, the justices of the court were all Germans and the defendants were all non-Germans. Werewolf trials were a method by which Germans performed their moral superiority. Thiess, in essence, sabotaged the political function of the werewolf trial. Not only did he frame werewolves as courageous and committed to justice, but the witches in his confession, who served Satan and stole the abundance that belonged to the peasants, functioned as stand-ins for the German nobility. Lincoln concludes:

> Werewolves proper are not at issue anywhere. Rather the discourse of both contesting parties takes "werewolf" as a trope and there's a struggle going on about how to define what it is to be a werewolf and the struggle is really about how different are the *undeutche* peasantry and the *deutche* nobles. Who are the real humans, who are the real animals? Who are the criminals? Who are the forces of justice? And the way they talk about the werewolf is the ground on which they weigh that struggle.[5]

Furthermore, he argues, if we find confessions from "good witches" in Italy and "good werewolves" in Latvia, this is because both societies exerted similar social pressures and provided the structure for similar strategies of resistance.

TST's claim to be "good Satanists" can be read as another manifestation of this strategy, which I call "appropriating the discourse of evil." Like Old Thiess, they are openly identifying—and even dressing as—what their culture understands to be the embodiment of evil. They then "flip the script" by arguing that it is the Satanists who believe in compassion and justice, while their opponents promote intolerance and authoritarianism. Identifying the forces of evil is always an exercise in power. David Frankfurter wrote, "Evil is a *discourse*, a way of representing things and shaping our experience of things, not some force in itself."[6] Hijacking the discourse of evil is an attempt to unsettle the dominant cultural logic—what Foucault called an *épistémé*—and effect a reassessment of what is possible. Just as Thiess subtly undermined the idea of German moral superiority, TST tries to undermine the assumption that the dominant religious group—American Christians—are inherently more moral. Instead, TST proposes, Satanists and Christians should be judged alike by their actions and values. Greaves sums up this strategy, "If people can see that Satanists aren't immoral or criminal or cruel, we have forced them to judge others based on real-world actions rather than maintain some obscure out-group standard by which unjustified purges have always taken place."[7]

One might think that coexisting with "good Satanists" would be preferable to "evil Satanists." However, responses from TST's opponents frequently demonstrate just the opposite. Charities and government agencies have blocked some of their efforts to do philanthropic work. Their Christian opponents have even accused them of not being "proper Satanists," to the extent that their actions are morally defensible. There is a need, it seems, for Satanists to be evil. I argue that these responses betray a recognition that TST is appropriating a discourse that has long been used to support certain types of Christian hegemony—namely the imagined religion of Satanism. Since the early modern period, stories about Satanists have been used to reinforce a Christian ethos by conjuring images of an inverted Christian world. In this sense, Satanism has not really served as the opposite of Christianity, but an adjunct to its authority. Both TST and their opponents seem to understand intuitively that the ability to define this inverted order has consequences for the uninverted order.

However, appropriating the discourse of evil is a risky strategy. To succeed, it is necessary to strike a careful balance between identifying with the imagined forces of evil and redefining those forces. On the one hand, it is easy to end up inadvertently reinforcing existing power structures by providing evidence that evil conspirators such as Satanists actually exist. On the other, there is a risk of sanitizing identification with the evil other to the point where the entire strategy appears disingenuous or silly. Attempting to negotiate this problem has become increasingly difficult for an organization where chapters spread across regional and political contexts share a single brand. One of the divisive issues within TST concerns the correct amount of transgression that can best leverage the discourse of evil to effect social change. Just how much shock is effective yet sustainable? TST has produced a variety of strategies for appropriating the discourse of evil. Those who have remained with TST seem to be converging toward a long-term strategy of community building and philanthropy. This strategy recognizes that as communities are exposed to the presence of "nice Satanists," the discourse of evil, and the moral authority of those who invoke it, is gradually weakened.

For some, however, such a strategy is unworthy of the name "Satanist." An essay by the CoS dismissed TST's activism stating, "We don't have bingo games and bake sales."[8] After her departure from TST, Jex Blackmore explained, "Bake sales don't empower people as much. They don't have 'bite' to them."[9] Some TST chapters have held literal bake sales. (For the two-year anniversary of TST-San Marcos, I was treated to homemade cupcakes. They were delicious, although the cream-cheese frosting was a disturbing shade of mauve.) But more broadly, "bake sale" has become shorthand for forms of activism deemed insufficiently transgressive or Satanic. These critiques demonstrate how efforts to appropriate the discourse of evil are still being renegotiated and finessed.

Appropriating the Inverted Order

Legends of Satanists are part of a larger cultural pattern that Frankfurter calls "the myth of the evil conspiracy." These conspiracies are said not only to defy social norms but also to deliberately invert them: cursing God instead of praising God, murdering babies instead of nurturing them, and so forth. Stories about conspiracies of witches and Satanists are not so much intellectual propositions as powerful symbols: They appeal to a deeper stratum of thought than logical persuasion. Frankfurter writes, "The capacity to imagine inversions lies at the very roots of social thought marking off cultural territory on every plane. . . . And ultimately a realm of pure evil verses the realm of civilization and morality."[10] Fantasies of inversion function such that "the moral rightness of the *un*inverted world is preserved as the center of all things."[11] We see this dynamic, for example, in Catholic blogger Mark Shea's analysis of TST's proposed black mass at Harvard University. Shea referred to host desecration as a "backhanded compliment" to Jesus Christ, noting, "the blasphemy is directed, not toward Zeus, Quetzelcoatl or Mars, but toward the one true God."[12] The actions and motivations of the Satanists—at least as Shea imagines them—function to affirm to truth of Catholicism.

Sometimes sufficient discussion of an imagined evil other will bring it into being. In October 2014, Pazuzu Algarad (née John Lawson) of Clemmons, North Carolina, and his girlfriend were arrested for murdering two people and burying them in their backyard. Church of Satan leader Peter Gilmore explained that Algarad had been a "devil worshipper" and not a Satanist, but for many people this seemed like a distinction without a difference.[13] Algarad had changed his name to reference the demon from *The Exorcist*, and his face was heavily tattooed. The walls of his home were covered in swastikas, pentagrams, and Halloween decorations. Algarad essentially lived out horror-movie tropes of evil Satanists in what Frankfurter calls the "mimetic performance of evil."[14] While transgressive, these performances empower certain moral entrepreneurs who claim to be combating a conspiracy of criminal Satanists.

But if Algarad's mimetic performance strengthened the utility of the inverted order, another kind of performance can problematize it. In *The Politics and Poetics of Transgression*, Peter Stallybrass and Anton White draw a distinction between "transgression from" and "transgression to."[15] Algarad's mimesis of the inverted order was "transgression from." Performing the role of a Satanic murderer reversed the values of a Manichaean order, but without altering them. By contrast, TST's mimesis of Satanism is "transgression to." It seeks to unsettle the order by calling us to reassess who is good and who is evil. In an interview for the blog *Friendly Atheist*, Greaves offered a more explicit theory of "transgression to." Hemant Mehta asked, "I don't get how a Satanic Temple could encourage benevolence. Can you fix my ignorance here?" to which Greaves replied:

We feel that by forcing people to look beyond superstitious out-group categorizations—to judge people for their concrete actions, we naturally encourage benevolence. There is a term in social psychology, moral self-licensing, that refers to the phenomenon in which those who define themselves in terms of moral superiority tend to act more brazenly in an immoral manner. We are happy to confuse and upset simplistic White Hat/ Black Hat Good Guy/Bad Guy notions that serve to ignore one's real-world deeds in favor of their symbolic fealty to social norms.[16]

While TST has refined this tactic, they hardly invented it. Anton LaVey wrote, "Experts will tell you, you can't have the Satanists win, they can't be the good guys. Why not? What rules are there that say that I can't? It's simply a given that it can't be done—it's one of those unwritten laws that says that all Satanists must advocate evil and must perform evil acts."[17] Blanche Barton further elaborates CoS's strategy of "transgression to": "An accomplished Satanist takes what is considered 'evil' by mainstream Judeo-Christian society, turns it upside down in unexpected ways and gives it back in spades. By applying LaVey's rule of 'nine parts social respectability to one part outrage,' Satan, church, religion, Bible must all be re-defined in the post-1966 era."[18] LaVey called his axiom of "nine parts respectability and one part outrage" a Satanic "magical formula." It acknowledges the balancing act required to appropriate the discourse of evil.

These challenges to the imagined moral order elicit a repertoire of defense mechanisms. To preserve the idea of an inverted world, the paradox of the "benevolent Satanist" must be dismantled. One way to do this is to simply deny the transgressors their identification with Satan and insist that the true conspiracy of evil exists elsewhere. LaVey described his frustration at encountering this attitude during the height of the Satanic Panic:

> Once others say, "We'll that's not real Satanism, you're not real Satanists— —you're just religious Satanists. The real Satanists are out killing babies and sacrificing cats"—that's our cue to start knocking heads. We have to be prepared to say "God damn it, you rotten sons of bitches! Don't tell me what Satanism is. I'm a 'real' Satanist and I'm proud of it."[19]

Chris Matthews argues that "Satanism" is such a heavily loaded term that its meaning can no more be redefined than the word "child abuser" and that LaVey was being "disingenuous" by even claiming this was his goal. Matthews writes, "In all matters semantic, the majority—aka the *herd*—gets the final say."[20]

In contrast to Matthews, some of TST's critics have expressed alarm that Satanists really *can* change the way we talk and think about Satanism if they are not stopped. This defense mechanism invokes a "declension narrative" in which tolerance for Satanists represents the final defeat of traditional Christian values. An article for *The Federalist* condemning TST's "Afterschool Satan Program," announced:

> The story deserves far more attention than it has received thus far. It shows that our civilization has lost the capacity to make even the most elementary moral and social distinctions. Despite what the half-witted sophists buzzing around such issues often say, there is nothing complicated about the distinction between God and Satan. There is not the least difficulty, to a sensible person, deciding which of these two names ought to have a place in the education of young children, or on the statues in our public squares. Even to the thoroughgoing atheist who regards these names as nothing more than mere symbols, *what they symbolize* is a matter of clearest preference: a matter of good over evil.[21]

Similarly, John Horvat II, vice president for the American Society for the Defense of Tradition, Family, and Property, wrote that the true goal of TST's presence in the public square is "to create a sense of normality around the abnormal Satan." He called on Christians to protest TST in order to "maintain the natural barrier of horror that has always stood and must continue to stand between the devil and humanity."[22]

These jeremiads seem self-refuting. If any "sensible person" can tell that symbols of God are better than symbols of Satan, why is it necessary to say so? If the "barrier of horror" around Satan is "natural," why are protests and other forms of social action necessary to maintain it? These responses to TST reveal not only that the meaning of Satanism is fluid and socially constructed but also that something bigger is at stake. The idea of Satanism is worth fighting over because it is a resource for moral entrepreneurs who employ the discourse of evil. To paraphrase George Orwell, "He who defines the inverted world can define the uninverted world."

Edgelords vs. the Goth ACLU: Optimizing Transgression

Jesper Aaagard Petersen described LaVey as engaging in a double move of "'sanitizing' Satanism and 'satanizing' the modern to obtain an optimal balance of satanic 'bite' and popular appeal.' "[23] Ruben van Luijk characterizes LaVey's Satanic balancing act as "a paradoxical and potentially self-defeating position."[24] If LaVey had truly succeeded in persuading the public that Satanists are law abiding and "harmless," then the transgressive element that makes Satanism attractive in the first place would have been lost. TST wrestles with this same dilemma. How is the discourse of evil best harnessed and manipulated?

In 2016 writer Christopher Knowles mocked TST in an essay called "Safe-space Satanists" writing, "When reading of the caffeine-free rites of the Neo-Not-Satanists, I can't help but think of the rites of Cybele, the Queen of Heaven in the ancient world, whose blood-frenzied priests would hack these not-Satanists to dogmeat just on account that they were so unspeakably lame."[25] Former TST members such as Shane Bugbee and Brian Werner have similarly accused TST of being insufficiently sinister.[26]

But others found TST's take on Satanism refreshing. Ash Astaroth was drawn to TST after watching Werner's resignation speech.[27] He responded to critiques that TST is insufficiently transgressive:

> While many Satanists are still convinced that spookiness is an inherent power they weild [sic], and complaints surface that The Satanic Temple is "defanging" Satan, those complaints expose the fear that the only Satanic power they've ever imagined they master is being stripped away. But, nobody interesting thinks Satanism is scary anymore. . . . Sorry bout it. Smart people who don't know much about Satanists more often imagine us as LARPers than demons or "the alien elite."[28]

Here the problem is turned on its head: those who feel that TST has become overly sanitized mistake "spookiness" for power and fail to see how foolish they appear.

In interviews with current and former TST members, I encountered two pejorative labels that came to mark the contours of this debate. "Edgelord" is a term adapted from Internet forums referring to individuals who enjoy making nihilistic or shocking statements. To call a Satanist an Edgelord is essentially to accuse them of pretentiousness. Conversely, TST members have been called "the Goth ACLU," implying that they pursue their goals only through mainstream "safe" methods and that the only thing "Satanic" about them are their sartorial choices. These two labels form a Procrustean bed that contains TST's efforts to appropriate the discourse of evil.

TST's tactics have changed over time, reflecting different approaches to this problem with various members and factions departing to pursue their agenda in their own way. I present three "ideal types" of social action employed by TST that leverage the discourse of evil in different ways. The most spectacular is "culture jamming," or guerrilla theater meant to reframe cultural debates by shocking the audience. TST-Detroit led by Jex Blackmore pioneered this approach. A drawback to culture jamming is that the non-discursive nature of art makes it easy for cultural opponents to impose whatever narrative they want onto transgressive performances. Less spectacular is a more legalistic strategy sometimes described as "the poison pill," or "Lucien's Law." This tactic involves claiming the same privileges for Satanists that are afforded to Christians, knowing that the public will find this intolerable and retreat to a more universally applied principal of secularism where no religion benefits from government resources. A drawback to this approach is that it can require serious legal and financial resources to execute effectively. The third tactic is to serve the local community through philanthropy. This is "the bake sale" approach. Philanthropy allows TST chapters to raise their profile in the community, undermining claims that they are "outsiders" who deserve no say in community affairs. Paradoxically, for Satanists, being "nice" *is* transgressive because it disrupts the discourse of evil that supports the established moral order. This disruption is evidenced by reactionary efforts to stop TST from performing their charity work. These three strategies are often used in concert, depending on the objectives and the resources available. Shiva Honey, a founding member of TST's National Council, described a "portfolio" of actions that includes performance art, legal action, and community building.[29]

Satanic Culture Jamming

The term "culture jamming" was first used in 1984, by Negativland, an experimental music group from the San Francisco Bay Area. It refers to the band's practice of disembedding media and repurposing it to subvert the original message. In 1987 Negativland released a song called "Christianity Is Stupid." It consisted of slow, foreboding music overlaid with a recording of a man with a heavy southern accent saying, "Christianity is stupid. Communism is good. Give up."[30] This speech was sampled from the film *If Footmen Tire You, What Will Horses Do?* (1971) narrated by Estus Pirkle, a

Baptist pastor from Mississippi. Pirkle's film depicts a hypothetical future where communism has defeated Christianity and consists of graphic scenes of American Christian families being raped and tortured by communists. Pirkle had been describing propaganda that defeated Americans would be forced to listen to, but Negativland took this speech out of context so that the audience simply heard Pirkle proclaiming that "Christianity is stupid" over and over again.

In 1988, the band was forced to cancel a national tour due to financial difficulties. Instead of admitting the reason for the cancellation, they released a phony press release claiming they had been advised by federal officials not to leave town because a teenage boy in Minnesota had listened to "Christianity Is Stupid" before murdering his family with an axe. The axe murders really occurred, but there was no connection to Negativland. The media never bothered to verify the press release with law enforcement, and there was a surge of sensationalized coverage. In 1989 the band sampled news coverage about their prank for a new album called *Helter Stupid*.[31]

By repurposing media, Negativland undermined both Pirkle's call to defend Christian America from communists and the credibility of media stories about dangerous music. Mark Dery has described such acts as "ontological sabotage."[32] Of course, Negativland did not invent this tactic. In the 1950s, Guy Debord's Letterist International movement in Paris formulated the theory of *détournement*. Kembrew McCleod writes, "The closest English translation of *détournement* falls somewhere between 'diversion' and 'subversion.' Another translation might be 'un-turning' or 'de-turning'—where the culture is turned back on itself, against itself."[33] Debord's book *Mémoires* (1959), produced with Danish artist Asger Jorn, consisted of collages of mass media text and images arranged into disturbing juxtapositions. The cover was made from sandpaper so that *Mémoires* would destroy other books it contacted. The purpose of this was to shock the reader into a reassessment of culture. Greil Marcus explains, "The détournement of the right sign, in the right place at the right time, could spark a mass reversal of perspective."[34] Unsurprisingly, David Guinan and Malcolm Jarry both described themselves as fans of Debord. Jarry composed several songs for his band inspired by the work of the Situationists.[35]

The 1960s—the decade that introduced religious Satanism to the world—were replete with experiments in culture jamming. Yippie leaders, such as Abbie Hoffman, attempted to change how the public perceived institutions through such stunts as exorcizing the Pentagon or dumping dollar bills on the New York Stock Exchange. The feminist collective WITCH actively combined these tactics with a mimetic parody of evil. WITCH was an acronym, although what the acronym stood for changed depending on the situation. Most often, it stood for Women's International Terrorist Conspiracy from Hell. On Halloween 1968 WITCH members staged a hex ritual at the Stock Exchange declaring, "You have a fiend at Chase Manhattan."[36] In 1969 when radical feminist professor Marlene Dixon was not rehired by the University of Chicago's sociology department, local WITCH members showered the sociology department with nail and hair clippings.[37] While LaVey despised the leftist radicals of the 1960s, he too was recontextualizing Christian elements to suit his own purposes.[38]

TST is a direct heir to these techniques of culture jamming and political theater. Several TST members have attempted to combat Christian opponents by appealing to their fears of supernatural evil. Lilith Starr explained, "That fear is a power for us, especially over evangelicals. It can really expose the hypocrisy of 'religious freedom only for us.'"[39] In March 2016, North Carolina held a special legislative session in which it introduced and passed HB2, a bill that rolled back local ordinances expanding anti-discrimination protection for LGBT people and decreed that people may use only those restrooms corresponding with their biological sex. In response, Satanic Bay Area, a group allied with TST, mailed a "hex of obsolescence" to every member of the North Carolina legislature who voted for HB2. The hex of obsolescence designed by artist Eliza Gauger includes an occult sigil and a message that reads in part:

> Warning: The image is a curse. By glancing at this sigil you invited it into your prefrontal cortex, where it will remain, working until such time as its work is done. This sigil curses your ideas. This sigil protects trans kids. This sigil harms the bodies, minds, and concepts of those who refuse to mind their own fucking business, and by business I mean gender.[40]

I asked organizer Daniel Walker why he would do this. He explained that state representatives are required to open their mail and added, "This makes a longer lasting impression than just another angry letter."[41] Satanic Bay Area now mails hexes to politicians to express their displeasure about once a year.

TST-Detroit, which formed in August 2014 and disbanded in 2016, excelled at transgressive performance art. Jex Blackmore, the chapter's charismatic director, brought a background in art history and opera. Shiva

Honey, another prominent chapter member, had a background in music and dance and was a political science major who studied protest movements including the Yippies.

In 2016, A24 studios approached TST about promoting their new horror film *The Witch*. Blackmore saw the Puritan family portrayed in the film as "a microcosm of a patriarchal theocratic society" that forces a young woman to rebel by becoming a Satanic witch.[42] Her "promotion" of the film consisted of a tour of New York, Los Angeles, Austin, and Detroit called "the Sabbath Cycle" in which screenings of the film were followed by a ritual performance and incitement to "Satanic revolution." I attended the Sabbath Cycle in Austin. A Facebook page for the event declared, "Texas is a stronghold of regressive theocratic, persecutory legislation which targets freethinking, godless Texas citizens." Upon arrival at the venue I was given a "grayscale" American flag. As the crowd waited for the ritual to begin, the voice of a southern preacher came on the speakers declaring, "Satan does not want you to do what he wants you to do. Satan wants you to do what *you* want to do." This was sampled from a speech by Baptist pastor Dr. Jeff Owens. Like Negativland, Blackmore recontextualized the pastor's words, turning a warning about out how Satan exploits selfish desires into an endorsement of Satan as an agent of moral autonomy.

The lights went up and on stage knelt a long-haired, athletic-looking man from TST-Detroit wearing a leather jacket over his bare torso. His right hand was bound to the floor by a length of chain, but he methodically pounded against the chain with his fist. Behind him was an ensemble of performers, including a nude man and woman. Their placement on the stage, alongside the chains, was meant to invoke "The Devil" card from the Rider-Waite tarot deck.

The hooded figure was revealed to be Blackmore, who took to a podium to deliver what can only be described as a "Satanic jeremiad." She warned that Christian theocrats were taking over America and that those present were allowing it to happen. The ensemble performed during her speech, and at one point the nude performers guzzled large containers of wine. Much of the fluid missed their mouths causing them to appear as though covered in blood. Blackmore accused the audience of "tweeting your indignation from the comfort of your own filthy nests" instead of engaging in real resistance. "We do not seek followers," she said, "but collaborators." Collaborating with TST meant embracing the demonizing language of the Christian right and using it against them to effect political change. Blackmore declared, "If they fear apocalypse, then we will deliver it!" This line was met with a roar of enthusiasm from the crowd. Several people raised their hands to give "the horns," as they would at a metal concert. In closing, Blackmore discussed the flags everyone had received. "These are not party favors," she said. She instructed the crowd to hang them in courthouses and other places where their message of Satanic resistance could be received, "Place them at 1100 San Jacinto [the address for the governor's office]. Where your governor Greg Abbot is finding a new way to spit in your face."

These kinds of performances can be emotionally powerful and several TST members I interviewed expressed that Blackmore was the one who first attracted them to TST. One of the chapter's most successful projects was a series of counter-protests in Michigan over reproductive rights. In July 2015, a covertly recorded video was released suggesting that Planned Parenthood "sells" aborted fetuses to laboratories at a profit. While the edited video was misleading, this triggered nationwide demonstrations in front of Planned Parenthood. Blackmore attempted to reframe the debate by applying détournement to familiar symbols such as babies, mothers, and Christ. They also leveraged the discourse of evil by using performers in transgressive, black clothing bearing Satanic flags.

In August, the Detroit chapter responded to a national day of protest in front of a Planned Parenthood with a "milk boarding" held in front of pro-life demonstrators. Two female performers knelt in prayer with their wrists bound while performers dressed as priests poured gallons of milk over them, causing them to cough and gasp for air. Blackmore stood behind this tableau with a sign that read, "America is not a theocracy. End forced motherhood!" The performers continued even after the chief of police—who arrived out of uniform—attempted to confiscate their milk. Their performance was met with applause by other counter-protestors. The intended message of the "milk boarding" was that the pro-life movement amounts to religious persecution of women. Significantly, when protestors attempted to drown out the spectacle by loudly intoning the Prayer to Saint Michael (a Catholic prayer invoked to oppose spiritual evil), this only enhanced the impression of women being tormented by Church authorities.[43]

In November, Blackmore published a blog called *Unmother* describing her experience of abortion, including the logistics, the physical side effects, and the hate mail she received online from anonymous men. It was posted to a website called crisispregnancymichigan.com. The website was another act of détournement. Its name suggests it is a "crisis pregnancy center" (CPC).

CPCs are nonprofits, typically run by conservative Christians, that pressure women not to seek abortions. Many CPCs attempt to attract pregnant women by deliberately presenting themselves as a women's health clinic that provides abortions. By imitating this tactic, Blackmore's website siphoned attention from Michigan CPCs while simultaneously drawing attention to this deceptive practice.[44]

On Good Friday, 2016, TST-Detroit arrived at a Planned Parenthood in Ann Arbor where the Pro-Life Action League (PLAL) was holding its annual "Way of the Cross for Victims of Abortion" protest. Blackmore wore a false belly to portray a pregnant woman. She also wore a crown of thorns and dragged a heavy wooden cross. Following her were chapter members in black suits who scourged her with whips. On their backs were written the names of Michigan legislators who had signed anti-abortion bills. This performance received significant coverage from Christian news sites. One pastor called it "a display of abject evil and apostasy" and a sign of the end times.[45] Blackmore's purpose, of course, was to suggest that women, and not the unborn, were being "crucified" in the abortion debate.[46]

On April 23, 2016—during another nationwide protest of Planned Parenthood—the chapter enacted a counter-protest called "The Future of Baby Is Now."[47] A van pulled up in front of the protest and dropped off six performers wearing rubber baby masks and bondage gear, including whips, collars, and leashes. The "babies" carried bottles, baby powder, pacifiers, and other props. Some wore diapers. They proceeded to flounder and cry in front of the protestors, whipping each other and spraying each other with milk and powder. A TST member began covering them with gold spray-paint while another member dressed as a priest appeared to worship them. Over this bizarre tableau, Blackmore stood with a sign that read, "No more lives sacrificed to fetal idolatry." Another TST member bore a sign that read, "Your fetish is not my command."[48] Blackmore explained the logic behind this protest to me, "There's no changing someone's mind at a protest that's anti-choice. What we want to do is characterize their whole protest as ridiculous. Holding up doctored pictures of mutilated fetuses *is* ridiculous. We want to mirror back their own fetishization of the fetus. . . . If this is disturbing and upsetting to you, you should look at yourself."[49]

In video of this performance, many pro-life demonstrators appear shocked and confused, but their attitudes seem unchanged. A writer for Lifesitenews used the protest to make a metaphysical argument that Satanists cannot challenge the symbolic order because it is mandated by God:

If the Satanists sought to provide repulsive street entertainment they certainly succeeded. But if this was a message in support of abortion and aimed to deride the pro-life cause, the message was essentially incoherent. . . . The Satanists' lack of coherency may actually itself stem from their allegiance to the Father of Lies. Symbols and images are things of the earth that express an objective meaning, indeed they are created by God who imbued them with an order, truth and beauty—but in the hands of the enemies of God they become convoluted, twisted and distorted—those symbols of communication lose their sense.[50]

The weakness of the protest is not, of course, that symbols express "an objective meaning," but rather the opposite: art is inherently polysemous and subject to interpretation. This makes culture jamming a high-stakes strategy in which the opportunity to reframe the debate comes with the risk of ridicule. When I spoke with Damien Blackmoor, a co-head from TST-Indiana, he said, "TST has calmed down as far as 'outrageous antics.' There's no more pouring milk on fetish babies. I had a reluctance to join at first, and I think a lot of that had to do with the spectacles."[51] The pace of the chapter's activism also proved unsustainable. Honey remarked that there had been constant action but not enough community building, which ultimately led to the "implosion" of the chapter.[52]

Two of Blackmore's projects fomented a parting of ways with TST. In November 2016, Texas passed a law requiring fetal remains from abortions and miscarriages to be either buried or cremated. This law, versions of which are still being reviewed in federal courts, was another consequence of the allegation that Planned Parenthood sells fetal tissue. Blackmore responded with a campaign called "Cumrags for Congress" that encouraged people to mail used condoms, semen-soaked socks, or simply lotions suggestive of semen to the office of Texas governor Greg Abbott. A photo promoting the campaign showed an envelope addressed to Abbot along with a sock and a note reading "These r babies. Plz bury." Blackmore explained, "The action was intended to be crass, humiliating, disgusting, a waste of resources, and absurd, just like the Texas regulation."[53] TST leadership was concerned that this was illegal and could bring prosecution on TST. Blackmore said that she called the post office and was told that mailing semen is legal so long as it is shipped in a sealed container.[54] On February 10, 2018, Blackmore held a performance in Detroit called the "subversive autonomous Satanic ritual." As discussed in chapter 2, TST's National Council was not informed about this ritual, and they feared that statements made during it could be misinterpreted as threats of literal violence. Blackmore parted ways with TST soon afterward.

Blackmore explained her decision, "I'm not going to change because the Temple isn't OK with what I'm doing. How do we unite people who identify as outsiders if we're not doing outsider actions?"[55] She argued that activism is about a transference of power and that by limiting oneself to "safe" activism you are already assenting to rules created by an oppressive system. Blackmore quoted civil rights activist Audre Lorde, "The master's tools will never dismantle the master's house."[56] She also felt that the tactics preferred by the National Council did not empower ordinary people who could not afford lawyers and PR agents. Her methods, however, which involved performance art and culture jamming, could be employed by anyone at any level. Blackmore plans to continue her transgressive work independently of TST and feels that socially engaged Satanism will continue to be a political force, with or without TST.

Lucien's Law: Leveraging the Discourse of Evil

If Blackmore is the consummate performance artist, TST founder Malcolm Jarry is the ultimate legal strategist. He once told me, "I'm a tactician. And I steal tactics that work."[57] Jarry wrote a master's thesis deconstructing protest literature in which he argued that protest movements should be analyzed in terms of what their ultimate aims are. He felt that the Occupy Wall Street protests and the Black Lives Matter movement were failures not because their causes were unworthy but because they lacked concrete, attainable goals. Protest movements, Jarry argues, must be clear about what they want to achieve and formulate strategies that will reach these goals. He cited Martin Luther King Jr.'s bus boycott as an example of a goal-oriented tactic.

Jarry's document, "The Satanic Temple's Guidelines for Effective Protest," calls for more targeted actions rather than generalized calls for revolution. It states, "Raising consciousness can be legitimate if it is part of a well-conceived broader strategy, but it is not legitimate as a goal because awareness of injustice does not lead to ending injustice without a strategy." Instead, proposed actions should be checked against a formula:

Effective protest is founded on a legitimate theory of change that is exemplified by the structure of *IF* I do X, *THEN* Y will happen *BECAUSE* Z.

For example, *IF* TST forms a Satanic organization with sincerely held beliefs and demands the same rights that are granted to other religious entities, *THEN* either a broader range of people will also be able to enjoy these privileges or certain privileges will no longer persist for an arbitrary elite *BECAUSE* of the legal protections and rights under the First Amendment and the 1964 Civil Rights Act.[58]

This example also attempts to leverage the discourse of evil but in a more focused way than the non-discursive style of performance art. It assumes that the "arbitrary elite" (Christians) would rather forfeit privileges than share them with Satanists because Satanists are understood to be "evil" and therefore intolerable. Thus, the quality of being intolerable can be a tool for cornering opponents.

A classic example of this tactic of leveraging the discourse of evil involved *The Satanic Children's Big Book of Activities*, which Jarry designed. Jarry began work on a Satanic children's book without any real idea of what it would be used for. He looked at activities from children's placemats at restaurants and then showed puzzles he designed to his wife. Despite featuring obviously Satanic symbols such as pentagrams and goat heads, nothing in Jarry's book is morally objectionable. A word jumble contains words like "respect" and "empathy." Jarry described it as providing "an ironic friendly face to Satanism."[59]

The children's book ended up playing a key role in a controversy in Orange County, Florida, where the public school district had allowed a Christian ministry called World Changers of Florida, Inc. to distribute Bibles in school. In January 2013, the Freedom From Religion Foundation (FFRF) complained to the school district that this was unconstitutional. The school district responded that the Bibles were not an endorsement of Christianity by the school because the school provided an open forum where anyone could distribute literature. So David Williamson of the Central Florida Free Thought Community attempted to use the open forum to distribute Robert Price's mythicist essay *Jesus Is Dead* and the anti-Muslim polemic *Why I am Not a Muslim*. But the school board censored these texts claiming their distribution would cause disruption. Williamson sued, claiming that the freedom of speech of atheists was being infringed.[60] The school board agreed to allow the distribution of atheist material, and Williamson's case was dismissed. But on January 3, 2014, the school district informed the atheists that any materials had to be submitted for approval by the school board by December 31, 2013—three days *before* the atheists were informed of the policy.

In July 2014, the FFRF reached out to TST. There was finally a chance to do something with Jarry's children's book. Jarry also felt that the FFRF miscalculated by choosing inflammatory anti-religious polemics and argued that it would be harder to justify censorship of his book, which featured only constructive children's activities. In February 2015, the school board voted 7-1 to ban all outsiders from distributing religious material rather than expose children to a Satanic coloring book. This victory, after years of effort, caused David Williamson to coin the phrase "Lucien's Law," which states that "governments will either (1) close open forums when The Satanic Temple asks to speak, or (2) censor The Satanic Temple, thereby opening itself to legal liability."[61] (Jarry expressed that the law should have been named after him but conceded that Lucien Greaves is the public face of TST.)[62]

A similar example is worth discussing. In 2015, Joe Kennedy, a football coach for Bremerton High School in Washington, had come under scrutiny for publicly praying at football games. As soon as the game ended, Kennedy would kneel on the fifty-yard line where players and parents would join him in prayer. The school district sent Kennedy a series of letters explaining that the football field was not an "open forum" for the expression of religious viewpoints. Furthermore, Kennedy's prayer sessions were interfering with his job duties, which did not end immediately after the game. A number of accommodations were suggested, but Kennedy's lawyers responded that anything short of praying on the fifty-yard line immediately after the game would be regarded as a violation of his religious freedom. After games on October 23 and 26, Kennedy held prayer sessions on the field in direct defiance of the district's orders.[63] This inspired several students from Bremerton—including the 2016 class president—to invite TST-Seattle to also hold public prayers during the game. The class president explained, "The main reason I did it is to portray to the school district that I think we should either have a policy that we're not going to have any religious affiliation or public religious practices, or they should say people are going to be allowed to practice their religion publicly whatever their beliefs."[64] On October 27 the Seattle chapter filed a formal request to hold Satanic prayers at a Bremerton home game.[65] On October 28, Kennedy was placed on paid leave, although it is unclear whether TST played a factor in the school board's decision.

On October 29, TST-Seattle arrived at Bremerton's final home game in full Satanic regalia. They did not go onto the field but held a brief ceremony outside the fence that enclosed the stadium. Chapter head Lilith Starr recalled that some students were enraged and threw what she thought might have been holy water over the fence. They also screamed at one of the students who had invited TST and identified as non-gender-binary, shouting "Dyke!" and "Everyone hates you!" Despite this, Starr remembers the night as "a really good time." The chapter met their student allies and exchanged hugs. After graduating, one of the students who invited TST went on to join the chapter.[66]

Kennedy did not reapply for a coaching position in 2016 and sued the school district. His case became a cause célébre with conservative politicians, including Donald Trump. The Ninth Circuit Court of Appeals sided with the school district. Significantly, the court's decision discussed "members of a Satanist religion" that offered to attend the game. The fact that Satanists could not take the field to pray but Kennedy could was cited as evidence that Kennedy was not exercising his rights as a private citizen: "The precise speech at issue—kneeling and praying on the fifty-yard line immediately after games while in view of students and parents—could not physically have been engaged in by Kennedy if he were not a coach."[67]

Lucien's Law relies on Satanism being intolerable even in its most sanitized form. Andrew Siedel of the FFRF wrote, "Apparently, The Satanic Temple's coloring book is scarier than atheist literature. Perhaps we atheists are not the most hated group in America. Or, perhaps we're the most hated, but less feared. After all, Satan does run hell."[68] Siedel's observation speaks to the power of the discourse of evil. While atheist literature deals with assessing intellectual propositions, Satanism and its allusions to an inverted world appeal to a deeper stratum of meaning, one that that lies close to "the roots of social thought."

This strategy also has weaknesses. School boards and other government institutions can often thwart these actions by simply not responding to requests. Even in the most egregious cases of discrimination, it takes resources to make a lawsuit a credible threat. Damien Ba'al was a chapter head for TST-St. Louis before departing to form his own movement, United Aspects of Satan. Ba'al felt that the "poison pill" strategy had played out, in part because "Christians have no problem being hypocrites."[69] The strategy also depends on a legal system that will take the principle of religious neutrality seriously. Since the controversial appointment of Brett Kavanaugh to the Supreme Court, Lucien Greaves has expressed worry that it might be better not to file suits that could wind up in federal courts stacked with conservative judges and appealable to a Supreme Court with a majority of very conservative judges. However, Malcolm Jarry felt that judicial hypocrisy comes with a heavy price: unjust decisions can expose the biases of those claiming to serve justice and ultimately erode hegemonic forces.

Satanic Philanthropy

Most of the TST chapters I interviewed were not engaged in transgressive performance projects or "poison pill" actions. This was partly the result of the National Council's policy that chapters must submit projects for approval before proceeding. Instead, most chapters expressed that they were focused on building a local community of Satanists and doing charitable works. Nearly all chapters are engaged in some sort of philanthropy such as gathering supplies for shelters or making care packages for the homeless. Others partner with charities that support survivors of domestic abuse or LGBT youth. Satanic donation drives often have names such as "Socks for Satan" or "Warmer than Hell." TST-Boston created a program called "Menstratin' with Satan" that collects feminine hygiene products for homeless women. Many chapters have done "Menstratin' with Satan" drives and some shelters have expressed gratitude to TST or even sent thank you notes because feminine hygiene products are such a needed yet overlooked donation item. Highway adoption has been another form of philanthropy. TST first attempted to raise money for a highway adoption program in 2013. Since then, TST chapters and allied Satanic groups in Arizona, Indiana, Arkansas, and Albany, New York, have experimented with adopting highways, and TST-Santa Cruz has adopted a beach.

When I asked members *why* a Satanic organization would engage in philanthropy, I received a variety of answers. Several pointed out that the Temple's first tenet demands "compassion and empathy." Donny of TST-Springfield simply answered, "Because it's the right thing to do."[70] Chris Turvey of TST-Colorado added that while Satanism is often associated with a philosophy of self-interest, helping others *is* an act of self-interest because philanthropy makes one feel good. But some added that public philanthropy also advances the interests of the chapter by raising their public profile and demonstrating that TST is not a nefarious organization. Some chapters found these actions also attracted new people interested in membership. Members of TST-Boston noted that philanthropy also strengthens their other endeavors by tying TST to the community.[71] A common response when TST offers to give prayer invocations before government meetings or erect monuments on government property is that the Satanists are "outsiders" who are "meddling" with the community's affairs. When local chapters form partnerships with shelters and other local philanthropic institutions, it becomes harder to dismiss them as foreign agitators.

Philanthropy would seem to be the least transgressive activity TST does, but paradoxically it is also the activity that does the most to disrupt the social order because it confounds popular ideas of "evil." It was for this reason that Satanic philanthropy was one of the first things Malcolm Jarry wanted TST to do. If black masses and other forms of blasphemy are a "transgression from," philanthropy is a "transgression to" that proposes a reassessment of our assumptions about good and evil. A member of TST-Austin called it "a slap in the face" to Christians when Satanists do charity work because it challenges the assumption that Christians are inherently more moral than other people. Simone of Satanic Bay Area commented, "Terms like good and evil lack the nuance that we need. We're trying to put up a challenge to norms that people don't really think about."[72]

These challenges to the moral order are ultimately what is at stake when people attempt to stop TST from doing charitable work. In 2017, TST-Arizona's "Menstratin' with Satan" drive was so successful that they were awarded "Best Community Service Project" by the *Phoenix New Times*. They donated so many supplies to the YWCA that the chapter had to build a shed to store them in. But in 2018, the YWCA corporate office received a phone call from a Christian who was upset that the YWCA was cooperating with Satanists.[73] The supervisor of the YWCA of Southern Arizona sadly informed the chapter that their partnership must be dissolved. Lucien Greaves opined, "Our charitable works are being inhibited by the religious prejudice of those who simply can't tolerate us doing good works because it conflicts with their narrative, and those in need of feminine hygiene products be damned. The corporate office of YWCA should be ashamed."[74] After the media picked up the story, the YWCA seemed to backpedal and issued a press release announcing that ending the partnership had been a miscommunication.[75]

Highway adoption programs have proved especially contentious, in part because groups are granted an official sign announcing them as benefactors of the highway. In 2018, TST-Arizona adopted a stretch of I-10, which they cleaned using special black pitchforks forged by a chapter member who is an ironworker. A news article on the clean-up featured a comment from a Christian who reacted, "This is offensive and the state needs to be forced to take it down I don't care how much money they gave the state. Arizona don't need money that bad."[76] TST-Indiana also adopted a highway in 2018, naming their project "Inverted Crossroads"—a play on Indiana's title as "the crossroads of America." Chapter co-head Mara Gorgo described the state as "really wonderful to work with."[77] However, people living near the chapter's highway sign expressed their displeasure. One resident was quoted, "It's like advertising a Satanic church in, you know, in front of our home. We raised our sons here."[78] Satanic Arkansas, an independent Satanic group allied with TST, successfully adopted a highway in February 2019.

TST-Albany's attempt to adopt a highway proved especially frustrating. They made a standard agreement with the New York Department of Transportation (DOT) to clean a stretch of highway for two years in exchange for a sign. But their sign never went up. Eventually they received a letter announcing that "it was not in the interest of the state of New York" to grant their highway adoption. The chapter made a series of phone calls and even sent a certified letter inquiring why their arrangement was cancelled. So far, these have gone unanswered. Chapter co-head Dex Desjardins felt that the DOT probably had nothing against them personally but knew that Christians would be angry over their highway sign and saw rejecting TST's proposal as "the path of least resistance": it would be less of a headache to deal with a few upset Satanists than many upset Christians. Desjardins explained, "They think we're the 'Hot Topic Army' and that we probably weren't even serious about this. But it turns out we're the sort of people who will haul a giant demon statue halfway across the continent just to make a point!"[79]

Entities such as the New York DOT or the YWCA of Southern Arizona probably do make these kinds of political calculations when deciding whether to work with TST. But the underlying issue is the fear of a backlash if Satanists—imagined as the antithesis of the good society—are given public recognition as community stakeholders. For some, the fact that Satanists are helping the needy or cleaning litter only makes the situation *worse* because this is seen as an assault on the moral order. A key example occurred in 2017 when TST organized a fundraiser for Valentine's Day. An editorial for RedState.com opined:

> A liberal, anti-Christian, anti-life group called A Satanic Temple, while ludicrously claiming to stand for "compassion and empathy," are having a Valentine's Day fund raiser to help raise funds for several pro-abortion lawsuits that were filed against the state of Missouri. Specifically, these poor,

twisted, lost souls are offering hugs and kisses, in exchange for donations. . . . Satanism is selfish humanism, and rejects anything that reflects true giving or compassion for "the least of these."[80]

Redstate was opposed to TST's pro-choice stance, but the author seemed more upset that self-described Satanists were engaged in the innocuous exchange of hugs and kisses instead of criminal violence. It was not sufficient to show that Satanists oppose pro-life Christians: the editorial attempts to restore the moral order by defining what Satanists believe and do over and against the words and actions of actual Satanists.

Similarly, when Satanic Australia and Satanic New Zealand—organizations allied with TST—announced a blood drive in 2018, a swarm of YouTube videos appeared condemning the drive and warning audiences not to donate blood. A YouTuber called "MomsOnAMission" repeatedly described Satanists donating blood as "insane" and quoted Isaiah 10:20:

> Woe to those who call evil good
> and good evil,
> who put darkness for light
> and light for darkness,
> who put bitter for sweet
> and sweet for bitter.

She added, "I can't even wrap my mind around it, but I know that Satan is the great deceiver and that's how he works—he wants to make everything look good because he wants to take the place of God."[81] Sociologist Peter Berger observed, "To go against the order of society as religiously legitimated . . . is to make a compact with the primeval forces of darkness."[82] In this sense, being nice may be the most "Satanic" activity that TST does.

Managing the Spectacle of Satanism

Hijacking the discourse of evil is inherently precarious. Joshua Gunn concluded that Anton LaVey attempted to "resignify" Satanism as "kitsch" but ultimately failed as moral entrepreneurs piled accusations of murder and child abuse onto his efforts. Gunn writes, "Although he was the architect of a successful Satanic spectacle, LaVey was incapable of controlling that spectacle once it was released into the popular media and, by extension, the popular imaginary."[83] Compared to accusations about CoS in the 1980s, few people claim that TST is secretly abusing children or part of a criminal conspiracy. Instead, TST's opponents are more likely to dismiss them as "just trolls" who merely pretend to be Satanists. For purposes of dispelling the paradox of "benevolent Satanist" and thereby preserving the imagined moral order, it is just as efficient to claim a group like TST are "not really Satanists" as it is to claim they are "not really benevolent."

I asked Lilith Starr whether there was a danger of TST becoming too domesticated or losing its transgressive qualities. She answered, "Our rituals are dark and solemn. They have nudity and blood!"[84] The best argument that TST are not merely "pretending" to be Satanists is that they hold private black masses and similar rituals that often involve such elements as blasphemy and nudity. A black mass performed in Salem involved urinating into a vessel and then dropping an (unconsecrated) communion wafer into the urine.[85] But these transgressions return TST to the first problem in which it becomes easier for cultural opponents to claim their blasphemy makes them incompatible with a tolerant society.

Van Luijk suggested that combining respectability with outrage is a self-defeating position for Satanists for this very reason—there is a constant balancing act between being overly domesticated and being the target of criminal prosecution. This is not to say that TST's strategy of harnessing embedded cultural fears of Satanism while simultaneously redefining the popular understanding of Satanism is doomed to failure. But it is a risky strategy with a potential for backfiring. Shiva Honey felt that as TST became better known, she encountered fewer reactionary responses to Satanism. It may be that as the public becomes more familiar with TST and its members, it will become harder to make sweeping generalizations about the nature of Satanism. If so, it may be that small incremental actions—even those as simple as holding a Satanic bake sale—ultimately prove the most effective at changing the way we talk and think about good and evil.

7

"Taking Equality Too Far"

How the Satanic Temple Is Changing the Way We Talk About Pluralism

> Harvard should learn that religious freedom is not just for the center, but also the margins.
>
> —Michael Muhammad Knight[1]

> The most serious attacks on the dignity of religious communities are invariably accompanied by the silencing of their members.
>
> —Cherian George, *Hate Spin*[2]

In the summer of 2003, I received a grant from the Pluralism Project at Harvard University to map out religious diversity in Austin, Texas. It was my first experience doing ethnography with religious communities. The following fall, I began my master's program at Harvard Divinity School where "pluralism" and "interreligious dialogue" were heady words. This was due not only to the progressive spirit that dominated the place, but also because about 20 percent of the students were preparing for the ministry and wanted to cultivate an empathetic understanding of other faiths. While I have never stopped supporting the work of the Pluralism Project or Harvard's Center for the Study of World Religion, by my second year I began to have doubts about the way my classmates talked about pluralism. Those doubts crystalized when I took a course on Afro-Atlantic religions in the College of Arts and Sciences and learned about practitioners of the Afro-Cuban religion of Palo Mayombe, living in Chelsea, Massachusetts.

Palo Mayombe practice revolves around a special cauldron called an *nganga* or *prenda*. The *nganga* is filled with a variety of objects to create a microcosm of the world. The world within the cauldron becomes home to certain elemental spirits as well as spirits of the dead, believed to be especially

Speak of the Devil. Joseph P. Laycock, Oxford University Press (2020). © Oxford University Press.
DOI: 10.1093/oso/9780190948498.001.0001

fierce. The *palero*, or practitioner, can summon the spirits of the *nganga* and command them, either for good or evil. The relationship between the *palero* and the spirits has been variously imagined as one of mutual respect, priestly veneration for the sacred, or one in which the spirits are subservient as a dog is to its master. Some scholars have speculated that the idea of the *palero* commanding spirits like dogs betrays a vestige of the slave culture of colonial Cuba.[3] The *nganga* traditionally contains human remains, either purchased through legal channels or taken from a cemetery. In 2012 an *nganga* was dredged from a canal in western Massachusetts containing a human skull as well as the remains of sacrificed animals.[4]

While I found Palo Mayombe fascinating, I tried to imagine a *palero* attending an interfaith function at the Divinity School and I could not. This is partly because our ideas about interfaith dialogue are often informed by what scholars call "the world religions paradigm," which tends to overlook smaller, emerging, or localized forms of religion.[5] J. Z. Smith wrote:

> A World Religion is a religion like ours; but it is, above all, a tradition which has achieved sufficient power and numbers to enter our history, either to form it, interact with it, or to thwart it. . . . We recognize both the unity within and the diversity between the "great" World Religions because they correspond to important geo-political entities with which we must deal.[6]

Palo Mayombe is a small tradition with no geopolitical power. But more importantly, it is not a religion "like ours." While none of my classmates would have dared to say that Palo Mayombe is not a *real* religion or that they found practices like animal sacrifice and commanding spirits of the dead abhorrent, I sensed that just beneath the rhetoric of celebrating diversity lay unstated rules about what "true religion" looks like and Palo Mayombe broke most of them. Robert Orsi, whose lectures I attended at the Divinity School, boldly attempted to codify these hidden criteria:

> True religion . . . is rational, respectful to persons, noncoercive, mature, nonanthropomorphic in its higher forms, mystical (as opposed to ritualistic), unmediated and agreeable to democracy (no hierarchy in gilded robes and fancy hats), monotheistic (no angels, saints, demons, ancestors), emotionally controlled, a reality of mind and spirit not body and matter. It is concerned with ideal essences not actual things, and especially not about presences in things.[7]

The problem, as I saw it, was not that my classmates who were preparing for the ministry were too bigoted to assist in summoning wrathful spirits from an *nganga*. Rather, Palo Mayombe made me realize that engaging with *actual* religious difference is a difficult, anxiety-producing undertaking. Yet we often talked about pluralism at Harvard as if all it entailed was not being deliberately close-minded. We could not grapple with the challenges of religious pluralism because we arrogantly believed we had already overcome them.

I was reminded of this problem on May 12, 2014, when TST, having been founded less than two years earlier, attempted to hold a re-enactment of a black mass under the auspices of the Harvard Extension School Cultural Studies Club. Here at last was a group that significantly challenged the invisible criteria of "true religion" yet demanded a seat at the table. The result was both predictable and disappointing. Almost no one attempted to find out what TST believed or what their black mass was about. Instead, it was framed as "hate speech" against Christians. A statement submitted by the Harvard chaplains to the *Harvard Crimson* admitted that they had no details about what the performance would entail but nevertheless proceeded to declare that it was "targeting" Catholics and ridiculing their faith. The chaplains added that they represented "most of the major Western and Eastern religious traditions, as well as the perspectives of atheists, agnostics, and those genuinely uncertain about what they believe." It never occurred to them that there were no Satanists among them. They described their shared commitment to "engaging in discourse about life's 'big questions' in a manner that is open and honest, but also respectful." But they made no attempt to engage TST in discourse, respectful or otherwise. Instead, they urged TST not to hold their black mass and the community not to "dignify" it by attending.[8]

In the end, TST was cornered into holding their event off campus while an estimated 1,500 Catholics protested with a holy hour and a Eucharistic procession down Massachusetts Avenue. David Barnes, director of Boston University's Catholic Center, described the protest against the black mass as "a magnificent evening" and said he felt "grateful" that he could see the Catholic community out in force.[9] But to me, the response to the black mass felt like a defeat: Harvard's claim to engage in religious difference had finally been dealt a significant challenge and was found wanting.

A week before the Harvard black mass, the Supreme Court ruled in *Greece v. Galloway* that towns may hold public invocations with sectarian prayers provided no one is overtly coerced to participate and minority faiths who wish to offer invocations are not discriminated against. Following the decision, TST again challenged our society's claim to religious tolerance by offering to hold Satanic prayer invocations in Austin, Boston, Phoenix, Scottsdale, Arizona, the Kenai Peninsula in Alaska, and Pensacola, Florida. Some of these requests were simply ignored. A few communities allowed Satanic prayer invocations, which caused a brief media sensation and then were forgotten. Arizona, home to TST's attorney Stu de Haan, became a major battleground on this front. The town of Scottsdale scheduled (and then rescheduled) a prayer invocation by TST but then cancelled it, claiming they were ineligible. TST sued for religious discrimination. Using the Freedom of Information Act, they also uncovered an email in which a Scottsdale councilwoman described their request to speak as "taking equality too far."[10] Much as the black mass was framed as an assault on the dignity of Catholics, Phoenix City Council member Sal DiCiccio decried TST's proposed prayer invocations in his city not as a legitimate expression of faith but as "social engineering for political correctness." He stated, "The goal of the satanic group has always been to ban all prayer. If the Mayor and Council were to give into [sic] the satanists; then they would be granting them their wish."[11]

The institutions that nominally support religious diversity justify their intolerance for TST by claiming TST is itself intolerant. According to this argument, TST does not act in good faith but rather seeks to "ruin it for everyone" by turning interfaith functions into a forum for insulting other religions or delivering deliberately offensive prayers in order to end the tradition of prayer invocations. But I do not believe this is what TST is trying to do. Malcolm Jarry, one of the organizers behind the Harvard black mass, conceded that the black mass was meant as a provocation, stating, "It was a catalyst for the worst components of the worst people to come forth."[12] However, I think the intent behind the black mass was not to hurt the feelings of Catholics but rather to reveal that behind our self-congratulatory claims of religious tolerance lie unstated rules about what religious people may or may not say and do. Stephen Prothero describes the problem of "pretend pluralism" in which we claim to tolerate all religions while actually believing (or perhaps hoping) that they share a common essence and that any apparent differences are insignificant.[13] But as soon as the spirit of inclusion and dialogue is extended to groups beyond the invisible boundaries of "true religion," it is liable to be seen as "taking equality too far." The response that such demands for inclusion amount to "intolerance" is actually a strategy of maintaining these subtle forms of exclusion.

It should be noted that Satanists have long questioned the sincerity of those claiming to be tolerant. In a ceremony on August 8, 1969, Anton LaVey allegedly put forth a curse on the hippies, declaring, "Beware you psychedelic vermin! Your smug pomposity with its thin disguise of tolerance will serve you no longer!"[14] Where LaVey simply assumed claims of tolerance are a ruse, TST provides opportunities to prove claims of tolerance are sincere. By defiantly insisting that we take their difference seriously, TST calls us to approach the challenge of religious pluralism with humility.

Pretend Pluralism and Radical Pluralism

In the strictest sense, religious pluralism simply refers to the condition of religious diversity within a political community. The First Amendment inscribes such diversity as a principle of our democracy. However, theorists such as Diana Eck, who founded Harvard's Pluralism Project, suggest that pluralism means more than just diversity: whereas diversity is a given, pluralism is an achievement. Eck's brief essay "What Is Pluralism?" presents a four-point model. First, pluralism means active engagement with diversity. Second, pluralism exceeds mere tolerance for difference in favor of actively seeking understanding across lines of difference. Third, pluralism does not entail moral relativism as some conservative critics have claimed. Pluralism means that commitments and identities are taken seriously. Fourth, pluralism is based on dialogue about differences, which includes both criticism and self-criticism.[15]

Eck's vision of an America where religious differences are explored and celebrated is not without its scholarly critics. In her seminal book *A New Religious America*, she noted that many critics and theorists regard this idea as "wholly sentimental."[16] Responding to Eck's model of engaging difference, Russell McCutcheon writes:

> But it's not—nor ever was—as simple as this, is it? Precisely what does it mean to "encounter" each other? What undisclosed ground rules stipulate the nature and extent of this encounter? More than likely, the soap box isn't open to just anyone. After all, to participate in any so-called public space, one must already be operating by a set of sociopolitical values and rhetorical standards that make it possible, attractive, meaningful, and compelling

to "encounter," "understand," and "appreciate" the other in just this manner, in just this context, for just this end.

How, McCutcheon asks, do we engage with the religious commitments of people whose religion demands that they murder doctors who provide abortions? And if we are not willing to engage with this religious murderer, then pluralists are only really interested in dialogue concerning "the leftover, minor differences."[17]

While pluralists may roll their eyes at McCutcheon's objection that engaging the religious commitments of murderers or terrorists is impossible, he has a larger point that the language of tolerance and pluralism often conceals a power dynamic in which the tolerant wield the power to set the terms by which the less powerful may be tolerated. He writes, "By definition, politically oppositional, as well as socially marginalized, groups cannot be expected to tolerate anything since they do not set the standards for what gets to count as a real commitment nor can they change their situation, even if they wanted to. Tolerance does not take place on their terms. Instead, they are themselves tolerated. Seemingly benign discourses on tolerance therefore have a subtle irony at their very core: they are discourses of the powerful."[18]

When I interviewed Lucien Greaves during the build-up to the Harvard black mass, this power dynamic was very much at stake. He was not prepared for how upset the Catholic community was, and he expressed some willingness to assuage their fears that he was planning to publicly attack their religion. But he resented the demand that reconciliation be done *on their terms.* No one seemed interested in whether the Satanists felt offended or persecuted by the controversy: total deference to Boston's powerful Catholic community was a prerequisite before the Satanists could make any public expression of their viewpoint.

An essay by Tim Murphy noted that Satanism is the religion par excellence where scholars often abandon their professed commitment to engaging religious difference. He noted that in the wake of religious violence, scholars often defend religious communities from backlash, noting that the perpetrators are an extremist minority. "One the other hand," he writes, "We *never* (nor are we ever likely to) see a scholar of religion on Nightline or CNN saying, '*True* Satanism has been misrepresented here.'" This double standard when it comes to Satanism leads Murphy to demand, "Is the study of religion really an exercise in self-absorption where liked-minded, 'faith-based' liberal religious intellectuals find a kind of simpatico they cannot find in their home communities?"[19]

Murphy does not go as far as McCutcheon in critiquing the idea of pluralism. Rather he makes a distinction between pluralism as it is often practiced, where difference is celebrated only when it is cosmetic rather than substantive, and a position of "radical pluralism" that views religious commitments as a right to be defended, whether we find these commitments tasteful or not. Murphy points out that the Pluralism Project's database of religious communities contains no entries for Satanism. Despite this detail, I think this radical form of pluralism *is* what Eck had in mind when she wrote, "Pluralism is the dynamic process through which we engage with one another in and through our very deepest differences."[20] While McCutcheon points out that engaging with some religious commitments is "downright impossible," as a practical matter, we cannot achieve anything like real pluralism until we are willing to question preconceived notions of "true religion." A Satanic Harvard student holding a black mass is a far cry from an abortion-clinic bomber. The religious commitments of the Satanist are not "un-engageable," but there is a strong temptation to declare them so, especially because the Satanists lack the political clout of the "world religions." On the other hand, if we can overcome our deep-rooted horror of Satanism and ask the Satanists to explain themselves, then perhaps we have achieved a feat of pluralism worth bragging about.

Hate Speech or Hate Spin?: The Harvard Black Mass

TST's attempt to hold a black mass at Harvard University escalated into a fiasco that attracted national attention. It was also a case study in the hidden obstacles to pluralism that TST reveals: religious differences that are truly significant can appear as intolerance or hate speech, and social actions mounted in the name of defending religious tolerance can actually be a strategy for silencing minorities.

In one of the first ethnographies of religious Satanism, Edward Moody wrote, "It is ironical that a good part of the Satanic practice used today may be the product of the overactive imagination of overzealous inquisitors rather than duplication of the 'real' activities of the Devil worshipers of the time."[21] The black mass—a blasphemous ceremony that inverts Catholic worship—has its origins in Catholic legend. In the early modern period, details of the black mass legend, including orgies, the sacrifice of babies, and the abuse of communion wafers were collected from the testimony of accused heretics and demoniacs, but there is little evidence such events actually occurred.[22] David Frankfurter has theorized how stories about "rituals of inversion" function to reinforce the social order.[23] Ruben Van Luijk notes that tales of host desecration helped support the doctrine of transubstantiation promulgated by the Fourth Lateran Council: the host *must* contain the presence of God or the Satanists would not seek to harm it.[24]

The most influential black mass legend is Joris-Karl Huysmans's novel *La-bas* (1891). The denouement of Huysmans's story features a fallen priest, Canon Docre, performing a black mass in a ruined convent for a congregation of prostitutes and homosexuals. After performing the miracle of transubstantiation, Docre throws the bread to the congregation to defile and an orgy ensues. Durtal, a character who serves as a stand-in for Huysmans, witnesses the black mass and afterward muses that the actions of the Satanists suggest the doctrine of transubstantiation may be true.

Huysmans's novel is a "legend" in the sense used by folklorists of a story that someone, somewhere believes to be true.[25] Like his character Durtal, Huysmans was actively exploring Paris's occult underground, and it was widely rumored that he was describing a ritual he had actually witnessed.[26] At any rate, the *La-bas* legend *became* true through a process folklorists call "ostension."[27] From the late nineteenth century until the 1950s, tourists to the red-light districts of Paris and Rome could pay to see a "genuine" black mass. Some were even listed in tourist guidebooks.[28]

LaVey understood that the black mass was a legend and consciously repurposed it as a form of therapy used to de-condition the participants from the stifling effects of a Christian upbringing. He wrote, "The prime purpose is to reduce or negate stigma acquired through past indoctrination."[29] For non-theistic Satanists, including CoS and TST, the black mass celebrates autonomy from the religious majority and aids recovery from religious socialization that they never asked for. The fact that blasphemy is inherently upsetting to Christians is, in essence, a side effect of this process. LaVey stated, "Any ceremony considered a black mass must shock and outrage, as this seems to be the measure of its success."[30]

Significantly, Satanists are not the only religious movement to view blasphemy as a religious practice for undoing harmful socialization. Sangharakshita (née Dennis Lingwood) was a British convert to Buddhism as were most of his followers. He prescribed what he called "therapeutic blasphemy," claiming it was necessary for ex-Christians to reject Christianity on a profound emotional level in order to develop their potential.[31]

Satanists may be less inclined to feel guilty about offending Christians because they believe that Christians invented these blasphemous rituals themselves for propaganda purposes. In his essay "What Is a Black Mass?," Lucien Greaves wrote:

> Now, the Black Mass, when it is performed, is a repurposing of the mythology into a declaration of personal independence on the part of its participants. It's an act of liberation from stifling and oppressive superstitious precepts that were likely instilled at a young age. It's usually something people feel motivated to do somewhere in the introductory stages of Satanism, when they are just feeling empowered by the fact that they can engage in blasphemy—these forbidden symbolic acts—without consequence.[32]

In fact, when the Catholics first objected to the black mass, Greaves reportedly remarked, "This is not about them! This has absolutely nothing to do with them!"[33]

TST's black mass, presented through the Cultural Studies Club, would have been a two-hour presentation consisting of a lecture on the history of the black mass legend in early modern Europe followed by a heavily sanitized performance of the ritual described in La-bas. In New York, David Guinan was tapped as the "producer" for the ritual. He hired a play director to design the performance and recruited performers, including Michael Wiener who had played the "high priest" at the Rick Scott rally.[34] The Cultural Studies Club foresaw that this might be controversial and submitted their poster for approval to the Office of Student Affairs. It was Student Affairs who asked the Cultural Studies Club to specify that this was only a "re-enactment" of a black mass. But neither TST nor Student Affairs anticipated the vociferous response from Catholic students, who drew national attention to the event. The Cultural Studies Club reported that 700 people attempted to register to watch the black mass before their website was shut down—far more than could fit in the venue. They estimated that twice this many planned on attending but were unaware they had to register.[35] This attention fueled further backlash. A petition signed by 60,000 students, faculty, and alumni demanded the black mass be shut down. (Oddly, this petition was never presented to the

Cultural Studies Club). Harvard President Drew Faust and the Archdiocese of Boston both released statements condemning the event.

Although documented black masses were almost unheard of in 2014, opponents of the Harvard black mass seemed confident that they knew exactly what this ritual would entail. Cardinal Sean Patrick O'Malley, archbishop of Boston, simply told reporters to look up "black mass" on Wikipedia.[36] Two Catholic students wrote an op-ed for the *Harvard Crimson*, entitled "Hatred at Harvard," in which they claimed, "Historically, black masses have involved desecrating the Eucharist, which Catholics believe is the real body of Jesus Christ, by placing it on the genitals of a naked woman, urinating on it, and slitting an infant's throat to pour blood over it."[37] Presumably no one actually believed TST would commit infanticide, but many Catholics assumed the ritual would involve acquiring a consecrated host and desecrating it. As materialists, TST had little interest in obtaining a consecrated host because they do not believe that bread can contain holy presence. But when they tried to explain this, Catholic critics either misunderstood or assumed they were lying. Elizabeth Scalia, a conservative Catholic blogger, repeatedly called TST's headquarters to ask whether they planned to steal and desecrate a consecrated host. She initially spoke with a recently hired PR representative who apparently answered "yes" when asked whether TST would use a consecrated host. This confusion seems to have originated with Guinan. Guinan is a secular Jew with no training in Catholic theology. He told me, "I thought 'consecrated host,' meant a person who would lead the ritual, like an emcee."[38] Scalia subsequently got in touch with Lucien Greaves, who explained that their PR representative was unfamiliar with Catholic doctrine and had not understood her question. Greaves tried to explain what the black mass means to atheistic Satanists and that they had no interest in consecrated hosts. But Scalia seemed convinced this explanation was a cover-up.[39] Similarly, C. J. Doyle, executive director of the Catholic Action League, opined, "As the entire purpose of a Black Mass is to debase the Blessed Sacrament, assertions by the organizers that unconsecrated bread will be used ought not to be taken at face value."[40] St. Paul's, the parish closest to the Harvard campus, publicly announced that Satanists were attempting to steal a consecrated host and required everyone to consume the host directly in front of the Eucharistic minister.[41]

There were some efforts to talk about the religious differences at stake. Francis X. Clooney is a Jesuit priest and Hinduism scholar, and in 2014 he was the director of Harvard's Center for the Study of World Religion. An important insight into Clooney's intervention in the black mass comes from a 2011 editorial he published criticizing Catholic exorcist Gabrielle Amorth for his claim that practicing yoga causes demonic possession. Clooney noted that this claim is not only offensive to Hindus, but that it also mirrors anti-Catholic claims that Catholics practice "priestcraft" rather than Christianity. Pithily, Clooney ended his essay, "If the devil is anywhere in this, he surely finds to his liking careless words that sensationalize rather than shed light."[42] Clooney obtained Greaves's email from the Cultural Studies Club and simply asked whether he was going to use a consecrated host, pointing out that this was traditionally the sin qua non of a black mass. Greaves reemphasized that he would not and sarcastically asked Clooney whether he could tell a consecrated host from an unconsecrated one in a blind experiment. While the email exchange did not resolve anything, unlike every other Catholic and Harvard leader, Clooney demonstrated a desire to understand what TST was doing.

As the controversy built, the head of the Cultural Studies Club was asked to meet with the Extension School's dean of alumni and student affairs and explain in detail every prop and costume that would be used in the ritual. The dean's assistant found it objectionable that some of the performers would be dressed in sexualized nun's habits. However, the dean countered that this was unfair as no one would object to such a costume on Halloween. They suggested that the re-enactors desecrate a piece of broccoli, rather than bread, so that no one watching need worry whether a consecrated host was involved. This suggestion was related to Greaves, who found the idea amusing, but saw the proposed accommodation as one sided: the Satanists were expected to compromise their religious performance while the Catholics remained free to publish that Satanists murdered babies in the *Harvard Crimson*.

As the black mass became national news, Harvard leaders found themselves in a bind: on the one hand, they did not want to censor the Satanists' freedoms of speech and religion; on the other hand, they were under tremendous pressure to do exactly that. President Drew Faust released a statement framing the issue as balancing free expression and debate against civility. She did not censor TST but condemned their ceremony as "abhorrent" and "flagrantly disrespectful." She also announced her intention to participate in a Eucharistic holy hour that was being held in protest.[43] Leaders of the Harvard Extension School threaded this needle by offering the Cultural Studies Club a deal: if they would move their event to a private venue off campus, they would reimburse them for the cost of booking fees and a security detail. The Cultural Studies Club and TST agreed since far more people had registered for the event than their venue could hold. Guinan booked a nightclub near campus called the Middle East, but he never discussed a cancellation policy for the booking. Hours before the performance was to begin, the Middle East cancelled the event, explaining that negotiations with the Harvard Extension School had "fallen through."[44] Malcolm Jarry spoke with the owner of the Middle East for thirty minutes but could not get a straight answer as to why the event was cancelled. It was rumored that well-connected opponents of the black mass had threatened to revoke the club's liquor license if the Satanic performance were allowed.[45] Refusing to admit defeat, about fifty people, including the organizers and performers, went to a nightclub across the street from Harvard Yard called the Hong Kong. There, while Catholic demonstrators and counter-demonstrators from Boston's punk rock scene dominated Harvard Square, the Satanists performed their re-enactment as best they could. The media contacted the club's owner, who claimed he had no idea a black mass was being held there. Following the ritual, the Hong Kong received a phone call from management: the Satanists were all asked to leave, and the employee who had seated them was informed that he was fired. Feeling bad, the Satanists emptied their pockets and collected a few hundred dollars for the fired employee.[46]

Hate Speech and Hate Spin

The dominant narrative surrounding the black mass, emphasized by the Catholic community and Drew Faust, was that this was an unmitigated act of hatred toward Catholics, and that any claim of religious or academic freedom was a charade. James Bretzke, a Jesuit priest from Boston College, told the *Boston Globe*, "It is not educational, and anyone who believes it is displays a lack of understanding of the deeper message of this practice."[47] The "Hatred at Harvard" article alleged that TST was "guilty of greater fundamentalism than any group it intends to mock. Any notion that the Satanic Temple is simply a cultural group is nonsense."[48] Critics seemed certain that the issue was uncomplicated and that their assessment of the black mass as hate speech was self-evident. Michael Drea, the pastor of St. Paul's stated:

> The university is allowing this under the guise that it is educational, but anything rooted in hatred is not something that should be put in the same category as academic freedom and academic expression. There is no way to

misunderstand a satanic act that degrades the Catholic liturgy. There is no misunderstanding; it is just a fact.[49]

Many Catholics also complained that Harvard's "multiculturalism" amounted to a double standard in which everyone had to be tolerated *except* Catholics. In an open letter to Drew Faust, a priest from Fall River, Massachusetts, wrote, "Harvard simply would never allow itself or its properties to be associated with events that mock the religious beliefs, desecrate the sacred texts, or insult the spiritual sensitivities of Jews or Muslims."[50] Several critics called TST a "hate group" and compared the ceremony to a KKK rally or burning a Quran.[51]

However, supporters of the black mass felt this narrative demonstrated ignorance of TST and its motives. Michael Muhammad Knight is a Muslim writer and a Harvard Divinity School graduate. He saw TST not as hateful aggressors but as an embattled religious minority. In a response to an essay by Francis X. Clooney, Knight accused Clooney of

> a general failure to ask these people what their outrageous, offensive beliefs, and behaviors actually mean to *them*. Reducing the Satanic mass to a parody of the Catholic mass, he assumes that the Satanists involved must have no personal conviction that might endow the act with meaning, and discusses the act without any engagement of the human beings for whom it matters. In his editorial, they remain faceless, nameless, and voiceless.[52]

Supporters pointed out that TST and the Cultural Studies group had tried repeatedly to explain themselves, but that critics refused to listen. The president of the Extension School's Cultural Studies Club stated, "Any offense taken was largely based on willed ignorance or religious bigotry against Satanists."[53]

Supporters also noted that the alleged victims of the black mass were, in fact, a powerful majority. Massachusetts is 45 percent Catholic, and Boston has the highest percentage of Catholics of any US city.[54] This power differential is important to consider when comparing the black mass to a KKK rally or an American burning a Quran. These examples involve groups attempting to intimidate a minority, not dissenting against a majority. Opponents of the black mass had the political resources to intimidate venues hosting the black mass, while the Satanists received numerous death threats for their activities. Knight wrote, "What bothers me the most about the official quashing of the

Satanic Temple's mass by Harvard is that it is being hailed as a victory for religious tolerance—it's not. Instead, it's a case of a small group getting bullied
into submission because it offended a big religion."[55]

For Guinan, the backlash against the black mass led to a sort of epiphany
about his involvement with TST. Guinan had always been more drawn to the
prankish element of TST, which appealed to his skill set as a producer. The following morning as he rode the Amtrak from Boston back to New York, he felt re-
morse over how upset the Catholics had been. "I felt almost like crying," he said,
"I felt like the entire city of Boston was against us. I felt ashamed. I felt guilty."
But then he remembered that this was the city where Cardinal Bernard Law
had protected predator priests such as John J. Geoghan and paid settlements to
victims in exchange for non-disclosure agreements. He suddenly felt that the
Catholic Church of Boston had no moral authority and no right to judge him.
He recalled thinking, "Fuck them. And fuck them for making me feel that way."
He added, "I felt like this [TST] wasn't a Debordian Situationist prank anymore.
That's when I really started to think of TST as my religion."[56]

Journalism professor Cherian George coined the term "hate spin" to describe the sort of "bullying" described by Knight and Guinan. George writes,
"If conventional hate speech is strategic offense-*giving* by those who are intol-
erant of diversity, this other type of aggression comprises indignant offense-
taking. The former overtly victimizes a target community; the latter is about
playing the provoked victim, with malicious intent."[57] "Hate spin agents"
claim offense and demand respect while simultaneously denying others the
right to participate in society as equals. George regarded the "Ground Zero
Mosque" controversy as a classic example of a hate spin campaign, in which a
non-Muslim majority effectively blocked Muslims from constructing a community center by framing their building as a monument to hatred toward
Americans. The lens of "hate spin" highlights several factors of the black
mass controversy.

First, George challenges "the myth of spontaneous rage" in which certain
actions naturally incite populations to anger in a manner akin to a chemical
reaction. Instead, he suggests that hate spin agents coach the public in both
why they should be offended and how they should express their indignation.
Consider the following statement put out by the Archdiocese of Boston:

> When engaging with others on this topic, make sure first they understand
> what a black mass is and isn't. It is not a religious rite on its own, and just a
> ceremony developed by the practitioners of a different faith. It is by design

and intent a mockery of the Mass, every Catholic prayer turned into its inverse, culminating in the desecration of a consecrated Host, the Body, Blood, Soul and Divinity of Our Lord in the Eucharist, in acts that are too foul and disgusting to write here.

You may find that people who are defending the carrying out of this act do not understand what it actually is.[58]

This statement not only encourages Catholics to feel "disgusted," but it inoculates them against any information that might make them feel less upset. They are instructed *not* to entertain the idea that Satanists have religious freedom. It is suggested that the Satanists cannot even explain or defend their own actions because they themselves do not understand them. Finally, the reader is coached how to spread this view to others.

Second, the expressions of triumph following the "defeat" of the black mass were more suggestive of a group exulting in its own political power than a celebration of tolerance. The Catholic Action League's Joe Doyle called the episode "an example of and an instruction on what might be accomplished if the slumbering Goliath of American Catholicism might be aroused from its torpor."[59] Aurora Griffin, a Catholic student who was instrumental in mobilizing against the black mass, wrote an essay for the *Catholic Herald* entitled "How We Stopped a Black Mass at Harvard." Griffin's essay literally dehumanizes her opponents, writing, "Looking into their dead eyes and beholding their inhuman expressions, I felt a combination of fear and pity. These poor souls were in the grip of an otherworldly evil, not the spirit of rational or political protest." Griffin's essay also presents one of the starkest examples of "pretend pluralism":

If religious freedom means allowing people to practice and preach whatever evil things they will, it is no ideal to be defended. Furthermore, if we, as Christians, allow atrocities to happen in the name of religious freedom and think that our enemies will leave us be, we are sorely mistaken. Evil will not let us alone in the name of fairness.

Religious freedom is about people's ability to pursue the good as they rationally perceive it, and what constitutes the good can and should be a matter of public discussion. The Satanists fell outside of this because they were pursuing evil as evil. And even were they so misguided as to think their Satanic worship good, as Catholics we should be unafraid to articulate why they are wrong—to call evil as we see it, and try to stop it.[60]

Griffin's position, if I understand it correctly, is that religious differences may be discussed so as long as Catholics do not deem the other religion "evil," in which case it is undeserving of public discussion and Catholics should challenge it or possibly take more drastic efforts to "stop" its evil. Alternative interpretations of religious freedom are undesirable and enable "evil." These paragraphs demonstrate how it is possible to pride oneself on being tolerant while simultaneously denying others the right to act as equals.

Other agendas were also apparent in condemnations of the Harvard black mass besides the stated concern of offending Catholics. Campus Reform, a conservative news site dedicated to demonstrating "liberal bias" on college campuses, reported on the black mass controversy.[61] Rebecca Hamilton, a congresswoman from Oklahoma, wrote an editorial on the black mass urging readers not to send their children to Harvard and to lobby their senators to deny Harvard government research grants. Hamilton added, "We need to do this anyway, you know. Harvard and its little troupe of elite schools are not healthy for this country. They create a 1% that is disconnected from and hostile to the rest of us. They are, in many ways, predatory."[62] For Hamilton, stoking rage toward Satanists was conducive to an anti-intellectual political platform.

Aftermath

Writing for the Jesuit magazine *America*, Francis X. Clooney mused, "Perhaps, in the long run, the whole affair will have some good consequences, if it leads to a conversation at Harvard on religions, lived, real and present." On this much, Clooney and TST were in agreement. On September 22, 2014, Clooney hosted a discussion at Harvard's Center for the Study of World Religion called "What Was That All About? Revisiting the Black Mass Controversy." Lucien Greaves attended, as did the dean of the Divinity School and representatives from the Cultural Studies Club. Tellingly, no one from St. Paul's parish came, even though this parish had been the most vocal in opposing the black mass.

I reached out to all the priests who wrote publicly about the Harvard black mass, but Clooney was the only one who responded to my inquiries. When I asked Clooney about the discussion in September, he provided me with the following account:

At the time of the controversy, in the days before the announced performance, my goal was to try to understand the situation, and thus cool
it down a bit. I was on email with a dean at the School of Education several times. I had some contact with Catholic faculty around the University.
I wrote an email to Drew Faust expressing my concern about the matter,
which in my view the university could hardly write off as a "student matter."
Thus too my initial contact too with the resolutely anonymous Harvard
sponsors and then with Lucien Greaves, via an email address of his that
I discovered online.

As a scholar of religion who has studied rituals in both India and the
West, I was interested in what would be the structure of the performance,
and whether, as many of us feared, a consecrated host would be used. I was
promised, but never received, the ritual/rubrics of the planned rite, which
at one point I was told were "from the Latin." To this day I do not know what
actually was the form of the practice, planned or carried out. Perhaps it was
merely an implementation of that vivid chapter from the French novel, *Là-
Bas* by Joris-Karl Huysmans?

As the scene heated up, the Christian rhetoric too became unhelpful,
more heat than light, and aimed more at shouting down the Satanists than
in understanding what was going on. Some of the rhetoric seemed only to
feed into the TST hope to gain attention and cause a bit of havoc.

In September of that year, I hosted a discussion of the event at the Center
for the Study of World Religions. Lucien Greaves and one of the campus
sponsors were among those in attendance. No official from the university
or School of Education came, nor did anyone from St. Paul's parish, which
had led the charge against the May event. Nothing was resolved, and we did
not come to agreement on what should have happened in May, but it was
good to sit in a civil manner to discuss what had happened.

On another level, I fear that the proponents of TST are playing with fire,
so to speak. Mr. Greaves and his companions are not malicious or evil, as
far as I can see, but are seeking rather to provoke. But there are real and dark
forces of malice in the world that are nothing to be toyed with. Even if one
does not believe in the standard portrayals of Satan, what "Satan" stands
for is real and dangerous. The Satanic oughtn't casually to be thought of as
friendly to the human, a remedy for institutions, etc.

There was a real point to the novel, *Là-Bas*, that need be remembered: Catholics and old-fashioned Satanists are those who take evil very

seriously, just as they take the presence of Christ in the Eucharist very seriously. If nothing is sacred, nothing can be profaned or blasphemed. If Satan ends up seeming to be a nice guy, a banality simply intended to annoy, then the Satanists also make their own project banal as well. Better if we all face up to "performances" of evil in our world and ground ourselves in sacred truths and realities that can resist the real evil that we see every day.[63]

Malcolm Jarry felt that while Clooney had entered dialogue in good faith, he never truly understood what TST was doing. For Jarry, TST's project is neither banal nor devoid of the sacred: TST fights for reason and empathy because they hold these values as sacred. The purpose of blasphemy is not to embrace nihilism by destroying the sacred, but to take those things alleged to be sacred and hold them to scrutiny.[64] But the fact that Clooney organized this discussion a full semester after the controversy shows, I think, a sincere desire to understand TST. Greaves seemed to appreciate this gesture and expressed some regret about responding sarcastically to Clooney's initial email. Jarry was less impressed and expressed his surprise that few people condemned the intolerance of Boston's Catholic community during the episode.

Clooney stated that "nothing was resolved," but why should anything be "resolved" when a Catholic priest and a Satanist discuss religion? Clooney raised his concern that TST is inadvertently invoking supernatural evil, despite their materialism. But if pluralism means not leaving religious commitments behind, then he could do no other. While some might regard this meeting as pointless or even farcical, I think this is what "radical pluralism" looks like in practice. If the black mass affair caused some at Harvard to be more self-critical about their understanding of religious pluralism, then Clooney was correct, and the affair did have good consequences.

Unbowed and Unfettered: Satanic Invocations

TST's practice of offering to hold prayer invocations before city council meetings served much the same function as the Harvard black mass. But whereas the black mass challenged the sincerity of an allegedly tolerant academic community, Satanic prayer invocations test the sincerity of a nation that claims not to have an established religion or to engage in religious discrimination. The catalyst for TST's prayer invocations was *Greece v. Galloway* (2014).

The plaintiffs in that case—a Jewish woman and an atheist woman—objected that the town of Greece, New York, began town council meetings with sectarian invocations. They argued this practice violated the establishment clause and wanted ecumenical prayers that would not alienate religious minorities who needed to conduct business at these meetings. In a 5-4 decision, the Supreme Court ruled that Greece was not violating the establishment clause so long as no one was coerced to participate in the prayer and religious minorities who wished to offer the invocation were not discriminated against. In a dissenting opinion, Justice Elena Kagan noted that all of Greece's prayers had been delivered by Christians, save for a brief period after the plaintiffs threated their suit when a Jew, a Wiccan priestess, and a Baha'i minister were allowed to offer the invocation. Kagan opined, "[T]he majority misjudges the essential meaning of the religious worship in Greece's town hall, along with its capacity to exclude and divide."[65] Significantly, the five justices in the majority were Catholic, while three of the four dissenters were Jewish.

TST followed *Greece v. Galloway* with interest. However, the outcome sought by the plaintiffs—that Greece allow only inclusive, ecumenical prayers—was the only solution deemed unacceptable by TST. During arguments in 2013, Justice Alito asked whether any religious prayer could be given that would not exclude religious minorities. Douglas Laycock suggested that prayers invoking "the almighty" might be acceptable. This immediately raised challenges that "the almighty" excludes atheists and polytheists. Justice Scalia piled on, asking, "What about devil worshippers?" Laycock responded, "Well, if devil worshippers believe the devil is the almighty, they might be OK. But they're probably out." In an interview for *The Atlantic*, Lucien Greaves commented on this exchange:

> The discussion regarding some type of all-inclusive public prayer naively assumes one type of religious construct (that of servitude and supernaturalism) while seemingly disregarding not only other religious conceptions, but the presence of those who don't wish to associate themselves with any type of religion whatsoever.[66]

TST's view is that there must either be no prayers at all or all religious minorities must be allowed to give invocations. On this much, the majority of the Supreme Court agreed with TST. But critics of the *Greece v. Galloway* decision noted it was easy to *say* anyone could give an invocation, but that in practice this stacked the deck against minorities. Law professor Ira Lupa stated, "The majority faith in a particular community can dictate the prayers and minority faiths could be left out if they don't step up and say, 'Hey, what about us?' "[67] "Stepping up" was exactly what TST planned to do.

In his majority opinion, Justice Kennedy specified that prayers must "lend gravity" to the occasion and should not threaten damnation or preach conversion. Lucien Greaves wrote a Satanic invocation he felt fell within these parameters. The day of decision, it appeared in the *Los Angeles Times*:

> Let us stand now, unbowed and unfettered by arcane doctrines born of fearful minds in darkened times. Let us embrace the Luciferian impulse to eat of the Tree of Knowledge and dissipate our blissful and comforting delusions of old. Let us demand that individuals be judged for their concrete actions, not their fealty to arbitrary social norms and illusory categorizations. Let us reason our solutions with agnosticism in all things, holding fast only to that which is demonstrably true. Let us stand firm against any and all arbitrary authority that threatens the personal sovereignty of One or All. That which will not bend must break, and that which can be destroyed by truth should never be spared its demise. It is Done. Hail Satan.[68]

Within two years, TST members were offering to give this invocation in towns across the country. In many cases, this resulted in exactly the kind of division and political turmoil that Kagan had warned about. It also caused these communities to reexamine their policies on prayer invocations. In fact, many communities had no policies regulating prayer invocations until TST's intervention.

Arizona

In December 2015 TST members filed their first request to give a prayer invocation in Phoenix, Arizona. Phoenix was chosen in part because in 2012 the city had barred Dianne Post, a human rights attorney and member of the Freedom from Religion Foundation, from offering a secular humanist invocation. She had threatened to sue, and some of the attorneys involved, including Andrew Siedel, moved in the same circles as TST. (Post was allowed to give an invocation on February 4, 2015.) In September 2015, Greaves connected two TST members living in Tucson to spearhead a Satanic invocation in Phoenix—Michelle Shortt, an alternative model, would deliver the invocation, and Stu de Haan, a criminal defense attorney, would provide legal representation.[69] In a 2018 interview, Shortt said she had no regrets but remarked, "Looking back I feel so naive making a decision that would change everything about my life."[70]

Their request was initially granted at the recommendation of the city's attorney, and Shortt was scheduled to deliver a prayer invocation on February 17, 2016. But almost immediately some members of the City Council objected that this was "a gimmick" meant to stop all prayer invocations and suggested the city face a lawsuit rather than capitulate.[71] Four members of the City Council, led by Sal DiCiccio, set to work drafting new rules for prayer invocation with an emergency clause that would make them go into effect immediately in order to "disinvite" TST.

On February 3 a televised City Council meeting was held to discuss ending the tradition of prayer invocations and replacing them with a moment of silence. The meeting lasted three hours in which over fifty people, including numerous pastors, gave public testimony. De Haan compared the meeting to "a medieval witch hunt happening before my eyes."[72] Many speakers claimed that the United States was founded as an explicitly Christian nation and that there was no requirement to tolerate other religions. Some wept and described the situation in overtly supernatural terms, warning that the land would be "cursed" if Christian invocations stopped. Cindy Petkovich, founder of a deliverance ministry that practices "strategic level" spiritual warfare, claimed to have spent thousands of hours ministering to people who have been damaged by Satanists.[73] She urged the Council to continue offering Christian prayers out loud and not to invite in a "strange God."

Several speakers and Council members challenged whether TST had standing to offer an invocation. They objected that Shortt and De Haan were "outsiders" from Tucson. Some claimed TST was not a religion, including Sal DiCiccio who opined, "It's a cult. It's not a real religion. It just isn't." Monica Dennington, who runs an evangelical YouTube channel, claimed TST is a hate group because modeling photos she had discovered on Shortt's social media constituted hate speech against women. Dennington told the Council, "You will see images of Michelle Shortt in bondage, in nudity, in all kinds of positions that are not appropriate and that are degrading to another minority group, which is women and girls. We cannot stand by while a hate group which promotes violence against women stands up and gives your invocation." Dennington was especially incensed by a photo taken for the "Tucson

Maidens of Metal" calendar in which Shortt appeared to cut the throat of an-other model. Although the photo had obviously been done with makeup and stage blood, Dennington equated it with actual decapitations perpetrated by ISIS stating, "It's [the photo] considered by a woman like me to be terrorism." DiCiccio furthered this comparison, telling local news, "Well, ISIS is evil. What is Satan?"[74]

A minority of speakers advocated for the moment of silence, including Dianne Post. A veteran explained that in Iraq he had seen people killing each other because they refused to accept religious difference. Another veteran cited survey data indicating that most Phoenix residents are not church-attending Christians and argued that those speaking amounted to an intol-erant minority. He added, "The Satanists want you to do what you're doing. They want you to show your true colors."

In the end, the Council voted in a 5-4 decision to adopt the moment of silence rather than allow Shortt to give the invocation. De Haan expressed surprise that the Council would really end a sixty-five-year-old tradition just to prevent one Satanic invocation. Shortt told reporters, "I think it's a little excessive."[75] The rightwing website *World Net Daily* framed the moment of silence as a victory, announcing,

> Satanists who thought they outsmarted the Phoenix City Council and cowed them with subtle threats of legal action into allowing them the right to deliver invocations, along with leaders of Christian churches, at the be-ginning of local government gatherings were thwarted at the last minute when governing officials decided to go with a moment of silence instead.[76]

But TST was anything but discouraged. De Haan offered to arrange Satanic invocations in the Arizona cities of Tucson, Sahuarita, Chandler, and Scottsdale. Soon the entire situation began to repeat itself in Scottsdale. The city initially scheduled a Satanic invocation for April 5, 2016.[77] But when Mayor Jim Lane began to receive thousands of emails condemning TST's in-vocation, he announced that the city was seeking "a clean path, one that is legal" that could reject the Satanists.[78]

Back in Phoenix, the city held another vote on March 3 and passed a new rule that only chaplains from the Phoenix police and fire departments may deliver invocations. With this move, which the city's attorney felt would prob-ably be declared constitutional, Phoenix was finally free to hold exclusively Christian prayers without having to allow prayers from Satanists or any other religious minorities.[79] TST initially threatened to sue, but Scottsdale became the focus of TST's legal resources.

The April 5 invocation in Scottsdale was rescheduled to July 6. In late May, Scottsdale cancelled the invocation, explaining that only institutions "with a substantial connection to the Scottsdale community" may offer prayers.[80] A student pastor from a local Baptist church was given the July 6 slot instead. This policy had not existed previously, and De Haan argued this was a clear case of religious discrimination. He began consulting with attorneys from the Freedom From Religion Foundation in preparation for a lawsuit. In November 2016, Mayor Jim Lane issued flyers for his re-election campaign. Among his five accomplishments was listed, "Stopped so called 'Satanists' from mocking City Hall traditions with a 'prayer.'"[81]

Florida

In Florida, TST's invocation drew the attention of a David Suhor, who had been protesting the Christian monopoly on local prayer invocations since 2014. In October 2015, Suhor attended a meeting of the Okaloosa County School Board that was preceded by a prayer meeting with five pastors. Suhor walked to the front of the room and interrupted the pastors by giving an eclectic invocation of his own, calling on Yahweh as well as numerous gods and mythological figures. For a moment Suhor's prayer was met with stunned silence. Then the room exploded into shouted impromptu prayers. A video showed the dueling invocations escalating for fifteen minutes: the audience began to sing hymns, clap, and even speak in tongues. Suhor continued to quietly recite his eclectic selection of prayers. Eventually two men began to shout prayers of exorcism in Suhor's face. Footage of the event reveals both Suhor's almost unfathomable tenacity and the incredible entrenchment of Christianity within the local Florida government.[82]

The following year Suhor co-founded TST-West Florida. After nearly six months of paperwork, Suhor was scheduled to give a Satanic invocation on July 14, 2016. As in Phoenix, a special meeting was held to discuss whether a Satanic invocation would actually be allowed. Once again, some citizens claimed the invocation would curse their town. Terrorism was invoked again with one woman pointing to Suhor and declaring, "That person right there is a representative of ISIS."[83] On July 14, Suhor arrived in a hooded black robe to a council chamber filled with Christian demonstrators who began shouting the words of the Our Father. Someone even splashed holy water on the podium.[84] Suhor waited for nearly two minutes for them to stop. When the Council president asked the crowd to be quiet, an elderly man responded, "No! He's gonna pronounce curses on us! And you!" The president then had police escort demonstrators who would not be quiet out of the room. One woman shouted, "This is not a constitutional right!" as she was ushered out.[85] Suhor is a musician and has a background in liturgical music. When he finally approached the podium, he blew a note on a pitch pipe before delivering Greaves's invocation to the tune of "The Lord's Prayer" composed by Albert Malotte. This was the first time TST's invocation was given at a public meeting. The remaining demonstrators kept prayers to a low mutter. The man who claimed Suhor was pronouncing a curse stood less than an arm's length behind him whispering, "I bind thee, Satan!" Council member Gerald Wingate walked out in protest. He later explained, "You've got somebody who is worshiping Satan and who is coming in when the majority of us in this area serve God."[86] When he finished, Suhor removed his robe, revealing a sensible T-shirt and khakis, sat down, and waited for an opportunity to speak. He also held up a sign that read "Matthew 6:5–6," a passage in which Jesus instructs his disciples not to pray "like the hypocrites." He later approached the podium and urged the Council to stop pushing "Christian privilege" and to adopt a moment of silence that would "let everyone pray— or not—according to their own conscience."[87] Like Scottsdale, Pensacola had no written policy for prayer invocations. In February 2017, the City Council voted to limit prayer invocations to a list of local religious organizations maintained by the city clerk. Suhor said that he must be put on the list or he would sue.[88]

Suhor has continued a series of provocations meant to call attention to the loopholes used to maintain a Christian monopoly over prayer invocations. He requested to give an invocation before a meeting of the Emerald Coast Utilities Authority (ECUA) but was told that only board members may give invocations. The ECUA's attorney advised that invocations be given *before* meetings are called to order. Chairwoman Louis Benson argued that this move accommodated Suhor because those who did not wish to hear a Christian invocation could still attend the full meeting. So, on August 24, 2017, Suhor arrived before a meeting wearing an inverted cross, stood at the front of the room, and began to deliver the TST invocation. When told to be silent, he asked whether the meeting had begun. After being told it had not, Suhor continued and explained that he was merely exercising his right to pray in a public place. A guard began to physically drag Suhor away, when Benson banged her gavel and said, "I call this meeting to order." At this, Suhor said, "Thank you, I will be silent," and sat down. But then Benson began giving an invocation, so Suhor stood back up and began to chant the "Hare Krishna" mantra. The guard again began trying to remove Suhor, who again asked whether the meeting was in order. Benson said that the meeting was currently in recess. Suhor refused to sit down and was dragged away by two guards. Suhor's point seemed clear: the prayer invocation was not technically part of the meeting, but in practice, it was impossible to tell when the meeting had begun and when it had not, making this distinction meaningless.[89] In February 2018, Suhor returned to an ECUA meeting and again prayed aloud—this time reciting the Our Father—explaining that he would sit down when the meeting was called to order. He was arrested and found guilty of trespassing and resisting arrest. Suhor announced plans to appeal and to sue the ECUA for violating his right to free speech.[90] In April 2019, Suhor's conviction was overturned although Benson insisted she was right to have him arrested.[91]

Other Invocations

In contrast to the turmoil that ensued in Florida, a community in Alaska allowed a TST member to give an invocation with minimal disruption. In August 2016, a month after Michelle Shortt had been scheduled to give an invocation in Scottsdale, college student Iris Fontana gave the TST invocation before the Kenai Peninsula Borough Assembly meeting. One assembly member walked out, but most were described as indifferent. Blaine Gilman, the head of the Assembly, explained that while he found the Satanic prayer "sort of offensive," it was important to protect the freedoms of speech and religion. Fontana told reporters, "I actually was very impressed at their reaction."[92]

There were attempts to stoke outrage over the invocation, but they gained little traction. Church Militant, a rightwing Catholic news group that reports frequently on TST, claimed the invocation was "using religion as a cloak" to "mock Catholic worship."[93] There were rumors that local Catholics would perform an exorcism to counteract the invocation. Instead, a small group of Catholic activists convened and protested a local Planned Parenthood where they clashed with counter-protestors. Catholic activist Toby Burk spoke of "the two evils" in the community of abortion and the invocation.[94] This response suggests an effort to channel excitement over a Satanic invocation into an existing pro-life agenda.

In October 2016, the Borough Assembly passed new rules stating that only local groups that meet for "the primary purpose of sharing a religious perspective" may gave invocations. This language appears to have been motivated by claims that TST is not *truly* religious but actually political. The ACLU of Alaska sued, pointing out that this language deliberately excludes atheists and similar minority groups, thereby failing to comply with *Greece v. Galloway*. In October 2018, an Alaska superior court struck down the new rules as unconstitutional and Fontana went on the schedule to give a second invocation.[95]

In October 2016, Boston became the next invocation battleground. The Boston city council uses a system in which each council member may invite two to three speakers a year to give the invocation. Ideally, council members invite leaders who have benefited their district. Travis LeSaffre of TST-Boston requested to give an invocation, but was rejected.[96] C.J. Doyle, who had spoken out against the Harvard black mass two years earlier, objected that *The Boston Globe* would even cover "the complaint by a fringe group of cultists" perpetuating "a series of attacks upon Catholics, who comprise, nearly, half the population of Massachusetts."[97] LeSaffre requested to give an invocation again in August 2017 but was ignored. In October the chapter threatened to sue.[98]

In November 2016, a TST member applied to give an invocation before a meeting of the Austin City Council. Once again, conservatives lobbied for new rules that would make it harder for minority groups to give invocations. Councilwoman Ellen Troxclair opined, "[TST] purposefully goes around to cities trying to get on the invocation list and if they're denied they seek to file a lawsuit."[99] By this time Stu de Haan had been promoted to TST's National Council. De Haan pointed out that TST was threatening more lawsuits over invocations than it had the resources to follow through on and the organization was in danger of earning a reputation for idle threats. He urged local chapters to *stop* requesting prayer invocations so that the national organization could focus on suing the city of Scottsdale. This effectively stopped the explosion of invocation cases. However, Malcolm Jarry decided to revisit the Boston chapter's case where Council members invite speakers. He attempted to explain to the City Council's attorney why their policy was discriminatory. After this failed, in February 2019, he filed a complaint with the

Massachusetts Commission Against Discrimination. Greaves noted that the Boston's City Council policy of "invitation only" invocations amounted to "the very definition of discrimination."[100] Malcolm Jarry explained that the complaint was necessary because he was simply tired of everything taking twice as long and costing twice as much because of discriminatory practices toward Satanists.

"Taking Equality Too Far"

In February 2018, TST finally filed suit against Scottsdale, alleging religious discrimination and citing the mayor and the members of City Council as defendants. They sought an injunction either preventing the city from denying the right to give invocations to non-Christians or, failing this, prohibiting invocations. They did not seek any specific financial compensation besides attorney's fees and other costs. By this time, TST had used the Freedom of Information Act to request internal communications from the City Council regarding their invocation. Their findings, cited in the complaint, strengthened their case significantly. After Shortt's invocation was scheduled, the mayor's office had attempted to fill as many slots as possible. An internal email explained, "Unfortunately, we weren't able to secure someone else to commit to the invocation on July 6th." Mayor Jim Lane had claimed that the invocations included "Christians, Jews, Muslims, Buddhists, Hindus and countless other faiths." But there was no record of Muslims, Buddhists, or Hindus ever having given invocations. TST also discovered an email exchange from February 11, 2016, in which an angry constituent wrote to Councilwoman Kathy Littlefield that she was "appalled" the city would allow Satanists to speak. As at the Harvard black mass, she compared TST to Nazis and the KKK. Littlefield responded, "Personally, I like having the prayers, do NOT want the Satanists, and I think this is taking equality too far. However, we are all sworn to uphold the law and cannot disobey it just because we find it undesirable and stupid."[101] Scottsdale attempted to have the case dismissed, but in August 2018 a federal judge for the district court in Arizona commented that *Satanic Temple v. Scottsdale* was a case of first impression, meaning that it raised a question about the interpretation of a law that had never arisen before. At the time of this writing, the case is expected to go before the Ninth Circuit Court of Appeals.

To raise legal funds, the Arizona chapter held a fundraiser in Tucson entitled, "Speak of the Devil: Equality Gone Too Far." The fundraiser included performances by several heavy metal bands as well as a Satanic ritual that functioned as a critique of the situation in Scottsdale through performance art. The ritual, which seemed influenced by ancient Greek theater, began with a performer dressed as the personification of Justice, inviting the audience to render judgment on what they saw. Next, Michelle Shortt took the stage and expressed her desire to speak on behalf of "reason and individual sovereignty." At this, other performers began to appear on the right half of the stage, arguing that only those submissive to God deserve the right to speak. A performer apparently dressed as Councilwoman Littlefield stepped forward and declared, "We may be equal and I cannot stop these Satanists from their misguided beliefs. But allowing them a platform is equality gone too far!" On the left side of the stage, performers began to gather dressed in black and fetish clothing, advocating for Shortt's right to speak. A chorus began in which performers on the left cried, "We speak too!" to which those on the right replied, "No, not you!" Finally, Shortt, who had become completely obscured by the arguing performers, parted the two sides and announced, "Enough! I need you not to speak for me! I need you not to silence me! I demand my right to speak to my beliefs, wherever such right exists." She then donned a Baphomet mask and was hoisted into the air by hooks that had been inserted into the flesh of her upper back. This is called a "suspension performance" and can be done relatively safely by trained professionals. Hovering above the stage, Shortt intoned Satan's lines from *Paradise Lost*:

> Turning our tortures into horrid arms
> Against the Torturer; when, to meet the noise
> Of his almighty engine, he shall hear
> Infernal thunder, and, for lightning, see
> Black fire and horror shot with equal rage
> Among his Angels, and his throne itself
> Mixed with Tartarean sulphur and strange fire,
> His own invented torments.

A heavy metal riff began, and performers spun Shortt about the stage, displaying the skill of Shortt and the suspensionist as the ritual's crescendo.

In 2019, the exact same pattern played out again when the town of Sahuarita, Arizona, scheduled a Satanic invocation for September 9. Once again, there were angry editorials about allowing Satanists to speak, and the town retroactively changed its policies on invocations. The mayor claimed the change was being made because of the town's twenty-fifth anniversary.[102] It is uncertain what will happen to TST's case in the Ninth Circuit. However, the short history of Satanic prayer invocations reveals several interesting insights. First, TST seems more sincere than their critics portray them. TST's opponents frequently claimed that TST's goal was to silence public prayer. In Phoenix, Monica Dennington claimed that TST's strategy was to force an "impossible choice" between stopping prayer and allowing an intolerable Satanic prayer. To some extent this is true: like the Freedom From Religion Foundation, TST has expressed that the simplest way to honor the establishment clause without excessive government entanglement over what sort of prayers may be said is to simply not have prayer invocations. TST's theory of "Lucien's Law" also demonstrates that they understand how to leverage intolerance toward Satanists to achieve their goals.

However, TST does not see this as an "impossible choice" at all. Greaves explained, "We're neither fighting solely for our presence in the public square, nor are we fighting to have public religious forums shut down. . . . What we're fighting against is a situation in which one religious voice assumes a place of privilege with Government sanction."[103] Significantly, Greaves was highly critical of Chaz Stevens, an activist not affiliated with TST, who organized a campaign in 2016 called "Satan or Silence." Stevens proposed a Satanic invocation that involved a mariachi band and twerking (a dance that involves wobbling the buttocks lasciviously). Greaves felt a Satanic invocation should be made in good faith and feature real religious commitments, rather than merely mocking prayer.[104] For TST, what is "impossible" is to claim freedom of religion while regularly holding prayers that are exclusively Christian and denying minority religions the same privilege. Shortt explained, "We call institutions on their bluff." When asked about Phoenix's initial decision to replace prayer invocations with a moment of silence, she responded, "*They* destroyed public prayer!," adding, "They're just mad that they're caught in their hypocrisy."[105]

Second, TST's "test" of these communities' claims to tolerate other faiths elicited some disturbing results. Responses from the community suggested that a large segment of the public had no comprehension of the constitutional issues at stake and understood only simplistic ideas of "majority rule." Public comments posted about TST's invocation included such statements as, "How about we get some red-blooded American children of God together and wipe these motherfuckers out!"[106] Such intimidation tactics are common when plaintiffs argue that prevailing norms and traditions violate the establishment clause, yet they often go unmentioned in court.[107] De Haan produced credible evidence that Mayor Jim Lane dishonestly exaggerated the level of diversity in the Scottsdale invocations. Finally, Phoenix's solution to allow only chaplains from fire and police departments, which has gone unchallenged, seems to have effectively thwarted *Greece v. Galloway*. Because marginalized religious groups are unlikely to ever have chaplains in these departments, this policy ensures that giving prayer invocations is a privilege reserved only for the most established religions.

These kinds of obstacles are common when minorities seek to exercise their rights, and it is because of this history that Harvard law professor Noah Feldman praised TST's efforts in Phoenix. He cited James Madison's concern that written guarantees of religious freedom amount to "parchment barriers" because the religious majority can effectively thwart the freedom of the minority. The only true protection was religious diversity that includes religious minorities willing to mobilize to defend their rights.[108] While the majority may roll their eyes at such "unreasonable" people as David Suhor and Stu De Haan, they serve an important function in a democracy.

Finally, the dynamic of "hate spin" repeatedly manifested in the discourse around many of these invocations as various actors attempted to generate outrage over the Satanists that could be harnessed into political action. Conservative Catholics continued to frame Greaves's Satanic invocation— which refrains from mentioning Christianity specifically and says nothing about Catholicism—as an attack on Catholics. At the close of the emotional Phoenix City Council meeting to discuss switching to a moment of silence, Mayor Greg Stanton stated, "I find it very sad that a member of this council is so small and desperate to score political points that he openly questions the faith of his colleagues by suggesting that members of this body were pushing—I quote—Satanic prayer. Frankly it's the most despicable thing that I have ever witnessed in my service to the city. This has gone over the line."[109] Although Stanton did not mention anyone by name, he was referring to Sal DiCiccio, a conservative Catholic, who used the episode to cast his opponents on the Council as sympathetic to Satanists and adversarial toward Christianity.

In an editorial discussing the Harvard black mass and Suhor's invocation in Pensacola, John Horvat II, vice president for the American Society for the Defense of Tradition, Family, and Property (TFP), provides a veritable blueprint for hate spin. He explains:

> When the protest is fervent enough, it has the effect of depriving the Satanists of the stage they demand to push their victim narrative. In fact, the victim game is reversed. People begin to see the townspeople, Catholics or other offended parties as the victims of authorities that deliver top-down decisions against the wishes of those they are supposed to represent.[110]

In other words, the TFP strategy is to protest so "fervently" that when minorities exercise their rights, they appear to be victimizing the majority. These sorts of maneuvers suggest that religious minorities not only have to fight for representation but must also thwart efforts to cast their struggle as an assault on the religious rights of the majority.

The Satanic Challenge to Pluralism

The claim has been made that TST does not really believe in religious pluralism or religious freedom but rather uses these concepts as a sort of Trojan horse to obtain a platform for "hate speech" against Catholics or to banish religion from the public square. I argue that this claim is not only inaccurate but is itself an attack on the ideals of pluralism and religious freedom. With little exception, every TST member I met expressed belief in the idea of a religiously plural society where no religion enjoys special privileges over others. Jon Winningham, co-head of TST-Houston stated bluntly, "I want my kid to grow up in a country where you can be whatever fucking religion you want."[111]

However, this does not mean that including Satanists—whether in pluralist dialogue or in rotating prayer invocations—is an easy task or one devoid of anxieties. Including a combative, non-theistic worldview such as TST is a *challenge* to any model of religious pluralism, but it is also *challenging* communities that claim to value religious freedom toward a form of pluralism that is more self-reflexive and more just. Responding to this challenge by claiming it is "self-evident" that TST is not a religion, or that it is a hate group, or making hysterical claims that TST are terrorists affiliated with ISIS amounts—at best—to intellectual laziness. At worst, this response devolves into hate spin that ultimately threatens the existence of religious liberty.

Whether or not Satanists deserve to be tolerated is a question for pretend pluralists. As McCutcheon pointed out, "tolerance" is a discourse of the powerful. The question for the radical pluralist is how we can accept and respond to the reality that members of our society—entitled to the same rights and freedoms as everyone else—practice Satanism. In the Book of Job, Satan appears as the accuser challenging Job's devotion to God. Satan tests just how much pain Job can bear before renouncing his core beliefs. TST adopts a similar role as accuser when American communities claim to support religious pluralism: How much discomfort can we tolerate before we abandon our professed values? The penultimate line of TST's prayer vocation reads, "That which will not bend must break, and that which can be destroyed by truth should never be spared its demise." If we cannot bear even a few black-clad gadflies before declaring that "equality has gone too far," then our claims of tolerance have broken, and the accuser has won his case.

8

Conclusion: Speak of the Devil

The Satanic Temple as American Counter-Myth

> During almost fifteen centuries has the legal establishment of
> Christianity been on trial. What have been its fruits? More or less in
> all places, pride and indolence in the Clergy; ignorance and servility
> in the laity, in both, superstition, bigotry and persecution.
> —James Madison, "Memorial and Remonstrance Against Religious
> Assessments"[1]

> Time is a continuing, unceasing series of alternating cycles. An Age
> of Ice is always followed by Age of Fire. When the pendulum swings
> too far in one direction, we act to swing it back the other way. That is
> Satan's function as the adversary.
>
> —Anton LaVey[2]

Satanism often appears as a sort of epiphenomenon in the sense that it is
a reaction to a Christian establishment and frequently an indictment of it.
I have tried to demonstrate that TST—and by extension religious Satanism—
matters because this reaction is part of a conversation in which the core
values of American society are negotiated. In the introduction I presented
TST as a manifestation of the "culture war cycle" described by Stephen
Prothero in which the right strikes out and the left strikes back. Somewhat
similarly, Massimo Introvigne has described a "pendulum theory" of
Satanic history that moves in three phases.[3] First, a small Satanic subculture
emerges and is discovered by the larger society. Second, established social
and religious forces respond with a wave of "anti-Satanism" that demonizes
Satanism and wildly exaggerates its scope in the form of a moral panic.
Third, the anti-Satanists are called out on their dishonesty and lose all credibility. (As the Satanic Panic was waning, theologian Ted Peters coined the

Speak of the Devil. Joseph P. Laycock, Oxford University Press (2020). © Oxford University Press.
DOI: 10.1093/oso/9780190948498.001.0001

term anti-anti-Satanism to describe this backlash.)[4] In the aftermath, those opposed to the dominant society acquire a renewed interest in Satanism, a new Satanic subculture organizes, and the cycle begins anew. TST is a good example of the third phase of Introvigne's theory as Malcolm Jarry, Lucien Greaves, and many other TST members were molded by the Satanic Panic of the 1980s and 1990s. This model of a cyclical struggle between Satanism and anti-Satanism is also reminiscent of a line TST members sometimes quote from *The Revolt of the Angels*: "God conquered, will become Satan; Satan, conquering, will become God."

In closing, I would suggest that the forces at play in the emergence of TST are much bigger than "Satanism" and "anti-Satanism." Talking about Satan—whether we condemn him as absolute evil or hail him as a fellow rebel—is ultimately a symbolic articulation of a deeper stratum of social thought. The cycle of Satanism and anti-Satanism is really a cycle of negotiating the narrative our society tells about itself. This is especially true in a nation that has historically imagined itself as a "city on a hill," predestined to defeat the forces of Satan. Sutekh, a member of Satanic Australia, commented that it is not a coincidence that America has been so influential in the development of religious Satanism because American identity is so closely tied to Christianity.[5] Indeed, further research is needed on groups like Satanic Australia and Global Order of Satan to explore how TST and adjacent groups are developing in nations that have a different relationship with Christianity.

Since Europeans first arrived in North America, Satan has been a key figure in the stories they have told about themselves and their relationship with other people. Jonathan Edwards, the father of the First Great Awakening, declared in one of his sermons, "It is certain that the devil did here quietly enjoy his dominion over the poor nations of Indians for many ages. But in later times God has sent the gospel into these parts of the world, and now the Christian church is set up here in New England and in other parts of America, where before had been nothing but the grossest heathenish darkness."[6] America's fascination with Satan has faded surprisingly little since colonial times. Surveys conducted in 2014 by Baylor University and Chapman University found that 58 percent of Americans "absolutely believe in Satan" and nearly 50 percent of Americans agree or strongly agree that "Satan causes most evil in the world."[7] If culture wars, as Prothero suggests, are really about classification, then Satan—whatever else he may be—is a master symbol that functions to speedily and irrevocably impose classifications of good and evil, us and the other. In his book *Satan in America*, W. Scott Poole describes how the Christian right spun a narrative of Christian values under assault by the devil in order to "fashion a sense of American identity that allows for no shadow, that asserts the reality of American innocence in the face of history." Poole adds, "The devil is the negation and hatred of the Other."[8]

It is into this context that TST inserts itself. In Penny Lane's documentary about TST, *Hail Satan?*, Stu de Haan describes TST as providing "a sociopolitical counter-myth" to the idea of America as a Christian nation. If Satan is the symbol that energizes the myth of America as a Christian nation and grants moral license to act against the other, it is predictable that those on the losing end of this myth will seek to hijack it by appropriating Satan for their own ends. Furthermore, the utility of Satan in constructing a counter-myth is directly proportional to how vehemently Satan is deployed to demonize the other. This dynamic creates the conditions of a cycle as described by Introvigne and alluded to in the writings of Anatole France.

LaVey often spoke in terms of cycles. Sociologist Randall Alfred was an early member of the CoS and one of the first academics to write on it. He remarked that a millennial idea of a coming "Age of Satan" was one of the biggest appeals of the church.[9] Like Marx, LaVey suggested the millennium would come about inevitably as Christianity essentially dug its own grave. In an essay written after the Satanic Panic of the 1980s, LaVey addressed conservative Christians, stating:

> Your Apocalypse is here. It arrived right on schedule. Just the way you like it, pickle in the middle with mustard on top. Credit me for the revolution, but credit yourselves for the forms that it has taken. I provided the reason and the rebellion. YOU provided the incentive and the weaponry[10]

The "weaponry," of course, is the myth of Satan that LaVey has turned back against its wielders. Presumably if this myth were not at hand, LaVey would have waged his revolution through some other means. For all his talk of misanthropy and isolationism, LaVey was quoted as saying, "If Satanists didn't care, they wouldn't be so dark and pessimistic."[11] This suggests he saw his Satanic counter-myth as doing something more important than just shocking people.

Another insight into what Satanists are "really" talking about when they talk about Satan comes from sociologist Kathleen Lowney, who conducted an ethnography of a group of teenaged Satanists in the 1980s. To preserve anonymity, she refers to her research subjects as "the Coven" and their small town in rural Georgia as "Victory Village." One of her informants explained he identified as a Satanist:

> Yeah, I know there's fucking no chance of changing this fucking town, [long pause] or even the damned school. But that doesn't mean I should just roll over and die—I am *here* and so long as I can dress this way, think this way.... Then they will *have* to deal with me, with us [the Coven]. It's fun to see them look scared, look the other way when I come down the hall.... Don't tell me I don't have power. So long as I'm in the Coven, so long as I believe, I have lots of power—least to rattle their chains. Not sure can ask for more.[12]

Lowney concludes that the Coven identifying as Satanists is a form of dissent against the values of their conservative Christian community. The statement above also indicates that they have resorted to this contrarian repurposing of the community's myths because of their subaltern status and their feeling of powerlessness.

Nor is the production of such counter-myths a modern phenomenon. An account by the Dominican friar Bartolomé de Las Casas of the execution of Prince Hatuey, a Native American, in Cuba, demonstrates how intuitive this semiotic reversal is. Early Spanish colonizers regarded indigenous people as agents of the devil and their religion as Satanic worship. Las Casas participated in the conquest of Cuba before he decided that Spain's actions in the New World were illegal and attempted to plead with King Ferdinand on behalf of the Native Americans. In his *A Short Account of the Destruction of the Indies* (1542), Las Casas wrote:

> [Prince Hatuey] was taken and they burned him alive. . . . When he was tied to the stake, a Franciscan, a holy man, who was there, spoke as much as he could to him of the teachings of our faith, of which he had never before heard. . . . After thinking a little, Hatuey asked the monk whether the Christians went to heaven; the monk answered that those who were good went there. The prince at once said, without any more thought, that he did not wish to go there, but rather to hell so as not be where the Spaniards were. . . . I was induced to write this work. . . . That God may not destroy my fatherland Castile for such great sins.[13]

Las Casas emphasizes that Hatuey had never heard Christian teachings before and did not need to think before responding: rearranging the Catholic doctrines of heaven and hell into a counter-myth where the worst possible afterlife is an eternity with the Spanish was an instantaneous mental process.

Three centuries later we find another manifestation of this counter-myth in the memoires of former slave William Wells Brown. In *My Southern Home: Or, the South and Its People* (1880), Brown tells an anecdote about a one-eyed slave named "Dinkie" who had a reputation as a "conjure man." Dinkie overslept and the overseer took him to the barn to be whipped. But Dinkie emerged unwhipped, and it was later rumored the overseer was stopped when Dinkie pointed to the east corner of the barn to reveal a vision of hell and the devil. In Brown's account, Dinkie prepared for his whipping with the following prayer:

> Now, good and lovely devil, for more than twenty years, I have served you faithfully. Before I got into your service, de white folks bought an' sold me an' my old wife an' chillen, an' whip me, and half starve me. Dey did treat me mighty bad, dat you knows. Den I use to pray to de Lord, but dat did no good, kase de white folks don't fear de Lord. But dey fears you, an' ever since I got into your service, I is able to do as I please. No white dares to lay his hand on me; and dis is all owing to de power dat you give me. Oh, good and lovely devil! please to continer dat power. A new oberseer is to come here to-morrow, an' he wants to get me in his hands. But, dear devil, I axe you to stand by me in dis my trial hour, an' I will neber desert you as long as I live. Continer dis power; make me strong in your cause, make me to be more faithful to you, an' let me still be able to conquer my enemies, an' I will give you all de glory, and will try to deserve a seat at your right hand.[14]

As with the trial of Old Thiess the werewolf discussed in chapter 6, the exchange between Hatuey and the Franciscan and Brown's account of a slave's pact with the devil are not really about the supernatural but a struggle over classification and moral license; hell and damnation provide a way of talking about which people represent the forces of evil and destruction. These dynamics are still at play in the ways we talk about Satan today. In this sense, TST has an antecedent in North America that dates back over four hundred years!

Satanic Patriots

Hatuey, Dinkie the conjure man, and the teenaged Coven reversed the myths of Satan and damnation to indict more powerful forces as unjust and hypocritical. In more developed forms of the Satanic counter-myth, Satanists not only critique the prevailing society but also demonstrate that they have their own values, which are superior to those of their opponents. In fact, the counter-myth suggests that its "Satanic" ideals are the true foundational values of the society, while its opponents have effectively perverted these ideals. For example, several TST members commented that TST was "more Christ-like" than many contemporary forms of Christianity.

In a 1971 tabloid column, LaVey wrote, "Satanism IS Americanism in its purest form. We do not advocate or even approve of denial or desecration of such sacred American traditions as home, family, patriotism, personal pride, etc. But instead champion these things."[15] Elsewhere, he explained, "I'm taking a thoroughly American thoughtform and seeing it for what it always was. When Satanism becomes the major religion in the United States, it will be complete with red, white and blue banners flying accompanied by the blaring trombones of John Philip Sousa."[16] Here, LaVey presents Satanism as a kind of hidden civil religion. The founding myth of America, after all, is a story of rebellion against tyranny, and LaVey's Satanism emphasized values Americans hold dear such as rugged individualism, self-reliance, and personal liberty. However, LaVey challenges the idea that these values are derived from or even compatible with Christianity.

While TST's values have little overlap with LaVey's, they understand their core beliefs inscribed in the Seven Tenets to be "Enlightenment values," essentially the same as those that informed the Constitution and the Bill of Rights. Conversely, they see their opponents as theocrats who seek to betray America's core values. Several TST members described their participation as an act of patriotism. The Sabbat Cycle performed by Jex Blackmore featured grayscale American flags, a symbol suggesting both patriotism and Satanism. Seraphina of TST-NYC said she was "standing up for what the founding fathers stood for."[17] When Lilim Camus, co-head for TST-San Marcos, explained her reasons for joining TST she said, "I consider myself a patriot. I believe in my country. I will try to protect everything about my country."[18] This project of articulating a counter-myth that renegotiates core societal values is largely what is at stake when TST chapters adopt highways, collect supplies for the needy, and otherwise attempt to be model citizens in the name of Satan.

The Reconciliation of Opposites

At TST's rally for religious liberty before the Arkansas capitol in Little Rock, Greaves began his speech, "Good people of Arkansas and supporters of religious liberty, I present to you Baphomet: a symbol of pluralism, legal equality, tolerance, free inquiry, freedom of conscience, and reconciliation."[19] While the statue was being designed, David Guinan suggested it should have bat wings, because bat wings "are scarier." But Greaves insisted that Baphomet have the feathery wings of an angel, in keeping with Eliphaz Levi's design.[20] Malcolm Jarry, who first conceived of building the statue and ended up footing most of the bill for its construction, agreed with Greaves. For Levi, Baphomet represented not evil but the reconciliation of opposites: male and female, matter and spirit, justice and mercy. In Arkansas, Greaves went on to explain that TST has never asked for the Ten Commandments monument in Little Rock to be taken down, only that Baphomet be installed beside it. It seems highly unlikely that this vision of Baphomet coexisting next to the Ten Commandments in front of some capitol or courthouse will ever come to pass. But this image serves as an apt metaphor for what TST's influence on American society could ultimately be—not a replacement for the myth of a Christian nation, but a corrective to it and a decentering of it. TST's actions are unlikely to result in the removal of Christian symbols from government buildings or obtain abortion on demand, but by persistently asserting their values, they elicit a renegotiation of the stories we tell about ourselves. Over time, these conversations can shift the center of gravity of a society.

Nor do such efforts amount to some sort of conspiracy to transform America. On the contrary, scholars of American religious history suggest that tolerance has always advanced when society fails to suppress minorities and finally adapts to coexisting with them. In his work *Religious Outsiders and the Making of Americans*, Lawrence Moore writes, "The full extension of religious tolerance, if indeed full tolerance describes the present state of religious affairs in the United States, was more the product of conditions of pluralism which no one sect had the power to over-come as of an abstract belief in the value of pluralism."[21]

Catherine Albanese frames American religious history as a "dance" in which different religious cultures exist side by side and exchange "gifts" of ideas, practices, and traditions. Despite this salubrious metaphor, this can be an ugly process. She writes:

> At other times the dance has looked more like a martial arts "push hands" demonstration between opposing but intimately connected actors: the harmony has arisen out of a balance of tensions. And still other times, one or another dancing partner has gone down. The gift has been smashed; "harmony" has become a pseudonym for hegemony; there are cuts and bruises, twisted knees, and more.[22]

It is possible that TST will exit the dance hall of American culture on a stretcher. But either way, in the foreseeable future, we are likely to be dancing with Satanists in one form or another. Could "moshing" with Satanists result in a balance of tensions as described by Albanese? And if so, what might this look like?

So far, the media has encountered TST in the places where such a harmony is least likely to manifest: in courtrooms, at political rallies, in intemperate editorials, and five-minute debates between "talking heads" on cable news shows. To find anything resembling harmony it is necessary to look at the sidelines. One surprising discovery of my ethnography is that many TST chapters had Christian allies and several members described having close friends who were Christian and with whom they discussed what Satanism means to them. These conversations over coffee or beer between Satanists and Christians, which appear to be occurring quietly and spontaneously across America, are the most likely channel through which the Satanic counter-myth might change the way Americans think about themselves.

There is at least one example where the media *did* note such a conversation taking place. In February 2017, dueling protests between pro-life and pro-choice activists were underway outside a Planned Parenthood in Dallas when a reporter for the *Dallas Morning News* noticed that two men—one from each side of the conflict—had wandered across the street and now appeared to be laughing and having a pleasant conversation. The men turned out to be a pro-life youth pastor named Robert Wetzel and Greg Stevens, a member of TST's National Council. After talking for half an hour, the two agreed on very little, but felt the conversation had been pleasant and worth having. Wetzel remarked, "These are the only conversations that are going to make a difference."[23] Indeed, these conversations are the reason scholars of American religion should think further about religious Satanism.

Notes

Chapter 1

1. Carl Sagan, *The Demon-Haunted World: Science As a Candle in the Dark* (New York: Random House, 1995), p. 429.
2. Douglas Laycock, "Government-sponsored religious displays: transparent rationalizations and expedient post-modernism," *Case Western Reserve Law Review* 61, no. 4 (Summer 2011): p. 1234.
3. *Van Orden v. Perry*, 545 U.S. 677 (2005), Breyer, J. concurring, p. 6.
4. Quoted in Jay Wexler, *Holy Hullabaloos: A Road Trip to the Battlegrounds of the Church/State Wars* (Boston: Beacon Press, 2009), p. 100.
5. Mike Ritze, "House Bill 1330" State of Oklahoma. 1st session of the 52nd legislature (2009). p. 3.
6. Ibid., p. 2.
7. Ibid., p. 2.
8. *Prescott v. Oklahoma Capitol Preservation Commission* OK 54, 373 P.3d 1032 (2015).
9. "Okla. Satanists seek monument by Statehouse steps," *USA Today* (December 8, 2013). Available online at http://www.usatoday.com/story/news/nation/2013/12/08/satanists-oklahoma-statehouse/3908849/ (Accessed January 9, 2017).
10. Lucien Greaves, letter to State Capitol Preservation Commission (November 17, 2013).
11. Daniel Burke, "Satanists want statue next to 10 Commandments," *CNN.com* (December 9, 2013). Available online at http://religion.blogs.cnn.com/2013/12/09/satanists-we-want-a-monument-in-oklahoma/ (Accessed January 9, 2017).
12. Barbara Hoberock, "State lawmakers slam proposed Satanist monument," *Tulsa World* (July 29, 2014). Available online at http://m.tulsaworld.com/news/government/satanists-seek-spot-on-oklahoma-statehouse-steps-next-to-ten/article_d7a11ac2-60dc-11e3-ac3b-0019bb30f31a.html?mode=jqm#.Uqc3ntfCx6s.twitter (Accessed January 20, 2017).
13. "Okla. Satanists seek monument by Statehouse steps," *USA Today* (December 8, 2013). Available online at http://www.usatoday.com/story/news/nation/2013/12/08/satanists-oklahoma-statehouse/3908849/ (Accessed January 9, 2017).
14. Ibid.
15. As the Oklahoma ACLU probably realized, the government *can* accept one monument and reject another. The government can also try to lead public opinion outside of religion. This very scenario was tested in the Supreme Court case *Pleasant Grove City v. Summum* (2009). That case concerned a park in Pleasant Grove City that allowed privately donated monuments, including a monument of the Ten

Commandments. When a new religious movement called Summum applied to erect a monument listing the "seven aphorisms" of their religion, the city rejected their proposal. Summum claimed that this was a violation of their freedom of speech. In a unanimous decision, the court ruled that the city had not violated Summum's freedom of speech because when the government accepts a monument as a donation, the monument's message becomes the speech of the government and not the individual donor. As Samuel Alito explained, when the United States accepted the Statue of Liberty from France, this did not obligate the government to also accept a "Statue of Autocracy" from the German Empire or Imperial Russia. For this reason, the ACLU preferred to focus on the issue at hand, which was not freedom of speech, but the separation of church and state. *Pleasant Grove City v. Summum*, 555 U.S. 460 (2009), Alito, J. opinion of the court, p. 17.

16. "Okla. imposes moratorium on capital monuments," *USA Today* (December 19, 2013). Available online at http://www.usatoday.com/story/news/nation/2013/12/19/oklahoma-capitol-statehouse-monuments/4134307/ (Accessed January 9, 2017).

17. K. Query and Courtney Francisco, "Temple seeks to build monument in 'homage' to Satan at State Capital," *KFOR.com* (January 6, 2014). Available online at http://kfor.com/2014/01/06/temple-seeks-to-build-monument-in-homage-to-satan-at-state-capitol/ (Accessed January 20, 2017).

18. Hoberock, "State lawmakers slam proposed Satanist monument."

19. Austin Petersen, "Satanic Church proposes demon statue Baphomet to be placed at Oklahoma state house," *The Libertarian Republic* (January 7, 2014). Available online at http://thelibertarianrepublic.com/satanic-church-proposes-daemon-statue-baphomet-placed-oklahoma-statehouse/#ixzz487a6A0hR (Accessed January 20, 2017).

20. Corey Robin, *The Reactionary Mind: Conservatism from Edmund Burke to Sarah Palin* (Oxford: Oxford University Press, 2011), p. 99

21. "Satanists plan statue to stand alongside Ten Commandments in Oklahoma," *The Guardian* (December 8, 2013). Available online at https://www.theguardian.com/world/2013/dec/08/satan-ten-commandments-oklahoma-city (Accessed January 20, 2017).

22. David Boroff, "Don Imus sidekick David McGuirk sorry for suggesting Satanists 'should be shot,'" *NYDaily News* (January 14, 2014). Available online at http://www.nydailynews.com/news/national/imus-sidekick-suggesting-satanists-shot-article-1.1579275 (Accessed January 20, 2017). Malcolm Jarry and Lucien Greaves felt that McGuirk was "sincerely contrite" and decided not to exploit this apology by boasting about it. (Electronic communication with the author, May 18, 2019.)

23. Hoberock, "State lawmakers slam proposed Satanist monument."

24. "Urgent voicemail for Beverly Hicks, Executive Assistant, Division of Capital Assets Management" (January 27, 2014, 12:37 p.m).

25. Philip Hamburger, *Separation of Church and State* (Cambridge, Mass.: Harvard University Press, 2002).

26. *Prescott v. Oklahoma Capital Preservation Commission*

27. Barbara Hoberock, "Ten Commandments decision likely to remain a monumental issue," *Tulsa World* (October 11, 2015). Available online at http://www.tulsaworld.com/news/government/ten-commandments-decision-likely-to-remain-a-monumental-issue/article_8e45374f-769c-53dc-8f96-f6192fc195cf.html (Accessed January 20, 2017).

28. "Opinion: Ten Commandments legislation misguided, opens door for Satanic monuments, too," *TulsaworldTV.com* (n.d.) Available online at http://www.tulsaworldtv.com/Opinion-Ten-Commandments-legislation-misguided-opens-door-for-Satanic-monuments-too-30362501?vcid=30362501&freewheel=91468&sitesection=tulsa (Accessed January 20, 2017).

29. Daniel Burke, "Satanists want statue next to 10 Commandments," *CNN Belief Blog* (December 9, 2013). Available online at http://religion.blogs.cnn.com/2013/12/09/satanists-we-want-a-monument-in-oklahoma/ (Accessed January 20, 2017).

30. Jonathan Smith, "Here's the first look at the new Satanic monument being built for Oklahoma's Statehouse," *Vice.com* (May 1, 2014). Available online at https://www.vice.com/en_us/article/heres-the-first-look-at-the-new-satanic-monument-being-built-for-oklahomas-statehouse (Accessed January 20, 2017). Malcolm Jarry estimates TST kept about $17,500 of this money after Indiegogo took their cut as well as other expenses. (Electronic communication with the author, May 19, 2019.)

31. Christina Hall, "Satanic Temple's monument to be unveiled Saturday in Detroit," *Detroit Free Press* (July 22, 2015). Available online at http://www.freep.com/story/news/local/michigan/2015/07/22/baphomet-monument-satanic-temple-detroit/30510369/ (Accessed January 20, 2017).

32. Malcolm Barber, *The New Knighthood: A History of the Order of the Temple* (New York: Cambridge University Press, 2012), p. 321.

33. David Guinan, interview with the author (March 6, 2019).

34. Dallas Franklin, "Man accused of destroying Ten Commandments monument talks about his mental illness," *KFOR.com* (March 5, 2015). Available online at http://kfor.com/2015/03/05/man-accused-of-destroying-ten-commandments-monument-talks-about-his-mental-illness/ (Accessed January 20, 2015).

35. Kim Hammer and Jason Rapert, "House Bill 1273." (January 24, 2017).

36. Alison Lesley, "Destruction of Arkansas Ten Commandments monument forces Satanic Temple to postpone lawsuit," *World Religion News* (June 29, 2017). Available online at https://www.worldreligionnews.com/religion-news/christianity/destruction-arkansas-ten-commandments-monument-forces-satanic-temple-postpone-lawsuit/ (Accessed February 8, 2019).

37. Christopher S. Queen and Sallie B. King, *Engaged Buddhism: Buddhist Liberation Movements in Asia* (Albany: State University of New York Press, 1996).

38. For a scholarly account of the Church of Satan and its history, see David Bromley's entry for "Church of Satan" in the World Religion and Spirituality Project (August 1, 2012). Available online at https://wrldrels.org/2016/10/08/world-religions-spirituality-church-of-satan/ (Accessed May 14, 2019). For a biography of founder Anton LaVey from the perspective of a Church of Satan member, see Peter H. Gilmore,

"LaVey, Anton Szandor," in James. R. Lewis, ed., *Satanism Today: An Encyclopedia of Religion, Folklore, and Popular Culture* (Santa Barbara: ABC-CLIO, 2001), 144–147.

39. Jesse Helms, "Helms Amendment No. 705," 121 Cong Rec S 12279. Vol. 131, no. 123, Pg. S12279 (September 26, 1985).

40. David G. Bromley, "Satanism: The New Cult Scare," in James T. Richardson, Joel Best, and David G. Bromley, eds, *The Satanism Scare* (Hawthorne, N.Y.: Aldine De Gruyter, 1991), p. 60.

41. Anton Szandor LaVey, *Satan Speaks!* (Venice, Calif.: Feral House, 1998), p. 5.

42. Bill Donahue, "Satanists surge at Christmastime," *Catholicleague.org* (December 16, 2015). Available online at http://www.catholicleague.org/satanists-surge-at-christmastime/ (Accessed January 20, 2017).

43. John Ritche, "Satan club for children opens at school amid strong opposition," *TFPStudentAction.org* (December 12, 2016). Available online at https://www.tfpstudentaction.org/news/satan-club-for-children-opens-at-school-amid-strong-opposition (Accessed February 8, 2019).

44. Asbjørn Dyrendal, "Darkness Within: Satanism as a Self-Religion," in Jesper Aagaard Petersen, ed., *Contemporary Religious Satanism: A Critical Anthology* (Farnham, UK: Ashgate, 2009), pp. 59–73. Blanche Barton, a former high priestess of the CoS and the mother of Anton LaVey's third child, acknowledges this connection in her biography of Anton LaVey, although she claims that LaVey's ideas came first. Barton explains, "Visit the 'New Age' section of your nearest bookstore. You'll see the entrepreneurs who have taken up LaVeyan ideas, slapping a more palatable name on them to their critical and financial profit." Blanche Barton and Anton Szandor La Vey, *The Secret Life of a Satanist: The Authorized Biography of Anton LaVey* (Los Angeles: Feral House, 1990), p. 14.

45. Participant observation, Austin, Texas (July 14, 2018).

46. Electronic communication with the author (December 14, 2018).

47. Daniel Burke, "Satanists square off on abortion (yes, really)," *CNN Belief Blog* (July 9, 2013). Available online at http://religion.blogs.cnn.com/2013/07/09/satanists-square-off-on-abortion-yes-really/ (Accessed January 20, 2017).

48. David Ferguson, "Florida pastor: First Amendment doesn't apply to 'malevolent, evil' faiths, like Satanism," *Raw Story* (December 18, 2014). Available online at http://www.rawstory.com/2014/12/florida-pastor-first-amendment-doesnt-apply-to-malevolent-evil-faiths-like-satanism/ (Accessed January 20, 2017).

49. Michael d'Oilveira, "Activist seeks satanic prayer to make a point," *South Florida Gay News* (November 21, 2015). Available online at http://www.edgemedianetwork.com//news/news/189497/activist_seeks_satanic_prayer_to_make_a_point#discussion (Accessed January 20, 2016).

50. Lisa J. Huriah, "Coral Springs ends public prayer rather than face the devil," *SunSentinal* (September 20, 2015). Available online at http://www.sun-sentinel.com/local/broward/fl-coral-springs-satan-chaz-20150910-story.html (Accessed January 20, 2017).

51. Jennifer Pierce, "Oklahoma City's civic center makes 'deal' with the devil," *News9. com* (August 31, 2010). Available online at http://www.news9.com/Global/story.asp?S=13074588 (Accessed January 20, 2017).

52. While working as a corrections officer, he had an illicit relationship with a female inmate. Jacqueline Sit, "OKC Satanic group says they 'don't deal with sex offenders,'" *NewsOn6.com* (September 17, 2010). Available online at http://www.newson6.com/Global/story.asp?S=13167040 (Accessed January 20, 2017).

53. Award-winning journalist John Thavis incorrectly reported that Daniels's black mass was sponsored by TST in his book *The Vatican Prophecies* (New York: Viking, 2015), p. 168.

54. Carla Hinton, "Prayer campaign continues against sold-out satanic 'black mass' in Oklahoma City," *NewsOK.com* (September 14, 2014). Available online at http://newsok.com/article/5341777 (Accessed January 20, 2017).

55. Roger J. Landry, "The fully Catholic response to black masses," *Catholic Herald* (September 21 2014). Available online at http://catholicpreaching.com/the-fully-catholic-response-to-black-masses-catholic-herald-september-12-2014/ (Accessed January 20, 2017); Michelle Martin, "Archbishop urges prayer to combat black mass," Our Sunday Visitor (September 7, 2014), 4A.

56. Susan Berry, "Only 42 attend 'black mass' in Oklahoma City, hundreds of Christians protest outside," *Breitbart.com* (September 22, 2014). Available online at http://www.breitbart.com/big-government/2014/09/22/only-42-attend-black-mass-in-oklahoma-city-with-hundreds-of-christian-protestors-outside/ (Accessed January 20, 2017).

57. Guy Birchall, "Satanic black mass sparks outrage with more than 100,000 signing petition to stop devil worshippers holding ceremony," *The Sun* (April 22, 2016). Available online at https://www.thesun.co.uk/archives/news/1140408/satanic-black-mass-sparks-outrage-with-more-than-100000-signing-a-petition-to-stop-devil-worshippers-holding-ceremony/ (Accessed January 21, 2017).

58. Paul Coakley, "Archbishop Coakley's statement on prayers of exorcism and cleanings," Archdiocese of Oklahoma City (n.d.). Available online at http://www.archokc.org/top-news/3808-archbishop-coakley-statement-on-prayers-of-exorcism-and-cleansing (January 21, 2017).

59. Stoyan Zaimov, "Satanists to pour blood over Virgin Mary, perform satanic ceremonies over Christmas," *The Christian Post* (December 18, 2015). Available online at http://www.christianpost.com/news/satanists-pour-blood-virgin-mary-satanic-ceremonies-christmas-152891/ (Accessed January 21, 2017).

60. Carla Hinton, "Catholic archbishop discourages focus on Satanists' Christmas Eve plans," *NewsOK.com* (December 17, 2015). Available online at http://newsok.com/catholic-archbishop-discourages-focus-on-satanists-christmas-eve-plans/article/5467358 (Accessed January 21, 2017).

61. Mary Anne Hackett, "Catholics defend the Virgin Mary in Oklahoma City as Satanists attack her," *CatholicCitizens.org* (December 30, 2015). Available online at http://catholiccitizens.org/news/63713/catholics-defend-the-virgin-mary-in-oklahoma-city-as-satanists-attack-her/ (Accessed January 21, 2017).

62. Lewis Bennett, "White evangelical Trump supporters OK with president's behavior," *Peninsula Daily News* (February 22, 2019). Available online at http://www.peninsuladailynews.com/letters/letter-white-evangelical-trump-supporters-ok-with-presidents-behavior/ (Accessed February 22, 2019).

63. James Martin, "Satanic group playing with fire," *America* (July 27, 2015). Available online at http://americamagazine.org/content/all-things/satanic-group-playing-fire (Accessed January 21, 2017).

64. Stephen R. Prothero, *Why Liberals Win the Culture Wars (Even When They Lose Elections): The Battles That Define America from Jefferson's Heresies to Gay Marriage* (New York: HarperOne, 2016), p. 18.

65. Robert P. Jones, *The End of White Christian America* (New York: Simon and Schuster, 2016), p. 50.

66. Pew Research Center, "Religious landscape study" (2019). Available online at http://www.pewforum.org/religious-landscape-study/religious-tradition/unaffiliated-religious-nones/#age-distribution-trend (Accessed February 25, 2019).

67. Prothero, *Why Liberals Win the Culture Wars*, p. 9.

68. Jones, *The End of White Christian America*, p. 211.

69. Robert P. Jones, "The rage of white, Christian America," *New York Times* (November 10, 2016). Available online at https://www.nytimes.com/2016/11/11/opinion/campaign-stops/the-rage-of-white-christian-america.html?_r=0 (Accessed January 17, 2017).

70. Sarah Pulliam Bailey, "How nostalgia for white Christian America drove so many Americans to vote for Trump," *Washington Post* (January 5, 2017). Available online at https://www.washingtonpost.com/local/social-issues/how-nostalgia-for-white-christian-america-drove-so-many-americans-to-vote-for-trump/2017/01/04/4ef6d686-b033-11e6-be1c-8cec35b1ad25_story.html?hpid=hp_hp-top-table-main_mayberry-prebuild%3Ahomepage%2Fstory&utm_term=.92999023bd14 (Accessed January 21, 2017).

71. Colin Campbell, "TRUMP: If I'm president, 'Christianity will have power' in the US," *Business Insider* (January 23, 2016). Available online at http://www.businessinsider.com/donald-trump-christianity-merry-christmas-2016-1 (Accessed January 21, 2017).

72. Reilly Capps, "Membership in satanic churches soars in Trump's America," *TheRooster.com* (November 11, 2016). Available online at http://www.therooster.com/blog/membership-satanic-churches-soars-trumps-america (Accessed January 21, 2017).

73. James R. Lewis, "Anton Lavey, the Satanic Bible, and the Satanist Tradition," in James R. Lewis, ed., *Legitimating New Religions* (New Brunswick, N.J.: Rutgers University Press, 2003), p. 115.

74. Tim Murphy, "Notes from the field: Religious defamation and radical pluralism as challenges to the scholar of religion," *The Council of Societies for the Study of Religion Bulletin* 34, no. 4 (November 2005): p. 83.

75. Hugh B. Urban, *The Church of Scientology: A History of a New Religion* (Princeton, N.J.: Princeton University Press, 2013), p. 4.

76. Michel Foucault, *The History of Sexuality* (New York: Pantheon Books, 1978), p. 86.

77. Christine Niles, "Liberty of perdition," *Church Militant.com* (April 26, 2016). Available online at http://www.churchmilitant.com/news/article/liberty-of-perdition (Accessed January 21, 2017).

78. David Feltmate, *Drawn to the Gods: Religion and Humor in The Simpsons, South Park, and Family Guy* (New York: New York University Press, 2017), p. 4.

79. Marci A. Hamilton, "What do the Satanic Temple and Jehovah's Witnesses have in common? They are champions against government inculcation of belief," *Verdict*.com (August 4, 2016). Available online at https://verdict.justia.com/2016/08/04/satanic-temple-jehovahs-witnesses-common-champions-government-inculcation-belief (Accessed February 25, 2019).

80. James A. Reichley, *Religion in American Public Life* (Washington, DC: Brookings Institution, 1985), pp. 127–129.

Chapter 2

1. George Bernard Shaw, *Man and Superman: A Comedy and a Philosophy* (New York: Brentano's, 1922), p. 238

2. Lucien Greaves, interview with the author (November 3, 2018).

3. Malcolm Jarry, "Educational mission: A report and plan of action" (December 12, 2012), p. 11.

4. Amy G. Bryant and Jonas J. Swartz, "Why crisis pregnancy centers are legal but unethical," *AMA Journal of Ethics* 20, no. 1 (2018): pp. 269–277. On funding for crisis pregnancy centers under both the Bush and Obama administrations, see Sarah Posner, "Crisis pregnancy centers and Obama's faith-based initiative," *Religion Dispatches* (March 29, 2011). Available online at http://religiondispatches.org/crisis-pregnancy-centers-and-obamas-faith-based-initiative/ (Accessed February 26, 2019).

5. David Guinan, interview with the author (March 5, 2019).

6. Malcolm Jarry, interview with the author (July 18, 2018).

7. Lucien Greaves, interview with the author (November 3, 2018).

8. Sally Morrow, "After school Satan? Church-state group plays devil's advocate in public schools," *Religion News Service* (October 18, 2016). Available online at http://religionnews.com/2016/10/18/after-school-satan-church-state-group-plays-devils-advocate-in-public-schools/ (Accessed February 9, 2018).

9. Lucien Greaves, interview with the author (November 3, 2018).

10. Paige Lavender, "Rick Scott praised by 'Satanists' at mock rally," *The Huffington Post* (January 26, 2013). Available online at http://www.huffingtonpost.com/2013/01/26/rick-scott-satanists_n_2559018.html (Accessed February 9, 2018).

11. Jarry, "Educational mission," p. 12.

12. David Guinan, interview with the author (March 6, 2019).

13. S.M.A.R.T., "Grey Faction, Satanic Temple and Lucien Greaves fact sheet," *Ritualabuse.us* (n.d.). Available online at https://ritualabuse.us/ritualabuse/grey-faction-satanic-temple-and-lucien-greaves-fact-sheet/ (Accessed February 9, 2018).

14. Christiana Ng, "Satanists plan rally in support of Florida Governor Rick Scott," *ABCnews.com* (January 15, 2013). Available online at http://abcnews.go.com/US/satanists-plan-rally-support-florida-gov-rick-scott/story?id=18219915 (Accessed February 9, 2018).

15. Malcolm Jarry, interview with the author (July 24, 2018).

16. Anna Merlan, "Trolling hell: Is the Satanic a prank, the start of a new religious movement or both?," *The Village Voice* (July 22, 2014). Available online at https://www.villagevoice.com/2014/07/22/trolling-hell-is-the-satanic-temple-a-prank-the-start-of-a-new-religious-movement-or-both/ (Accessed February 9, 2018). Shane Bugbee wrote that he was initially "offered the role" of Lucien Greaves. Greaves denies this, pointing out that Bugbee did not become involved with TST until the spring of 2013 and parted ways not long after. Shane Bugbee, "a master and slave relationship," *shanebugbee.com* (n.d.), http://www.shanebugbee.com/?p=2161 (website defunct).

17. The Huffington Post Staff, "'Satanists for Rick Scott' rally actually part of mockumentary (UPDATE)," *The Huffington Post* (January 14, 2013). Available online at http://www.huffingtonpost.com/2013/01/14/satanists-rally-for-rick-scott_n_2471328.html (Accessed February 9, 2018).

18. Malcolm Jarry, interview with the author (July 18, 2018).

19. Michael Wiener, interview with the author (March 6, 2019).

20. David Guinan, interview with the author (March 6, 2019).

21. On Jack Chick, see Jason Bivins, *Religion of Fear: The Politics of Horror in Conservative Evangelicalism* (Oxford: Oxford University Press, 2008).

22. Malcolm Jarry, interview with the author (March 3, 2019).

23. The group had not planned an exit strategy for when the rally was over. The performers, still clad in black robes, had to cross the street to get to their van but were unaware that the light to activate the crosswalk was operated by a button. Hostile observers and reporters surrounded the frightened performers, who awkwardly waited for a light that would never change. Later, there was an argument about who was to blame for this failure of planning. (Malcolm Jarry, interview with the author, March 3, 2019.)

24. John Morreall, *Taking Laughter Seriously* (Albany: State University of New York, 1998): pp. 15–16.

25. Leslie Rutledge, "Response in opposition to motion to intervene" (July 26, 2018), p. 9. There is some evidence that in writing this document Rutledge was coached by TST's rival, the Church of Satan. Rutledge submits to the court as evidence a "Fact Sheet" created by the Church of Satan purporting to expose TST's true motives.

26. Order, *Cave and Levy v. Martin,* No. 4:18-cv-00342-KGB. Dist. Ct. Eastern Dist of Ark. Western Div. (December 17, 2018), p. 25.

27. Malcolm Jarry, interview with the author (July 18, 2018).

28. Malcolm Jarry, electronic communication with the author (March 3, 2019).

29. Jonathan Smith, "Satanists turned the founder of the Westboro Baptist Church's dead mom gay," *Vice.com* (July 17, 2013). Available online at https://www.vice.com/en_us/article/5gwnj8/satanists-turned-the-founder-of-the-westboro-baptist-churchs-mom-gay (Accessed February 9, 2018). By this time, Jarry and Greaves were already moving toward a public position that they rejected the idea of an afterlife. Thus they did not claim that Catherine Johnston *is* gay in the afterlife, only that they believe her descendants now believe this claim. (Malcolm Jarry, electronic communication with the author, March 3, 2019.)

30. David Guinan, interview with the author (March 6, 2019).

31. Jonathan Smith, "Mississippi police want to arrest the Satanists who turn dead people gay," *Vice.com* (July 24, 2013). Available online at http://www.vice.com/read/mississippi-police-want-to-arrest-the-satanists-who-turn-dead-people-gay (Accessed February 9, 2018). Guinan wanted to turn himself in to further the absurdity of the situation. He proposed the group all arrive at jail wearing devil horns, accompanied by an attorney wearing slightly smaller devil horns. However, the only attorney Guinan could find willing to wear devil horns was not licensed in Mississippi. (Interview with the author, March 6, 2019.)

32. Malcolm Jarry, interview with the author (July 18, 2018).

33. Lux Arminor, interview with the author (July 5, 2018).

34. Malcolm Jarry, interview with the author (July 18, 2018).

35. Brittani Ferrendi, "Cakes, homo-erotic counter protests and a trans dance party: The Satanic Temple fighting for LGBT rights," *South Florida Gay News* (January 23, 2018). Available online at http://southfloridagaynews.com/National/satanic-temple.html (Accessed February 9, 2018).

36. Field notes, Salem, Massachusetts (July 14, 2018).

37. James R. Lewis, *Legitimating New Religions* (Piscataway, N.J.: Rutgers University Press, 2004), pp. 13–14.

38. Chris Turvey, interview with the author (June 23, 2018).

39. Asbjorn Dyrendal, James R. Lewis, and Jesper A. Petersen, "Old Nick on the 'net: Satanic politics," *OUPblog* (December 20, 2015). Available online at https://blog.oup.com/2015/12/satanist-politics/ (Accessed February 9, 2018).

40. Stu de Haan, interview with the author (September 29, 2018).

41. Michelle Shortt, interview with the author (September 30, 2018).

42. National Center for Education Statistics, "2014 tables and statistics," Available online at https://nces.ed.gov/programs/digest/d17/tables/dt17_233.28.asp (Accessed February 9, 2018).

43. Frances Locke, "The Satanic Temple's anti-spanking campaign is something we can all agree on," *Mommyish.com* (April 12, 2014). Available online at http://www.mommyish.com/2014/04/12/satanic-temple-anti-spanking-campaign/ (Accessed February 9, 2018).

44. Malcolm Jarry, interview with the author (August 16, 2018).

45. James A. McNaughton, interview with the author (July 23, 2018).

46. For more on the 2012 incident see Joseph Laycock, "Satanists take aim at school spanking," *Religion Dispatches* (March 20, 2017). Available online at http://religiondispatches.org/satanists-take-aim-at-school-spanking/ (Accessed February 9, 2018).

47. Hemant Mehta, "The Satanic Temple tackles corporal punishment with billboard: 'Never Be Hit in School Again,'" *Friendly Atheist* (March 16, 2017). Available online at https://friendlyatheist.patheos.com/2017/03/16/the-satanic-temple-tackles-corporal-punishment-with-tx-billboard-never-be-hit-in-school-again/ (Accessed February 9, 2018).

48. "DEMAND THE SATANIC CHURCH BILL BOARD BE TAKEN DOWN!!!," *Care2Petitions* (n.d.). Available online at https://www.thepetitionsite.com/830/977/

117/demand-the-satanic-church-bill-board-be-taken-down/ (Accessed February 9, 2018).

49. Bobby Ross, Jr., "Satanic Temple billboard protesting corporal punishment rankles Texas town," *Religion News Service* (November 2, 2017). Available online at http://religionnews.com/2017/11/02/satanic-temple-billboard-protesting-corporal-punishment-rankles-texas-town/ (Accessed February 9, 2018).

50. William J. Gibbs, Jr., "Three Rivers ISD responds to controversial billboard," *The Progress* (October 26, 2017). Available online at http://www.mysoutex.com/the_progress/news/three-rivers-isd-responds-to-controversial-billboard/article_afe17bbe-ba9f-11e7-84cb-43648d2c8abd.html (Accessed February 11, 2019).

51. Michael W. Chapman, "Satanic Temple: Gay marriage is 'a sacrament,'" *CNSnews.com* (June 11, 2014). Available online at https://www.cnsnews.com/news/article/michael-w-chapman/satanic-temple-gay-marriage-sacrament (Accessed February 11, 2019).

52. Shiva Honey, interview with the author (August 11, 2018).

53. Doktor Zoom, "Hero Michigan legislator will save baby Jesus from Satan, stuffed snake," *Wonkette.com* (December 18, 2014). Available online at http://wonkette.com/569609/hero-michigan-legislator-will-save-baby-jesus-from-satan-stuffed-snake (Accessed February 11, 2019).

54. Hermant Mehta, "Illinois GOP introduces resolution condemning Satanists' 'Snaketivity' display," *Friendly Atheist* (December 13, 2018). Available online at https://friendlyatheist.patheos.com/2018/12/13/illinois-gop-introduces-resolution-condemning-satanists-snaketivity-display/ (Accessed February 11, 2019).

55. John Counts, "Satanic group plans to resurrect holiday display at Michigan capitol," *Mlive.com* (December 7, 2018). Available online at https://www.mlive.com/news/2018/12/satanic-group-plans-to-resurrect-holiday-display-at-michigan-capitol.html (Accessed February 11, 2019).

56. Abby Ohlheiser, "The Florida capitol's holiday display will include a festive message from the Satanic Temple," *Washington Post* (December 11, 2017). Available online at https://www.washingtonpost.com/news/post-nation/wp/2014/12/04/the-florida-capitols-holiday-display-will-include-a-festive-message-from-the-satanic-temple/ (Accessed January 20, 2017).

57. Joy Davenport, interview with the author (March 8, 2019).

58. Michael Grybowski, "'Catholic warrior' who destroyed satanic display in Florida pleads for help in war against Lucifer," *Christianpost.com* (May 7, 2015). Available online at http://www.christianpost.com/news/catholic-warrior-who-destroyed-satanic-display-in-florida-pleads-for-help-in-war-against-lucifer-138810/ (Accessed January 20, 2017).

59. Lulu Ramadan, "Two Boca Raton schools become battle ground for religious debate," *Palm Beach Post* (January 4, 2017). Available online at http://www.palmbeachpost.com/news/two-boca-raton-schools-become-battle-ground-for-religious-debate/WrmywW2LLoGK0O4ogjs1lO/ (Accessed February 11, 2019).

60. Lulu Ramandan, "Teacher who erected Boca Satan display: This was social experiment," *Palm Beach Post* (January 5, 2017). [Website defunct].

61. Hemant Mehta, "A Florida pastor bragged on TV about his plans to vandalize a satanic display," *Friendly Atheist* (September 26, 2017). Available online at https://friendlyatheist.patheos.com/2017/09/26/a-florida-pastor-bragged-on-tv-about-his-plans-to-vandalize-a-satanic-display/ (Accessed February 11, 2019).

62. Mehta, "Illinois GOP introduces resolution condemning Satanists' 'Snaketivity' display."

63. Shiva Honey, interview with the author (August 11, 2018).

64. Bethania Palma Markus, "Satanic Temple to unveil statue in secret after Christians threaten to 'blow it up real good,'" *Raw Story* (July 14, 2015). Available online at http://www.rawstory.com/2015/07/satanic-temple-to-unveil-statue-in-secret-after-christians-threaten-to-blow-it-up-real-good/ (Accessed January 20, 2017).

65. Scott Eric Kaufman, "'Let's burn it down!': Detroit Christians conspire to prevent Satanic Temple from unveiling Baphomet statue," *Salon.com* (July 17, 2015). Available online at https://www.salon.com/2015/07/17/lets_burn_it_down_detroit_christians_conspire_to_prevent_satanic_temple_from_unveiling_baphomet_statue/ (Accessed February 11, 2019).

66. "The Satanic Temple unveils a massive statue of Baphomet in Detroit," *VigilantCitizen.com* (August 3, 2015). Available online at http://vigilantcitizen.com/latestnews/the-satanic-temple-unveils-a-massive-statue-of-baphomet-in-detroit/ (Accessed January 20, 2017).

67. Malcolm Jarry, interview with the author (July 24, 2018).

68. Jennifer Dixon, "Protestors: Don't turn Detroit over to Satanists," *Detroit Free Press* (July 25, 2015). Available online at http://www.freep.com/story/news/local/michigan/detroit/2015/07/27/baphomet-satanic-temple-detroit-preachers-prayers/30682409/ (Accessed January 20, 2017).

69. Christina Hall, "Satanic Temple's monument to be unveiled Saturday in Detroit," *Detroit Free Press* (July 22, 2015). Available online at http://www.freep.com/story/news/local/michigan/2015/07/22/baphomet-monument-satanic-temple-detroit/30510369/ (Accessed January 20, 2017).

70. "Shut down the Satanic Temple." Available online at https://petitions.whitehouse.gov//petition/shut-down-satanic-temple-detroit-mi (January 20, 2017).

71. "The Devil in Detroit," *Church Militant.com* (July 26, 2015). Available online at http://www.churchmilitant.com/news/article/the-devil-in-detroit (Accessed January 20, 2017).

72. Malcolm Jarry, interview with the author (July 26, 2018).

73. The Satanic Temple, "About us," *Thestanictemple.com* (n.d.). Available online at https://thesatanictemple.com/pages/about-us (Accessed February 11, 2019).

74. Corky Siemaszko, "Hate attacks on Muslims in U.S. spike after recent acts of terrorism," *NBCnews.com* (December 20, 2015). Available online at https://www.nbcnews.com/news/us-news/hate-attacks-muslims-u-s-spike-after-recent-acts-terrorism-n482456 (Accessed May 31, 2019).

75. Malcolm Jarry, electronic communication with the author (March 3, 2019).

76. Susan Du, "Boss orders Minneapolis Satanists to rescind offer to protect Muslims," *Citypages.com* (December 22, 2015). Available online at http://www.citypages.com/

news/boss-orders-minneapolis-satanists-to-rescind-offer-to-protect-muslims-7912462 (Accessed February 11, 2019).

77. Greg Stevens, interview with the author (January 8, 2019).

78. Shiva Honey, interview with the author (August 11, 2018).

79. Jennifer Swann, "Is a Trump presidency the Satanic Temple's chance to go mainstream?," *LAWeekly.com* (February 27, 2017). Available online at http://www.laweekly.com/arts/is-a-trump-presidency-the-satanic-temples-chance-to-go-mainstream-7975996 (Accessed February 11, 2019).

80. Hofman A. Turing, interview with the author (June 18, 2018).

81. Mara Gorgo, interview with the author (June 21, 2018).

82. Marius Omnes and Rose Vespira, interview with the author (July 17, 2018).

83. Malcolm Jarry, electronic communication with the author (January 2, 2019).

84. Katherine Stewart, "An After School Satan Club could be coming to your kid's elementary school," *Washington Post* (July 30, 2016). Available online at https://www.washingtonpost.com/local/education/an-after-school-satan-club-could-be-coming-to-your-kids-elementary-school/2016/07/30/63f485e6-5427-11e6-88eb-7dda4e2f2aec_story.html?tid=pm_local_pop_b (Accessed February 11, 2019).

85. A Cleveland school attempted to discourage the Good News Club by charging a "facility fee." They were sued by the Liberty Counsel and in 2016 ordered to pay $150,000 in nominal damages and attorney's fees. Liberty Counsel, "Child Evangelism fellowship wins major victory in Cleveland" (June 29, 2016). Available online at https://www.lc.org/newsroom/details/062916-child-evangelism-fellowship-wins-major-victory-in-cleveland (Accessed February 11, 2019).

86. Katherine Stewart, *The Good News Club: The Christian Right's Stealth Assault on America's Children* (New York: Public Affairs, 2012),p. 21.

87. Ibid., p. 55.

88. Ibid., p. 25.

89. Ibid., p. 99.

90. Ibid., p. 146.

91. Stewart, "An After School Satan Club could be coming to your kid's elementary school."

92. Patti Armstrong, "What to do about Satanic After-School Clubs?," *The National Catholic Register* (August 4, 2016). Available online at http://www.ncregister.com/blog/armstrong/what-to-do-about-satanic-after-school-clubs (Accessed February 11, 2019).

93. Amanda Whiting, "If you send your kids to After School Satan Club, they will most likely be bored as hell," *Washingtonian* (August 8, 2016). Available online at https://www.washingtonian.com/2016/08/08/send-kids-school-satan-club-will-likely-bored-not-learn-anything-satan/ (Accessed February 11, 2019).

94. The Satanic Temple, *After-School Satan Club Grades K-6 Curriculum* (n.d.).

95. Katherine Stewart and Moriah Balingit, "Educators say After School Satan clubs likely legal," *Washington Post* (August 1, 2016). Available online at http://www.miamiherald.com/news/nation-world/national/article93182387.html (Accessed February 11, 2019).

96. The Satanic Temple, *After-School Satan Club: Volunteer Handbook* (n.d.), p. 13.

97. Malcolm Jarry, interview with the author (August 16, 2018).

98. Mary De Young, *The Day Care Ritual Abuse Moral Panic* (Jefferson, N.C.: McFarland, 2004), p. 18.

99. Patricia Ramirez, "The Satanic Temple wants to bring Satanism to elementary schools," *Inquisitr* (August 1, 2016). Available online at http://www.inquisitr.com/ 3370543/the-satanic-temple-wants-to-bring-satanism-to-elementary-schools-video/ (Accessed February 11, 2019).

100. Q McCray, "After School Satan Club pushes for inclusion in Prince George's Co. elementary school," *WJLA.com* (August 2, 2016). Available online at http://wjla.com/ news/local/after-school-satan-club-pushes-for-inclusion-in-prince-georges-co-elementary-school (Accessed February 11, 2019).

101. Harry Farley, "The Satanic Temple opens 'After School Satan Clubs' for children young as five," *Christianity Today* (August 2, 2016). Available online at http://www. christiantoday.com/article/the.satanic.temple.opens.after.school.satan.clubs.for. children.young.as.five/92075.htm?email=1. (Accessed February 11, 2019).

102. Stewart and Balingit, "Educators say After School Satan clubs likely legal."

103. Derek Anderson, "After School Satan Club gets Christians to protest," *Midcountymemo.com* (December 8, 2016). Available online at https:// midcountymemo.com/2016/12/school-satan-club-gets-christians-protest/ (Accessed February 11, 2019).

104. Stewart, "An After School Satan Club could be coming to your kid's elementary school."

105. Liberty Counsel, "Satanist group has no right to disrupt school," *CanadaFreePress* (August 2, 2016). Available online at http://canadafreepress.com/article/satanist-group-has-no-right-to-disrupt-school (Accessed February 11, 2019).

106. Thomas Essel, "The Satanic Temple responds to claim that it has no right to after school clubs," *Danthropology* (August 4, 2016). Available online at http://www. patheos.com/blogs/danthropology/2016/08/the-satanic-temple-responds-to-claim-that-it-has-no-right-to-after-school-clubs/ (Accessed February 11, 2019).

107. The Satanic Temple, "Liberty Council bare their hypocrisy in satanic After-School Club controversy," *Digital Journal* (August 3, 2016). Available online at http://www. digitaljournal.com/pr/3028113 (Accessed February 11, 2019).

108. Amanda Whiting, "The leader of the Satanic Temple on why he's recruiting kids to join his club," *Washingtonian* (August 4, 2016). Available online at https://www. washingtonian.com/2016/08/04/after-school-satan-club-satanic-temple-lucien-greaves-evangelism-constitution/ (Accessed February 11, 2019).

109. Kera Wanielista, "Lawyer: After School Satan Club must be allowed to proceed," *Skagit Valley Herald* (September 22, 2016). Available online at http://www.goskagit. com/news/education/lawyer-after-school-satan-club-must-be-allowed-to-proceed/article_cccb1716-8e92-5f80-9e8c-13d1f5041677.html (Accessed February 11, 2019).

110. "Satanic group confronts Cobb school board," *Marietta Daily Journal* (August 26, 2016). Available online at http://www.mdjonline.com/news/satanic-group-

threatens-cobb-school-board-with-lawsuit/article_fc432ed6-6b94-11e6-bd53-779da70c9754.html (Accessed February 11, 2019).

111. Christopher Paul, interview with the author (June 21, 2018).

112. Mary Kate McGown, "The Satanic Temple to consider legal action against Cobb schools," *Marietta Daily Journal* (December 26, 2016). Available online at http://www.mdjonline.com/news/the-satanic-temple-to-consider-legal-action-against-cobb-schools/article_4353cb5c-cbdd-11e6-87ad-0b6125a0ad32.html (Accessed February 11, 2019).

113. Christopher Paul, interview with the author (June 21, 2018).

114. "Protests," *Americaneedsfatima.org* (n.d.). Available online at https://www.americaneedsfatima.org/protests.html?lang=en&limit=18&limitstart=36 (Accessed February 11, 2019).

115. Kera Wanielista, "Satanic Temple cancels plans for After School Satan Club," *Skagit Valley Herald* (October 11, 2016). Available online at http://www.goskagit.com/news/education/satanic-temple-cancels-plans-for-after-school-satan-club/article_9d33142e-02c8-51b0-9c95-d4d5d654fbcd.html (Accessed February 11, 2019).

116. Will James, "Satanic Temple leaders to Tacoma parents: We teach critical thinking, not child sacrifice," *KNKX.org* (December 15, 2016). Available online at http://knkx.org/post/satanic-temple-leaders-tacoma-parents-we-teach-critical-thinking-not-child-sacrifice (Accessed February 11, 2019).

117. Patranya Bhoolsuwan, "Satan After School Program ending for now," *KIRO7.com* (September 14, 2017). Available online at https://www.kiro7.com/news/local/tacomas-after-school-satan-club-is-on-pause-for-now-says-satanic-temple-of-seattle/608696599 (Accessed February 11, 2019).

118. Amber Cortes, "After-school Satan club tests the limits of church and state," *KALW.org* (September 12, 2017). Available online at http://kalw.org/post/after-school-satan-club-tests-limits-church-and-state#stream/0 (Accessed February 11, 2019).

119. Candice Ruud, "Tacoma's After-School Satan Club is on pause for now, says Satanic Temple of Seattle," *The News Tribune* (September 14, 2017). Available online at http://www.thenewstribune.com/news/local/article173005561.html (Accessed February 11, 2019).

120. Chalice Blythe, electronic communication with the author (December 19, 2018).

121. Malcolm Jarry, electronic communication with the author (December 27, 2018).

122. Chalice Blythe, electronic communication with the author (December 19, 2018).

123. Liz Sawyer, "Under pressure from town, Belle Plaine City Council votes to restore cross to vets memorial," *The Star Tribune* (February 7, 2017). Available online at http://www.startribune.com/under-pressure-from-town-belle-plaine-city-council-votes-to-restore-cross-to-veterans-memorial/413042913/ (Accessed February 11, 2019).

124. Hemant Mehta, "A MN town wants religious war memorials, so Satanists offer one with a Baphometic Bowl of Wisdom," *Friendly Atheist* (February 21, 2017). Available online at http://www.patheos.com/blogs/friendlyatheist/2017/02/21/a-mn-town-wants-religious-war-memorials-so-satanists-offer-one-with-a-baphometic-bowl-of-wisdom/ (Accessed February 11, 2019).

125. Koren Walsh (Jezebel Pride), interview with the author (December 28, 2018).

126. Matthew Davis, "Christians express concerns over proposed satanic memorial in Belle Plaine," *The Catholic Spirit* (June 6, 2017). Available online at http://thecatholicspirit.com/news/local-news/christians-express-concerns-proposed-satanic-memorial-belle-plaine/ (Accessed February 11, 2019).

127. Hemant Mehta, "Catholic priest: MN park's new monument will attract Satanists who want to molest kids," *Friendly Atheist* (June 7, 2017). Available online at https://friendlyatheist.patheos.com/2017/06/07/catholic-priest-mn-parks-new-monument-will-attract-satanists-who-want-to-molest-kids/ (Accessed February 11, 2019).

128. Catholic News Service, "After protests over satanic monument, city removes all religious symbols from memorial," *The Catholic Herald* (July 22, 2017). Available online at http://catholicherald.co.uk/news/2017/07/22/after-protests-over-satanic-monument-city-removes-all-religious-symbols-from-memorial/ (Accessed February 11, 2019).

129. William Siebenmorgen, "Rosary rally against first public satanic monument in history," *Standard Newswire* (July 10, 2017). Available online at http://www.standardnewswire.com/news/4610012716.html (Accessed February 11, 2019).

130. Web Desk, "Christians protest against installation of satanic monument," *Christians in Pakistan* (July 23, 2017). Available online at https://www.christiansinpakistan.com/christians-protect-against-installation-of-satanic-monument/ (Accessed February 11, 2019).

131. Thomas Craughwell, "Bedeviled, bothered, and bewildered in Minnesota," *The American Spectator* (July 26, 2017). Available online at https://spectator.org/bedeviled-bothered-and-bewildered-in-minnesota/ (Accessed February 11, 2019).

132. Hemant Mehta, "Satanists want $35,000 from MN town that changed policy to avoid their display," *Friendly Atheist* (December 11, 2017). Available online at https://friendlyatheist.patheos.com/2017/12/11/satanists-want-35000-from-mn-town-that-changed-policy-to-avoid-their-display/ (Accessed February 11, 2019).

133. Natividad Sidlangan, "Satanic Temple sues city after officials retract permission for devil statue," *SocialNewsDaily* (April 30, 2019). Available online at https://socialnewsdaily.com/86132/satanic-temple-sues-city/ (Accessed May 14, 2019).

134. Liz Sawyer, "Satanic Temple demands $35K after Belle Plaine cancels public space at veteran's park," *The Star Tribune* (December 11, 2017). Available online at http://www.startribune.com/satanic-temple-demands-35k-after-belle-plaine-cancels-public-space-at-veterans-park/463270723/ (Accessed February 11, 2019).

Chapter 3

1. Roger Finke and Christopher P. Schietle, "Understanding Schisms: Theoretical Understandings of their Origins," in James R. Lewis and Sarah M. Lewis, eds., *Sacred Schisms: How Religions Divide* (Cambridge: Cambridge University Press, 2009), p. 19

2. David Guinan, interview with the author (March 5, 2016).

3. Anna Merlan, "The Satanic Temple is engulfed in a civil war over a decisions to hire an attorney with a stable of alt-right clients," *Jezebel.com* (August 7, 2018). Available online at https://jezebel.com/the-satanic-temple-is-engulfed-in-a-civil-war-over-a-de-1828130997 (Accessed February 11, 2019).

4. Inemesit Udodiong, "Satanic Temple cries out on Twitter," *Pulse.ng* (January 22, 2018). Available online at http://www.pulse.ng/communities/religion/religious-discrimination-satanic-temple-cries-out-on-twitter-id7873921.html (Accessed February 11, 2019).

5. Madeleine Aggeler, "A guide to the all the drama roiling the satanic community," *The Cut* (August 10, 2018). Available online at https://www.thecut.com/2018/08/the-satanic-temple-drama-explained.html (Accessed February 11, 2019).

6. Madison Malone Kircher, "White nationalists and other extremists are disappearing from Twitter," *New York Magazine* (December 18, 2017). Available online at http://nymag.com/intelligencer/2017/12/twitter-purges-alt-right-nazi-accounts-like-jayda-fransen.html (Accessed February 11, 2019).

7. Ash Astoroth, electronic communication with the author (January 16, 2018). Astoroth left TST later that year and remains highly critical of it.

8. Andrew Hall, "The attack on the Satanic Temple headquarters," *Laughing in Disbelief* (January 14, 2018). Available online at https://www.patheos.com/blogs/laughingindisbelief/2018/01/the-attack-on-the-satanic-temple-headquarters/ (Accessed February 11, 2019).

9. Thomas J. Main defines the "alt-right" as a political ideology rather than a movement defined by four points: a rejection of liberal democracy, white racialism, anti-Americanism, and vitriolic rhetoric, see his *The Rise of the Alt-Right* (Washington, DC: Brookings Institution Press, 2018), p. 8.

10. Randazza has also represented left-leaning clients such as the Orbit, an atheist group committed to social justice, and the Muslim American Women's Political Action Committee.

11. Sebastian Simpson, interview with the author (November 18, 2018). I have not seen this leaked draft.

12. Matthew Gault, "Adam Parfrey's Feral House was the forerunner to Reddit and 4Chan," *Motherboard* (May 11, 2018). Available online at https://motherboard.vice.com/en_us/article/ywez7w/adam-parfrey-dies-feral-house (Accessed February 11, 2019).

13. "8/8/88 rally: Radio Werewolf, Boyd Rice, Zeena Schreck, Adam Parfrey." Available online at https://www.youtube.com/watch?v=vx0kRUOzrxI (Accessed February 17, 2017).

14. Chris Mathews, *Modern Satanism: Anatomy of a Radical Subculture* (Westport, Conn.: Praeger, 2009), p. 204.

15. Jesper Aagaard Petersen, "The Carnival of Dr. LaVey: Articulations of Transgression in Modern Satanism," in Per Faxneld and Jesper Aagaard Petersen, eds., *The Devil's Party: Satanism in Modernity* (New York: Oxford University Press, 2013), p. 172.

16. The Southern Poverty Law Center, "Atomawaffen," *splcenter.org* (n.d.). Available online at https://www.splcenter.org/hatewatch/2018/02/22/atomwaffen-and-siege-parallax-

how-one-neo-nazi%E2%80%99s-life%E2%80%99s-work-fueling-younger-generation (Accessed February 11, 2019); Jonah Engel Bromwich, "What is Atomwaffen? A neo-Nazi group, linked to multiple murders," *New York Times* (February 12, 2018). Available online at https://www.nytimes.com/2018/02/12/us/what-is-atomwaffen.html (Accessed February 11, 2019).

17. TST chapter heads, letter to the National Council and Executive Ministry of The Satanic Temple (July 5, 2018), p. 2.

18. Jack Matirko, "The Satanic Temple-UK helps to mail upside down crucifixes to Bavaria," *For Infernal Use Only* (May 31, 2018). Available online at https://www.patheos.com/blogs/infernal/2018/05/the-satanic-temple-uk-is-helping-to-mail-upside-down-crucifixes-to-bavaria/ (Accessed February 12, 2019).

19. Lucien Greaves, interview with the author (August 8, 2018).

20. Zeke Apollyon, interview with the author (September 10, 2018).

21. Lucien Greaves, interview with the author (August 8, 2018).

22. Statement from the Satanic Collective. Available online at https://www.instagram.com/p/BmFaw1WFO5i/ (Accessed February 11, 2019).

23. Bel Citoyen, interview with the author (August 8, 2018).

24. Jerilyn Jordan, "Satanic Temple announces mysterious 'ritual performance' slated for next week," *Detroit Metro Times* (February 2, 2018). Available online at https://www.metrotimes.com/the-scene/archives/2018/02/02/satanic-temple-announces-mysterious-ritual-performance-slated-for-next-week (Accessed February 11, 2019).

25. Quoted in Anna Merlan, "Satanic artist and activist Jex Blackmore on her controversial role in the documentary *Hail Satan?*" *Jezebel.com* (May 20, 2019). Available online at https://themuse.jezebel.com/satanic-artist-and-activist-jex-blackmore-on-her-contro-1834791520 (Accessed May 31, 2019).

26. Jex Blackmore, interview with the author (June 24, 2018); electronic communication with the author (February 19, 2019).

27. Merlan, "Satanic artist and activist Jex Blackmore."

28. Blackmore, "The struggle for justice is ongoing."

29. Shane Bugbee, Amy Bugbee, and Doug Mesner, "Might is right special," *Radio Satan* (September 11, 2002). Available online at https://archive.org/details/MightIsRightSpecial (Accessed February 11, 2019).

30. Jesper Aagaard Petersen, "'Smite Him Hip and Thigh': Satanism, Violence, and Transgression," in James R. Lewis, ed., *Violence and New Religious Movements* (New York: Oxford University Press, 2011), p. 352.

31. Lucien Greaves, interview with the author (November 3, 2018).

32. Malcolm Jarry, electronic communication with the author (March 3, 2019).

33. Blackmore, "The struggle for justice is ongoing." One group of former TST members divided the podcast amongst themselves, each volunteering to listen to a few hours of it, in order to discern the extent of objectionable content.

34. Autumn, "Yet another quitting The Satanic Temple post (YAQTSTP) updated: New information about Adam Parfrey," *Medium.com* (August 13, 2018). Available online at https://medium.com/@iNerdGirl/yet-another-quitting-the-satanic-temple-post-yaqtstp-ea4ad9a49c3d (Accessed February 12, 2019); Emma Story, "Why I'm leaving

The Satanic Temple," *Medium.com* (August 7, 2018). Available online at https://medium.com/@emmastory/why-im-leaving-the-satanic-temple-528bbc06432b (Accessed February 12, 2019); Schwarzer Teufel, "What would Satan do; knowing when to pull anchor and sail away," *Medium.com* (August 17, 2018). Available online at https://medium.com/satanic-collective/what-would-satan-do-knowing-when-to-pull-anchor-and-sail-away-f6d8249accaf; https://medium.com/satanic-collective/what-would-satan-do-knowing-when-to-pull-anchor-and-sail-away-f6d8249accaf (Accessed February 12, 2019); Nikki Moungo, "As witness and measure taken, to pronounce: The Satanic Temple—my experience," *Medium.com* (August 15, 2018). Available online at https://medium.com/@SistersSatanic/as-witness-and-measure-taken-to-pronounce-the-satanic-temple-my-experience-a1400928656f (Accessed February 11, 2019).

35. "Trident antifascism." Available online at https://tridentantifascism.blackblogs.org/ (Accessed February 11, 2019).

36. Zeke Apollyon, interview with the author (September 10, 2019).

37. Lucien Greaves, phone communication with the author (November 15, 2018).

38. Joseph Laycock, "Neo-Nazis call on 'white Christians' to oppose Satanic Temple Rally," *Religion Dispatches* (August 14, 2018). Available online at https://rewire.news/religion-dispatches/2018/08/14/neo-nazis-call-on-white-christians-to-oppose-satanic-temple-rally/ (Accessed February 11, 2019).

39. The presence of suspicious men with walkie-talkies was confirmed by a camera crew recording for *Vice*. Electronic communication with the author (August 18, 2018).

40. Amber, interview with the author (January 3, 2019).

41. Hemant Mehta, "After pushback, The Satanic Temple will revise its non-disparagement clause," *Friendly Atheist* (September 4, 2018). Available online at https://friendlyatheist.patheos.com/2018/09/04/after-pushback-the-satanic-temple-will-revise-its-non-disparagement-clause/ (Accessed February 11, 2019).

42. Ibid.

43. The Black Light Catechism, "The man in the high temple," *Medium.com* (November 16, 2018). Available online at https://medium.com/@blacklightcatechism/the-man-in-the-high-temple-3c463e4f8f41 (Accessed February 11, 2019).

44. Amber, interview with the author (January 3, 2019).

45. Sebastian Simpson, interview with the author (November 28, 2018).

46. Sekhmet Solas, interview with the author (September 15, 2019).

47. Lucien Greaves, "Down the spiral of purity," *Patreon.com* (August 7, 2018). Available online at https://www.patreon.com/posts/down-spiral-of-20599936 (Accessed February 11, 2019).

48. Bradley Campbell and Jason Manning, *The Rise of Victimhood Culture: Microaggressions, Safe Spaces, and the New Culture Wars* (New York: Palgrave Macmillan, 2018), p. 168.

49. Dex Desjardins, interview with the author (September 15, 2019).

50. Felix Fortunado, interview with the author (September 12, 2019).

51. Finke and Scheitle, "Understanding Schisms," p. 12.

52. Greg Stevens, interview with the author (January 8, 2019).

53. Jack Matirko, interview with the author (August 9, 2019).

54. Hofman Turing, interview with the author (September 23, 2018).

55. Dex Desjardins, interview with the author (September 15, 2018).

56. Felix Fortunado, interview with the author (September 12, 2018).

57. Lucien Greaves, "Lucien Greaves on The Satanic Temple and free speech," *For Infernal Use Only* (June 19, 2018). Available online at https://www.patheos.com/blogs/infernal/2018/06/lucien-greaves-tst-free-speech/ (Accessed February 11, 2019).

58. Amber, interview with the author (January 3, 2019).

59. Herbert Marcuse, "Repressive Tolerance," in Herbert Marcuse and Andrew Feenberg, eds., *The Essential Marcuse: Selected Writings of Philosopher and Social Critic Herbert Marcuse* (Boston: Beacon Press, 2007), p. 50.

60. Dan Pringle, "Cal Poly leftists plan 'Satanist' counter-event against Milo," *Brietbart.com* (January 17, 2017). Available online at https://www.breitbart.com/social-justice/2017/01/17/cal-poly-leftists-plan-satanist-counter-event-against-milo/ (Accessed February 11, 2019).

61. Dalila Johari Paul, "Protestors shut down Milo Yiannapoulos event at UC Davis," *CNN.com* (January 14, 2017). Available online at https://www.cnn.com/2017/01/14/us/milo-yiannopoulos-uc-davis-speech-canceled/index.html (Accessed February 11, 2019).

62. Dan Pringle, "The Satanic Temple disavows anti-Milo 'Satanist' event at Cal Poly, defends free speech," *Brietbart.com* (January 19, 2017). Available online at https://www.breitbart.com/social-justice/2017/01/19/the-satanic-temple-distances-itself-from-cal-poly-anti-milo-event/ (Accessed February 11, 2019). In the article, this quote is attributed to Lucien Greaves.

63. The Satanic Temple, "The Satanic Temple's guidelines for effective protest," *thesatanictemple.com* (n.d.). Available online at https://thesatanictemple.com/pages/the-satanic-temple-s-guidelines-for-effective-protest (Accessed February 11, 2019).

64. Emma Story, "Why I'm leaving The Satanic Temple."

65. Greg Lukianoff and Jonathan Haidt, *The Coddling of the American Mind: How Good Intentions and Bad Ideas Are Setting Up a Generation for Failure* (New York: Penguin, 2018).

66. Tara Isabella Burton, "The Satanic Temple is divided over its leader's decision to hire Alex Jones's lawyer," *Vox.com* (August 9, 2018). Available online at https://www.vox.com/2018/8/9/17669894/satanic-temple-alt-right-marc-randazza-lawyer-lucien-greaves (Accessed February 11, 2019).

67. Asbjørn Dyrendal, James R. Lewis, and Jesper Aagaard Petersen, *The Invention of Satanism* (New York: Oxford University Press, 2015), pp. 136–137.

68. Nelcitlaly, interview with the author (September 28, 2019).

69. Cara Jeanne, interview with the author (August 7, 2019).

70. Lex Manticore and Lux Armiger, interview with the author (July 5, 2018); Sekhmet Solas and Dex Desjardins (September 15, 2018).

71. Donny, interview with the author (September 15, 2018).

72. Steve Hill, interview with the author (August 11, 2018).

73. Greg Stevens, interview with the author (January 9, 2018).

74. Schwarzer Teufel, "What would Satan do."

75. Lux Armiger, interview with the author (July 5, 2018).

76. Lex Manticore, interview with the author (July 5, 2018).

77. Greg Stevens, interview with the author (January 8, 2019).

78. Donny, interview with the author (September 15, 2018).

79. Jesper Aagaard Petersen, "Satanists and Nuts: The Role of Schisms in Modern Satanism," in James R. Lewis and Sarah M. Lewis, eds., *Sacred Schisms: How Religions Divide* (Cambridge: Cambridge University Press, 2009), p. 243.

80. Steve Hill, interview with the author (August 11, 2018).

81. Jon Winningham, interview with the author (September 12, 2018).

82. Hofman Turing, interview with the author (December 29, 2018).

83. Damien Ba'al, interview the author (July 9, 2018). See also Damien Ba'al, *The Satanic Narratives: A Modern Satanic Bible* (St. Louis, Mo.: HLA, 2015).

84. Koren Walsh (Jezebel Pride), interview with the author (December 28, 2018).

85. Evyn and Thom of Satanhaus, interview with the author (January 14, 2019).

86. Malcolm Jarry, electronic communication with the author (March 3, 2019).

87. Jon Winningham, interview with the author (September 12, 2018).

88. Hofman Turing, interview with the author (September 23, 2018).

89. Damien Ba'al, interview the author (July 9, 2018).

Chapter 4

1. Josh Sanburn, "The new Satanism: Less Lucifer, more politics," *Time* (December 10, 2013). Available online at http://nation.time.com/2013/12/10/the-new-satanism-less-lucifer-more-politics/ (accessed February 11, 2019).

2. Lucien Greaves, "What is the difference between The Satanic Temple and the Church of Satan," *For Infernal Use Only* (January 21, 2019). Available online at https://www.patheos.com/blogs/infernal/2019/01/what-is-the-difference-between-the-satanic-temple-and-the-church-of-satan/ (Accessed February 11, 2019).

3. Blanche Barton and Anton Szandor La Vey, *The Secret Life of a Satanist: The Authorized Biography of Anton LaVey* (Los Angeles: Feral House, 1990), p. 77.

4. Nikolas Schreck, *The Satanic Screen: An Illustrated Guide to the Devil in Cinema* (London: Creation, 2001), p. 143. In Barton's account (*The Secret Life of a Satanist*), p. 80), this suggestion came from a police inspector LaVey was friends with named Jack Webb.

5. Barton and LeVey, *The Secret Life of a Satanist*, p. 82.

6. Arthur Lyons, *The Second Coming: Satanism in America* (New York: Dodd, Mead, 1970), p. 190.

7. Schreck, *The Satanic Screen*, p. 144; Ruben van Luijk, *Children of Lucifer: The Origins of Modern Religious Satanism* (New York: Oxford University Press, 2016), p. 297.

8. James R. Lewis, "Anton LaVey, The Satanic Bible, and the Satanist Tradition," in James R. Lewis, ed., *Legitimating New Religions* (New Brunswick, N.J.: Rutgers University Press, 2003): p. 112. In LaVey's (*Satan Speaks!* [Venice, Calif.: Feral House, 1998],

p. 5) own account, the idea was put forth by Fred Goerner, a writer. LaVey had met Goerner though his wife, Merla Zellerbach, who was a student in workshop for witches run by LaVey.

9. Owen Davies, *Grimoires: A History of Magic Books* (Oxford: Oxford University Press, 2009), p. 274.

10. Asbjørn Dyrendal, James R. Lewis, and Jesper Aagaard Petersen, *The Invention of Satanism* (New York: Oxford University Press, 2015), p. 75.

11. Lewis, "Anton LaVey, The Satanic Bible, and the Satanist Tradition," p. 113.

12. Marcello Truzzi, "The occult revival as popular culture: Some random observations on the old and the nouveau witch," *The Sociological Quarterly* 13, no. 1 (1972): p. 27.

13. Van Luijk, *Children of Lucifer*, p. 353.

14. Ibid., p. 363.

15. Per Faxneld and Jesper Aagaard Petersen, "Part Two: The Black Pope and the Church of Satan," in Per Faxneld and Jesper Aagaard Petersen, eds., *The Devil's Party: Satanism in Modernity* (New York: Oxford University Press, 2013), p. 81. Rodney Stark and Williams Sims Bainbridge put forward a model of "audience cults, client cults, and movement cults." In this model an "audience cult" refers to a group that shares common media but features little face-to-face interaction. See *The Future of Religion: Secularization, Revival, and Cult Formation* (Los Angeles: University of California Press, 1985), pp. 27–28.

16. David G. Bromley, "The Church of Satan," *World Religion and Spirituality Project* (August 1, 2012). Available online at http://www.wrldrels.org/profiles/ChurchOfSatan.htm (Accessed February 17, 2017).

17. Greg Stevens, "When Satanism met the Internet," *Breitbart.com* (October 31, 2015). Available online at https://www.breitbart.com/tech/2015/10/31/when-satanism-met-the-internet/ (Accessed February 11, 2019).

18. Seraphina, interview with the author (July 1, 2019).

19. "Lucien Greaves v. Tucker Carlson," July 20, 2017, full transcript. Available online at https://luciengreaves.com/lucien-greaves-v-tucker-carlson-20-july-2017-full-transcript/ (Accessed February 11, 2019).

20. Greg Stevens, "Politics, the Dark Lord, and Hobby Lobby: An interview with the Satanic Temple," *The Daily Dot* (August 13, 2014). Available online at https://www.dailydot.com/layer8/satanic-temple-interview/ (Accessed February 11, 2019).

21. Field notes, Austin, Texas (June 23, 2018).

22. Malcolm Jarry, electronic communication with the author (March 3, 2019).

23. Lilith Starr, electronic communication with the author (February 5, 2019).

24. Lucien Greaves, phone communication with the author (February 12, 2019).

25. David Frankfurter, "Review of *The Invention of Satanism*. Asbjorn Dyrendeal, James Lewis, and Jesper Peterson," *Journal of Religion and Violence* 5, no. 1 (2017): 111–112.

26. Benedict Anderson, *Imagined Communities: Reflections on the Origin and Spread of Nationalism* (New York: Verso, 2016). In a similar analysis, Rafal Smocyzynski has applied Max Weber's category of an "emotional community" and Michel Maffesoli's notion of "neotribalism" to encapsulate modern Satanism; see Smocyzynski, "Cyber-Satanism and Imagined Satanism: Dark Symptoms of Late Modernity," in Jesper

Aagaard Petersen, ed., *Contemporary Religious Satanism: A Critical Anthology* (New York: Routledge, 2016), pp. 141–152.

27. Peter H. Gilmore, "Full disclosure: The Snowman is a diabolical hit," *ChurchofSatan. com* (n.d.). Available online at https://www.churchofsatan.com/the-snowman-is-diabolical-hit/ (Accessed February 11, 2019).

28. Dyrendal, Asbjørn, "Devilish consumption: Popular culture in satanic socialization," *Numen* 55, no. 1 (2008): 86–87.

29. Daniel Walker, interview with the author (July 8, 2018).

30. Ann Swidler, "Culture in action: Symbols and strategies," *American Sociological Review* 51, no. 2 (1986): p. 277.

31. Ibid., p. 279.

32. Stevens, "Politics, the Dark Lord, and Hobby Lobby."

33. Greaves, "What is the difference between The Satanic Temple and the Church of Satan."

34. Peter H. Gilmore, "Satanism: The feared religion," *ChurchofSatan.com* (n.d.). Available online at https://www.churchofsatan.com/satanism-the-feared-religion/ (Accessed February 11, 2019).

35. Dyrendal, Lewis, and Petersen, *The Invention of Satanism*, p. 175.

36. Van Luijk, *Children of Lucifer*, p. 368.

37. Joel Ethan, "The Satanic Temple fact sheet," *ChurchofSatan.com* (n.d.). Available online at https://www.churchofsatan.com/the-satanic-temple-fact-sheet/ (Accessed February 11, 2019).

38. Peter H. Gilmore, "Mirror mirror," *ChurchofSatan.com* (n.d.) Available online at http://www.churchofsatan.com/mirror-mirror.php (Accessed February 17, 2017).

39. Anna Mertlan, "Trolling hell," *The Village Voice* (July 23, 2014). Available online at https://www.villagevoice.com/2014/07/23/trolling-hell/ (Accessed February 11, 2019).

40. Joel Ethan, "Third side Intelligence: Missouri abortions," *ChurchofSatan.com* (October 10, 2017). Available online at http://news.churchofsatan.com/post/166258537007/third-side-intelligence-missouri-abortions-an (Accessed February 11, 2019).

41. The Church of Satan tweeted at Josh Hawley on October 4, 2017, and reporter Grace Carr on October 11, 2017. These tweets were archived by TST and forwarded to me July 18, 2018.

42. Van Luijk, *Children of Lucifer*, p. 305.

43. Field notes, Salem, Massachusetts (July 13, 2018).

44. Davies, *Grimoires*, p. 274.

45. James R. Lewis, "Who serves Satan? A demographic and ideological profile," *Marburg Journal of Religion* 6, no. 2 (2001): p. 5.

46. Joshua Gunn, *Modern Occult Rhetoric Mass Media and the Drama of Secrecy in the Twentieth Century* (Tuscaloosa: University of Alabama Press, 2005), p. 188.

47. Seraphina, interview with the author (July 1, 2018).

48. Jon Winningham, interview with the author (September 12, 2018).

49. Greaves, "What is the difference between The Satanic Temple and the Church of Satan."

50. Mara Gorgo, interview with the author (June 21, 2018).

51. Greaves, "What is the difference between The Satanic Temple and the Church of Satan."

52. Merlan, "Trolling hell."

53. Gunn, *Modern Occult Rhetoric*, p. 184.

54. Gavin Baddeley, *Lucifer Rising* (London: Plexus, 1999), p. 67.

55. Chris Mathews, *Modern Satanism: Anatomy of a Radical Subculture* (Westport, Conn.: Praeger, 2009), p. 170.

56. Matthew Bagger, *The Uses of Paradox Religion, Self-Transformation, and the Absurd* (New York: New York University Press, 2012).

57. Lyons, *The Second Coming*, p. 180.

58. Barton, *The Secret Life of a Satanist*, p. 215.

59. Lawrence Wright, *Saints & Sinners: Walker Railey, Jimmy Swaggart, Madalyn Murray O'Hair, Anton LaVey, Will Campbell, Matthew Fox* (New York: Knopf, 1993), p. 138.

60. Anton LaVey, "Pentagonal revisionism: A five-point program" (1988). Available online at http://www.churchofsatan.com/pentagonal-revisionism.php (Accessed February 17, 2017).

61. Annette Lamoth-Ramos, "Beelzebub's daughter," *Vice.com* (April 25, 2012). Available online at https://www.vice.com/en_uk/article/beelzebubs-daughter-0000175-v19n4?Contentpage=-1 (Accessed February 17, 2017).

62. Lewis, "Anton LaVey, The Satanic Bible, and the Satanist tradition," p. 111.

63. The Church of Satan, "Satan wants you!" (n.d.) Available online at http://news.churchofsatan.com/post/84339903252/satan-wants-you (Accessed February 17, 2017).

64. Greaves, "What is the difference between The Satanic Temple and the Church of Satan."

65. Shane and Amy Bugbee, "The doctor is in . . ." *ChurchofSatan.com* (n.d.). Available online at https://www.churchofsatan.com/interview-mf-magazine/ (Accessed February 11, 2019).

66. Daniel Walker, electronic communication with the author (July 11, 2018).

67. Malcolm Jarry, personal communication with the author (March 3, 2019).

68. Arthur Lyons, *Satan Wants You: The Cult of Devil Worship in America* (New York: Mysterious Press, 1988), p. 84.

69. Quoted in Susan Roberts, *Witches U.S.A.* (New York: Dell, 1971), p. 228.

70. Anton Szandor LaVey, *Satan Speaks!* (Venice, Calif.: Feral House, 1998), p. 4.

71. Baddeley, *Lucifer Rising*, p. 67.

72. Barton and LeVey, *The Secret Life of a Satanist*, p. 115

73. Greaves, "What is the difference between The Satanic Temple and the Church of Satan."

74. Interviews with the author (January 6, 2014; November 3, 2018).

75. "The Satanic Temple library." Available online at https://thesatanictemple.com/pages/the-satanic-temple-library (Accessed February 11, 2019).

76. Lilith Starr, interview with the author (July 27, 2018).

77. Jacob Senholt, "Secret Identities in the Sinister Tradition: Political Esotericism and the Convergence of Radical Islam, Satanism and National Socialism in the Order of

Nine Angles," in Per Faxneld and Jesper Petersen, eds., *The Devil's Party: Satanism in Modernity* (New York: Oxford University Press, 2012), pp. 250–274.

78. Quoted in Guy Birchall, "DEVIL'S DANCE: Inside the Los Angeles Satanic Temple's biggest-ever 'black mass' with blood-letting, demonic cats and stand-up," *The Sun* (January 18, 2017). Available online at https://www.thesun.co.uk/news/2641653/black-mass-los-angeles-satanic-temple-pictures-blood-letting/ (Accessed February 17, 2017).

79. Jeffrey Burton Russell, *The Devil, Perception of Evil: Perceptions of Evil from Antiquity to Primitive Christianity* (Ithaca: Cornell University Press, 1982), pp. 195–196.

80. Bel Citoyen, interview with the author (July 10, 2018).

81. Peter A. Schock, *Romantic Satanism: Myth and the Historical Moment in Blake, Shelley, and Byron* (New York: Palgrave Macmillan, 2003), pp. 13–17.

82. Percy Bysshe Shelley, *A Defense of Poetry* (Charleston, S.C.: BiblioLife, 2009), p. 30.

83. Van Luijk, *Children of Lucifer,* p. 73.

84. Anatole France, *The Revolt of the Angels* (New York: Modern Library, 1914), p. 347.

85. Hofman A. Turing, interview with the author (December 29, 2018); Belle Phomet, interview with the author (January 6, 2019).

86. "High priest Brian Werner Resigns from the Satanic Temple" (December 23, 2014). Available online at https://www.youtube.com/watch?v=ZIN4aZ8IMz0 (Accessed February 11, 2019).

87. Joshua Gill, "Catholics to rally in prayer against first satanic monument on public land in U.S. History," *The Daily Caller* (July 10, 2017). Available online at https://dailycaller.com/2017/07/10/catholics-to-rally-in-prayer-against-first-satanic-monument-on-public-land-in-u-s-history/ (Accessed February 11, 2019).

Chapter 5

1. John Lardas Modern, "My evangelical conviction," *Religion* 42 (June 2012): p. 336.

2. Stu de Hann, interview with the author (September 29, 2018).

3. A notable exception occurred when Martin Lamers, a CoS member in the Netherlands, opened a Satanic "abbey" in Amsterdam. Visitors to the abbey paid to watch "Satanic nuns" perform sex acts. Lamers claimed his Abbey was tax exempt because the sex acts were religious services and the payments were actually donations. LaVey considered revoking Lamers's charter over his claim to be tax exempt. In 1987, after a decade of police raids and legal battles, the abbey was legally declared a sex club and not a religious institution, and Lamers was made to pay ten million guilders in back taxes. Gavin Baddeley interviewed a former performer at the abbey, who insisted that her performances had been acts of sexual magic, which is "one of the highest sexual ideals for Satanists." Arthur Lyons, *Satan Wants You: The Cult of Devil Worship in America* (New York: Mysterious Press, 1988), pp. 120–121; Gavin Baddeley, *Lucifer Rising* (London: Plexus, 1999), p. 110.

4. Bryn Alexander Coles and Melanie West, "Trolling the trolls: Online forum users constructions of the nature and properties of trolling," *Computers in Human Behavior* 60 (2016): pp. 232–244.

5. Russell McCutcheon, "'They licked the platter clean': On the co-dependency of the religious and the secular," *Method & Theory in the Study of Religion* 19, no. 3/4 (2007): p. 175.

6. Ibid., p. 191.

7. Stephen R. Prothero, *Religious Literacy: What Every American Needs to Know—and Doesn't* (San Francisco: HarperSanFrancisco, 2007), p. 29.

8. Hugh B. Urban, *The Church of Scientology: A History of a New Religion* (Princeton, N.J.: Princeton University Press, 2013), p. 17.

9. Joseph P. Laycock, "Is the Satanist behind 10 Commandments challenge sincere?," *Religion Dispatches* (January 8, 2014). Available online at http://religiondispatches. org/is-the-satanist-behind-10-commandments-challenge-sincere/ (Accessed February 11, 2019).

10. Damien Ba'al, interview with the author (July 9, 2018). This fundraising led to a falling out with TST's executive ministry, who had been planning their own media campaign about the case in advance of fundraising. The executive ministry felt far more money could have been raised if the St. Louis chapter had been more patient. Lucien Greaves, "The savage saga of Mary Doe," *The Lucien Greaves Archive* (n.d.). Available online at https://luciengreaves.com/the-savage-saga-of-mary-doe/ (Accessed February 21, 2019).

11. Callie Beusman, "A state-by-state list of the lies abortion doctors are forced to tell women," *Broadly* (August 18, 2016). Available online at https://broadly.vice.com/en_ us/article/nz88gx/a-state-by-state-list-of-the-lies-abortion-doctors-are-forced-to-tell-women (Accessed February 11, 2019).

12. Norman Solomon, *Judaism a Very Short Introduction* (New York: Oxford University Press, 2014), p. 129.

13. John Haldane and Patrick Lee, "Aquinas on human ensoulment, abortion and the value of life," *Philosophy* 78, no. 2 (2003): p. 266.

14. James McNaughton, interview with the author (July 23, 2018).

15. Hobby Lobby's health plan covered the birth control methods in question until they dropped this coverage to file their lawsuit in 2012.

16. *Kathleen Sebelius, Secretary of Health and Human Services, et al., v. Hobby Lobby Stores Inc., et al.* On petition for a writ of certiorari to the US Court of Appeals for the Tenth Circuit. Brief of amici curiae Physicians for Reproductive Health, American College of Obstetricians and Gynecologists, American Society for Emergency Contraception, et al., in support of petitioners. Docket No. 13-354 (October 21, 2013).

17. *Burwell v. Hobby Lobby* 573 U.S., 1, 5 (2014).

18. James McNaughton, interview with the author (July 23, 2018).

19. Malcolm Jarry, electronic communication with the author (March 3, 2019).

20. Avi Asher-Schapiro, "The Satanic Temple is suing Missouri over its abortion Law," *Vice. com* (June 24, 2015). Available online at https://news.vice.com/article/the-satanic-temple-is-suing-missouri-over-its-abortion-law (Accessed February 11, 2019).

21. The Satanic Temple, "Satanist religious exemption" (n.d.). Available online at https:// www.scribd.com/doc/263769869/Satanist-Religious-Exemption (Accessed February 11, 2019).

22. James McNaughton, interview with the author (July 23, 2018).

23. MO Rev Stat §1.205. (1986).

24. James McNaughton, interview with the author (July 23, 2018).

25. Missouri Department of Health and Human Services, "Missouri's informed consent booklet" (October 2017), p. 1. Available online at https://health.mo.gov/living/families/womenshealth/pregnancyassistance/pdf/InformedConsentBooklet.pdf (Accessed February 11, 2019).

26. Joe Ortwerth, "Satan worshippers lose lawsuit to stop pro-life law informing women about their unborn baby," *Lifesite News* (February 9, 2016). Available online at http://www.lifenews.com/2016/02/09/satan-worshipers-lose-lawsuit-to-stop-pro-life-law-informing-women-about-their-unborn-baby/ (Accessed February 11, 2019); Missouri Family Policy Council, "Guiding principles" (n.d.). Available online at https://www.missourifamily.org/guiding-principles/ (Accessed February 11, 2019).

27. Associated Press, "Lawsuit challenging 72-hour abortion waiting period heads to Missouri Supreme Court," *KSHB.com* (October 10, 2017). Available online at https://www.kshb.com/news/local-news/missouri-abortion-lawsuit-heads-to-state-supreme-court (Accessed February 11, 2019).

28. Alex Dobuzinskis, "Satanist group challenges Missouri law on abortions," *Business Insider* (January 24, 2018). Available online at http://www.businessinsider.com/r-satanist-group-challenges-missouri-law-on-abortions-2018-1?r=UK&IR=T (Accessed February 11, 2019).

29. Alex Stuckey, "Judge dismisses case claiming abortion restrictions violate religious beliefs," *St. Louis Post-Dispatch* (January 21, 2016). Available online at http://www.stltoday.com/news/local/govt-and-politics/judge-dismisses-case-claiming-abortion-restrictions-violate-religious-beliefs/article_4b2ed702-75e9-5eb6-9d7b-a256ddb861fd.html (Accessed February 11, 2019).

30. *Mary Doe v. Eric Greitens et al.* WD80387 (October 3, 2017). Available online at https://www.courts.mo.gov/file.jsp?id=118276 (Accessed February 11, 2019).

31. The Satanic Temple, "The Satanic Temple makes historic win for abortion rights" (January 24, 2018). Available online at https://www.scribd.com/document/369922123/Satanic-Temple-Press-Release (Accessed February 11, 2019).

32. James McNaughton, interview with the author (July 23, 2018).

33. Marci A. Hamilton, "What do the Satanic Temple and Jehovah's Witnesses have in common? They are champions against government inculcation of belief," *Justia.com* (August 4, 2016). Available online at https://verdict.justia.com/2016/08/04/satanic-temple-jehovahs-witnesses-common-champions-government-inculcation-belief (Accessed February 11, 2019).

34. *Mary Doe v. Parson et al.* Supreme Court of Missouri SC96751 (February 13, 2019), p. 2.

35. Hemant Mehta, "Missouri Supreme Court rejects Satanist's religious challenge to abortion laws," *Friendly Atheist* (February 14, 2019). Available online at https://friendlyatheist.patheos.com/2019/02/14/missouri-supreme-court-rejects-satanists-religious-challenge-to-abortion-laws/ (Accessed February 21, 2019).

36. Days after the ruling, the Ordo Sororitatis Satanicae (OSS) published a *Medium* article purporting to be an interview with Mary Doe in which Doe claimed TST had been using her as "a cash cow" and repeating rumors that TST is secretly allied with the alt-right. Lucien Greaves responded with his own essay about Mary Doe. One of the founders of OSS is Nikki Moungo, who had been a chapter head for TST-St. Louis and a member of the National Council before she had falling out with TST. Greaves reported that Mary Doe and her child had lived with Nikki Moungo for a time during the case and that Mary became an "abusive" houseguest due, in part, to an abusive ex-boyfriend and drug addiction. According to Greaves, Doe constantly threatened to withdraw from the case if Moungo stopped supporting her. After Doe moved to her own apartment, Moungo received a hoax text message claiming that Doe had been shot by a pro-life activist. Presumably, the text was sent by Doe herself. OSS responded with more *Medium* articles in which they accused Greaves of "gaslighting" his female critics. See Greaves, "The savage sage of Mary Doe"; Ordo Sororitatis Satanicae, "Pt. 2—The devil's in the details: A response to Lucien Greaves of The Satanic Temple," *Medium.com* (February 21, 2019). Available online at https://medium.com/@SistersSatanic/pt-2-the-devils-in-the-details-a-response-to-lucien-greaves-of-the-satanic-temple-812dc7a4d7dd?fbclid=IwAR2WBRL5AjQ4D1c42uBHsH0WzuaJ0oOnKOo_g_ZIn2ljFyLAwL-63EPZHqc (Accessed February 21, 2019).

37. Malcolm Jarry, electronic communication with the author (February 21, 2019).

38. The Satanic Temple, "The Satanic Temple declares its members to be immune from Indiana law regarding fetal remains" (May 28, 2019).

39. Jack Suntrup, "Missouri's high court tosses case alleging abortion law violated Satanic Temple member's rights," *St. Louis Dispatch* (February 13, 2019). Available online at https://www.stltoday.com/news/local/crime-and-courts/missouri-s-high-court-tosses-case-alleging-abortion-law-violated/article_ae0e57c3-305e-51e6-b6cd-28699d41fada.html (Accessed February 18, 2019).

40. James McNaughton, interview with the author (July 23, 2018).

41. Quoted in Mark Hodges, "Satanists sue Missouri: Pro-life laws violate our religious beliefs," *Lifesitenews.com* (July 10, 2015). Available online at https://www.lifesitenews.com/news/satanists-sue-missouri-pro-life-laws-violate-our-religious-beliefs (Accessed February 11, 2019).

42. *Mary Doe v. Eric Greitens et al.* SC96751 (p. 2). Available online at https://www.thomasmoresociety.org/wp-content/uploads/2017/11/171110-Amici-Brief-Assembled_FINAL-BRIEF-for-SAT.pdf. (Accessed February 11, 2019).

43. Emma Green, "Satanists troll *Hobby Lobby*," *The Atlantic* (July 30, 2014). Available online at https://www.theatlantic.com/politics/archive/2014/07/satanists-troll-the-hobby-lobby-decision/375268/ (Accessed February 11, 2019).

44. Mark Hodges, "Satanists to democrat Missouri governor: Abortion is a 'sacrament,'" *Lifesitenews.com* (October 6, 2015). Available online at https://www.lifesitenews.com/news/satanists-to-democrat-missouri-governor-abortion-is-a-sacrament (Accessed February 11, 2019).

45. Hodges, "Satanists sue Missouri: Pro-life laws violate our religious beliefs."

46. Carole Novielli, "Satanic Temple in Missouri raises funds for woman to have abortion," *Lifesitenews.com* (Mary 4, 2015). Available online at http://www.lifenews.com/2015/05/04/satanic-temple-in-missouri-raises-funds-for-woman-to-have-abortion/ (Accessed February 11, 2019).

47. Trey Elmore, "Satanists Sue over abortion law, go after Christian bakers," *Church Militant.com* (October 9, 2017). Available online at https://www.churchmilitant.com/news/article/satanists-suing-over-abortion-wait-period-in-missouri-going-after-christian (Accessed February 11, 2019).

48. Anna Merlan, "Satanic Temple says Texas's new rules on fetal burial violate their religious freedom," *Jezebel.com* (December 2, 2016). Available online at https://jezebel.com/satanic-temple-says-texass-new-rules-on-fetal-burial-vi-1789616487 (Accessed February 11, 2019).

49. Amanda Marcotte, "Satanists claim abortion waiting periods violate their religious beliefs," *Slate.com* (May 4, 2015). Available online at http://www.slate.com/blogs/xx_factor/2015/05/04/satanists_in_missouri_they_argue_that_the_state_s_waiting_period_for_abortion.html (Accessed February 11, 2019).

50. Green, "Satanists troll *Hobby Lobby.*"

51. Kimberly Winston, "Satanists' challenge to Hobby Lobby ruling may face legal hurdles," *Religion News Service* (February 13, 2019). Available online at https://religionnews.com/2014/07/31/satanists-challenge-hobby-lobby-ruling-may-face-legal-hurdles/ (Accessed February 11, 2019).

52. Doug Mesner, "Dispatch from the Satanists battle against anti-abortion laws," *DailyKos.com* (August 4, 2014). Available online at http://www.dailykos.com/story/2014/08/05/1319202/-Dispatch-From-the-Satanist-Battle-Against-Anti-Abortion-Laws (Accessed February 11, 2019).

53. Jonathan Z. Smith, *Relating Religion: Essays in the Study of Religion* (Chicago: University of Chicago Press, 2004), p. 389.

54. Joel Ethan, "The Satanic Temple fact sheet," *ChurchofSatan.com* (n.d.). Available online at https://www.churchofsatan.com/the-satanic-temple-fact-sheet.php (Accessed February 11, 2019).

55. Shane Bugbee, "Unmasking Lucien Greaves, leader of the Satanic Temple," *Vice.com* (July 30, 2013). Available online at https://www.vice.com/en_us/article/4w7adn/unmasking-lucien-greaves-aka-doug-mesner-leader-of-the-satanic-temple (Accessed February 11, 2019).

56. Melissa M. Wilcox, *Queer Nuns: Religion, Activism, and Serious Parody* (New York University Press, 2018), p. 2.

57. Steven Sutcliffe, and Carole M. Cusack, eds., *The Problem of Invented Religions* (New York: Routledge, 2016), pp. 5–6

58. Johan Huizinga, *Homo Ludens: A Study of the Play-Element in Culture* (Boston: Beacon Press, 2014); Robert N. Bellah, *Religion in Human Evolution: From the Paleolithic to the Axial Age* (Cambridge, Mass.: Harvard University Press, 2011).

59. Carole M. Cusack, *Invented Religions: Imagination, Fiction and Faith* (Farnham, Surrey, UK: Ashgate, 2010), p. 23.

60. Ruben Van Luijk, *Children of Lucifer: The Origins of Modern Religious Satanism* (New York: Oxford University Press, 2016), p. 13.

61. Anton LaVey, *The Satanic Rituals* (New York: Avon, 1972), p. 27.

62. Blanche Barton, and Anton LaVey, *The Secret Life of a Satanist: The Authorized Biography of Anton LaVey* (Los Angeles: Feral House, 1990), p. 88.

63. Blanche Barton, *The Church of Satan* (New York: Hell's Kitchen Productions, 1990), p. 157.

64. Per Faxneld, "Secret Lineages and De Facto Satanists: Anton Lavey's Use of Esoteric Tradition," in Egil Asprem and Kennet Granholm, eds., *Contemporary Esotericism* (Sheffield, UK: Equinox, 2013), p. 78.

65. Joseph Laycock, "Laughing matters: 'Parody religions' and the command to compare," *Bulletin for the Study of Religion* 42, no. 3 (2013): 19–26.

66. Lucien Greaves, "Religion as illusion," *The Lucien Greaves Archive* (n.d.) Available online at https://luciengreaves.com/religion-as-illusion/ (Accessed February 11, 2019).

67. Sadie Satanas, Facebook.com (November 11, 2018).

68. Shane Bugbee, "Religion: A master and slave relationship," *Shanebugbee.com* (February 14, 2014). [Website defunct].

69. Carole Cusack, "Play, narrative and the creation of religion: Extending the theoretical base of 'invented religions," in Sutcliffe and Cusack, eds., *The Problem of Invented Religions,* p. 10.

70. Debra Heine, "They weren't kidding: After-School Satan Clubs are now organizing," *PJMedia* (October 21, 2016). Available online at https://pjmedia.com/faith/2016/10/21/they-werent-kidding-after-school-satan-clubs-are-now-organizing-across-the-country/ (Accessed February 11, 2019).

71. Edward Burnett Tylor, *Primitive Culture: Researchers into the Development of Mythology, Philosophy, Religion, Language, Art, and Custom* (New York: G.P. Putnam's Sons, 1920 [1871]), p. 424.

72. *Torcaso v. Watkins,* 367 U.S. 488 (1961).

73. Quoted in Vincent Philip Munoz, *Religious Liberty and the American Supreme Court: The Essential Cases and Documents* (New York: Rowman and Littlefield, 2015), p. 140.

74. Lucien Greaves, "A Stone for a stone: the Baphomet & the decalogue," *The Lucien Greaves Archive* (Fall 2014). Available online at https://luciengreaves.com/a-stone-for-a-stone-the-baphomet-the-decalogue/ (Accessed February 11, 2019).

75. Daniel Walker, interview with the author (July 8, 2018).

76. Chris, interview with the author (June 21, 2018).

77. Smith, *Relating Religion,* p. 366; Winnifred Sullivan drew a similar conclusion in her work *The Impossibility of Religious Freedom* (Princeton, N.J.: Princeton University Press, 2005).

78. Cécile Laborde, "Religion in the law: The disaggregation approach," *Law and Philosophy* 34, no. 6 (2015): 581–600.

79. Jonathan Z. Smith, "Religion, Religions, Religious," in Mark C. Taylor, ed., *Critical Terms for Religious Studies* (Chicago: University of Chicago Press, 1998): 269–285.

80. Catherine L. Albanese, *America Religions and Religion* (Belmont, Calif.: Thomson/ Wadsworth, 2007), p. 7. Albanese cites Joachim Wach's *Sociology of Religion* (1947). Wach outlined a framework for analyzing religion in terms of its theoretical expression (doctrine), practical expression (cultus), and sociological expression (communion). This framework is the prototype for Albanese's "four 'c's."

81. Field notes, San Marcos, Texas (July 20, 2018).

82. Malcolm Jarry, interview with the author (July 18, 2018).

83. Malcolm Jarry, phone conversation with the author (January 12, 2019).

84. Chris Turvey, interview with the author (June 24, 2019).

85. Belle Phomet, interview with the author (June 25, 2019).

86. Tara Isabella Burton, "Take religion. Remove God. Add #resistance. Meet the Satanic Temple," *Vox.com* (October 31, 2017). Available online at https://www. vox.com/identities/2017/10/31/16560150/religion-god-resistance-satanic-temple (Accessed February 11, 2019).

87. Malcolm Jarry, electronic communication with the author (May 19, 2019).

88. Chris Turvey, interview with the author (June 24, 2018).

89. Rose Vespira, interview with the author (July 17, 2018).

90. Christopher Paul, interview with the author (June 21, 2018).

91. Marius Omnes, interview with the author (July 17, 2018).

92. Chris Turvey, interview with the author (June 24, 2019).

93. Jack Santino, *The Hallowed Eve Dimensions of Culture in a Calendar Festival in Northern Ireland.* (Lexington: University of Kentucky Press, 2015), p. 10.

94. Shiva Honey, interview with the author (August 11, 2018).

95. Field notes, Austin, Texas (June 23, 2018).

96. Adam B. Seligman, Robert P. Weller, Michael J. Puett, and Bennett Simon. *Ritual and Its Consequences: An Essay on the Limits of Sincerity* (New York: Oxford Univ. Press, 2008), p. 24.

97. Ibid., p. 22.

98. Greaves, "Religion as illusion."

99. There is a Facebook group called Raising Hell where TST members with children discuss parenting within TST; it would be a fascinating topic for future researchers.

100. Mara Gorgo, interview with the author (June 21, 2018).

101. Seraphina, interview with the author (July 1, 2018).

102. Amber, interview with the author (January 14, 2019).

103. Adam Reilly, "From Salem, Satanism (of a sort) goes national," *WGBH.org* (November 20, 2017). Available online at https://news.wgbh.org/2017/11/20/how-we-live/salem-satanism-sort-goes-national (Accessed February 11, 2019).

104. Ibid.

105. McCutcheon, "'They licked the platter clean,'" p. 196.

106. Tisa J. Wenger, *Religious Freedom: The Contested History of an American Ideal* (Chapel Hill: University of North Carolina Press, 2018).

107. Wenger, *Religious Freedom;* Sullivan, *The Impossibility of Religious Freedom;* Finbarr Curtis, *The Production of American Religious Freedom* (New York: New York University Press, 2017).

108. Curtis, *The Production of American Religious Freedom,* p. 153

109. Ibid.

110. David Ferguson, "Florida Pastor: First Amendment doesn't apply to 'malevolent, evil' faiths like Satanism," *Rawstory.com* (December 18, 2014). Available online at https://www.rawstory.com/2014/12/florida-pastor-first-amendment-doesnt-apply-to-malevolent-evil-faiths-like-satanism/ (Accessed February 11, 2019).

111. The Foundation for Economic Education, "A reasonable way to handle religious conflict on public property," *Valuewalk.com* (September 1, 2016). Available online at https://www.valuewalk.com/2016/09/public-property-cross/ (Accessed February 11, 2019).

112. Christine Niles, "Liberty of perdition," *Churchmilitant.com* (April 26, 2016). Available online at https://www.churchmilitant.com/news/article/liberty-of-perdition (Accessed February 11, 2019).

113. Craig Martin, *Masking Hegemony: A Genealogy of Liberalism, Religion, and the Private Sphere* (London: Equinox, 2010), p. 31.

114. Elizabeth Shakman Hurd, *Beyond Religious Freedom: The New Global Politics of Religion* (Princeton, N.J.: Princeton University Press, 2015); Winnifred Sullivan, Elizabeth Hurd, Saba Mahmood, and Peter G. Danchin, eds., *Politics of Religious Freedom* (Chicago: University of Chicago Press, 2015).

115. Malcolm Jarry, interview with the author (July 18, 2018).

116. Jill, interview with the author (July 8, 2018).

117. Donny, interview with the author (September 15, 2018).

118. Scott D. Peterson, Brockton District Court (December 17, 2018), pp. 4–5. In the copy I received of this document, the name of the plaintiff and the case number were redacted to protect the patient's identity.

119. The Church of Satan maintains that they are qualified to receive tax-exempt status but will not apply for it in keeping with their conviction that all churches should be taxed. However, former CoS member and critic Michael Aquino claims that the CoS applied for tax-exempt status multiple times and was denied it. Assuming this is true, LaVey made a virtue out of necessity. Michael Aquino, *The Church of Satan* vol. 1, 8th.ed (Michael Aquino, 2013), p. 428.

120. The Satanic Temple, "Trump's executive order and the future of the Satanic Temple" (2017). Available online at https://mailchi.mp/thesatanictemple/trumps-executive-order-a-new-religious-future-the-satanic-temple (Accessed February 18, 2019).

121. Life Petitions.com, "SIGN THE PETITION: Tell the IRS the Satanic Temple is not a 'church,'" (April 26, 2019). Available online at https://lifepetitions.com/petition/sign-the-petition-tell-the-irs-to-withdraw-satanic-temple-s-tax-exempt-status (Accessed May 15, 2019).

122. EWTN, "The Satanic Temple receives tax-exempt designation as a church by the IRS" (April 29, 2019). Available online at https://www.youtube.com/watch?reload=9&v=lLyeXHb4iCo&feature=youtu.be (Accessed May 15, 2019).

123. Jonathan Z. Smith, *Relating Religion: Essays in the Study of Religion* (Chicago: University of Chicago Press, 2004), p. 376.

Chapter 6

1. Monica Garcia, "Satanic Temple adopts Arizona highway," *12news.com* (January 28, 2018). Available online at https://www.obsev.com/life/satanic-temple-just-adopted-highway-highway-hell-seem.html (Accessed February 11, 2019).

2. John Horvat II, "A call to protest the growing threat from Satanism," *Crisis Magazine* (July 19, 2017). Available online at https://www.crisismagazine.com/2017/a-call-to-protest-satanism?utm_source=feedburner&utm_medium=feed&utm_campaign=Feed%3A+CrisisMagazine+%28Crisis+Magazine%29 (Accessed February 11, 2019).

3. Mark Dery, "The Merry Pranksters and the art of the hoax," *New York Times* (December 23, 1990). Available online at https://www.nytimes.com/1990/12/23/arts/the-merry-pranksters-and-the-art-of-the-hoax.html (Accessed February 15, 2019).

4. Carlo Ginzburg, T*he Night Battles* (Baltimore, Md.: Johns Hopkins University Press, 1983), pp. 29–31; *Ecstasies: Deciphering the Witches' Sabbath*, trans. by Raymond Rosenthal (New York: Pantheon, 1991), pp. 153–155; Bruce Lincoln, "The werewolf, the shaman, and the historian: Rethinking the case of 'Old Thiess' after Carlo Ginzburg." Paper presented at the Hayes-Robinson Lecture, Royal Holloway College, University of London (March 3, 2015). Available online at https://backdoorbroadcasting.net/2015/03/bruce-lincoln-the-werewolf-the-shaman-and-the-historian-rethinking-the-case-of-old-thiess-after-carlo-ginzburg-2/ (Accessed February 12, 2019).

5. Lincoln, "The werewolf, the shaman, and the historian."

6. David Frankfurter, *Evil Incarnate: Rumors of Demonic Conspiracy and Satanic Abuse in History* (Princeton, N.J.: Princeton University Press, 2006), p. 11.

7. Sally Morrow, "After School Satan? Church-state group plays devil's advocate in public schools," *Religion News Service* (October 18 October, 2016). Available online at https://www.religionnews.com/2016/10/18/after-school-satan-church-state-group-plays-devils-advocate-in-public-schools/ (Accessed February 12, 2019).

8. Peter Gilmore, "Mirror, mirror," *ChurchofSatan.com* (n.d.). Available online at http://www.churchofsatan.com/mirror-mirror.php (Accessed February 12, 2019).

9. Jex Blackmore, interview with the author (June 24, 2018).

10. Frankfurter, *Evil Incarnate*, pp. 153–154.

11. Ibid. p. 167.

12. Mark Shea, "Monstrous," *Catholic and Enjoying it* (May 7, 2014). Available online at https://www.patheos.com/blogs/markshea/2014/05/monstrous-7.html (Accessed 15 March 2018).

13. Abby Ohlheiser, "The Church of Satan wants you to stop calling these 'devil worshiping' alleged murderers Satanists," *Washington Post* (November 7, 2014). Available online at https://www.washingtonpost.com/news/national/wp/2014/11/07/the-church-of-satan-wants-you-to-stop-calling-these-devil-worshipping-alleged-murderers-satanists/ (Accessed February 15, 2019).

14. Frankfurter, *Evil Incarnate*, p. 176.

15. Peter Stallybrass and Allon White, *The Politics and Poetics of Transgression* (Ithaca, N.Y.: Cornell University Press, 1995), pp. 31–59.

16. Hemant Mehta, "The Satanic Temple wants to put a monument outside Oklahoma's capitol building. what could possibly go wrong?" *Friendly Atheist* (December 4, 2013). Available online at http://www.patheos.com/blogs/friendlyatheist/2013/12/04/the-satanic-temple-wants-to-place-a-monument-outside-oklahomas-capitol-building-what-could-possibly-go-wrong/ (Accessed February 12, 2019).

17. Anton LaVey, *Satan Speaks!* (Venice, Calif.: Feral House, 1998), pp. 61–62.

18. Blanche Barton, *The Church of Satan* (New York: Hell's Kitchen Productions, 1990), p. 136.

19. LaVey, *Satan Speaks!* p. 65.

20. Chris Mathews, *Modern Satanism: Anatomy of a Radical Subculture* (Westport, Conn.: Praeger, 2009), p. 96.

21. Mark A. Signorelli, "If we can't distinguish between God And Satan, society's going to hell," *The Federalist* (October 7, 2016). Available online at http://thefederalist.com/2016/10/07/distinguish-god-devil-societys-going-to-hell/ (Accessed February 12, 2019).

22. Horvat, "A call to protest the growing threat from Satanism."

23. Jesper Aagaard Petersen, "Contemporary Satanism," in Christopher Partridge, ed., *The Occult World* (New York: Routledge, 2015), pp. 396–404.

24. Ruben Van Luijk, *Children of Lucifer: The Origins of Modern Religious Satanism* (New York: Oxford University Press, 2016), p. 397.

25. Christopher Knowles, "Safe-space Satanists," *Disinfo.com* (April 2016). [Website defunct].

26. Shane Bugbee, "Religion: A master and slave relationship," *Shanebugbee.com* (February 14, 2014). [Website defunct]; "High priest Brian Werner resigns from the Satanic Temple" (December 23, 2014). Available online at https://www.youtube.com/watch?v=ZIN4aZ8IMz0 (Accessed February 11, 2019).

27. Kate Ryan, "How the Satanic Temple became a queer haven," *Vice.com* (July 24, 2017). Available online at https://www.vice.com/en_us/article/zmv7my/how-the-satanic-temple-became-a-queer-haven (Accessed February 12, 2019).

28. Ash Astaroth, "Satanic organizations: Inside the outsiders," *Ashastaroth.com* (January 3, 2016). Available online at https://ashastaroth.wordpress.com/2016/01/03/satanic-organizations-inside-the-outsiders/ (Accessed February 12, 2019). LARP is an acronym for "Live Action Role-Playing" games.

29. Shiva Honey, interview with the author (August 11, 2018).

30. Dery, "The Merry Pranksters and the art of the hoax."

31. Kembrew McLeod, *Freedom of Expression®: Resistance and Repression in the Age of Intellectual Property* (Minneapolis: University of Minnesota Press, 2007), pp. 114–117.

32. Dery, "The Merry Pranksters and the art of the hoax."

33. McLeod, *Freedom of Expression®*, p. 132.

34. Greil Marcus, *Lipstick Traces: A Secret History of the Twentieth Century* (Cambridge, Mass.: Harvard University Press, 1990), p. 158, 168.

35. Malcolm Jarry, electronic communication with the author (March 3, 2019).

36. Ralph A. Moellering, "The new quest for the sacred: The witchcraft craze and the lure of the occult," *The Springfielder* 35, no. 4 (1972): 277.

37. Kathryn Rountree, *Embracing the Witch and the Goddess: Feminist Ritual-Makers in New Zealand* (London: Routledge, 2004), p. 33.

38. Jesper Aagaard Petersen and Asbjorn Dyrendal, "Satanism," in Olav Hammer and Mikael Rothstein, eds., *The Cambridge Companion to New Religious Movements* (Cambridge: Cambridge University Press, 2012), p. 215.

39. Lilith Starr, interview with the author (July 27, 2018).

40. Daniel Walker, electronic communication with the author (July 11, 2018).

41. Daniel Walker, electronic communication with the author (July 8, 2018).

42. Field notes, Austin, Texas (February 16, 2016).

43. Gus Burns, "Detroit-area Satanists doused with milk at Planned Parenthood protest," *Mlive.com* (August 24, 2015). Available online at https://www.mlive.com/news/detroit/index.ssf/2015/08/detroit-area_satanists_doused.html (Accessed February 12, 2019).

44. Available online at https://broadly.vice.com/en_us/article/ezjedn/this-satanic-temple-leader-is-blogging-her-abortion (Accessed February 12, 2019).

45. Gabby Bess, "This Satanic Temple leader is blogging her abortion," *Broadly* (December 8, 2015). Available online at http://www.wnd.com/2016/03/pro-lifers-satanic-activism-proves-abortion-is-evil/#EtEj6QTYGLfvfjkm.99 (Accessed February 12, 2019).

46. Samantha Allen, "Michigan Satanists defend Planned Parenthood on Good Friday," *The Daily Beast* (March 25, 2016). Available online at http://www.thedailybeast.com/articles/2016/03/25/michigan-satanists-defend-planned-parenthood-on-good-friday.html (Accessed February 12, 2019).

47. Shiva Honey suggested that this counter-protest was precipitated after *Vice* contacted Jex Blackmore. The chapter organized the protest so that *Vice* would have something to cover. Interview with the author (August 11, 2018).

48. Bethania Palma Markus, "Detroit Satanists mock anti-abortion protestors' 'fetal idolatry' by dressing as leather-clad babies," *Raw Story* (April 26, 2016). Available online at https://www.rawstory.com/2016/04/watch-detroit-satanists-mock-anti-abortion-protesters-fetal-idolatry-by-dressing-as-leather-clad-babies/ (Accessed February 12, 2019).

49. Jex Blackmore, interview with the author (June 24, 2018).

50. Monica Miller, "Planned Parenthood protest disrupted by Satanists in bizarre street theatre spectacle," *Lifesitenews* (April 26, 2016). Available online at https://www.lifesitenews.com/opinion/protestpp-protested-by-satanists-in-convoluted-street-theatre-spectacle (Accessed February 12, 2019).

51. Damien Blackmoor, interview with the author (June 21, 2018).

52. Shiva Honey, interview with the author (August 11, 2018).

53. Jex Blackmore, "Cum rags for Congress," *jexblackmore.com* (2016). Available online at https://www.jexblackmore.com/#/cum-rags-for-congress/ (Accessed February 12, 2019).

54. Jex Blackmore, interview with the author (June 24, 2018).

55. Ibid.

56. Anna Merlan, "Satanic artist and activist Jex Blackmore on her controversial role in the documentary *Hail Satan?*" *Jezebel.com* (May 20, 2019). Available online at https://

themuse.jezebel.com/satanic-artist-and-activist-jex-blackmore-on-her-contro-1834791520 (Accessed May 31, 2019).

57. Malcolm Jarry, field notes, Little Rock, Arkansas (August 16, 2018). He qualified that he also invents his own tactics and does not borrow tactics he considers to be unethical (electronic communication with the author, May 30, 2019).

58. The Satanic Temple, "The Satanic Temple's guidelines for effective protest," *TheSatanicTemple.com* (n.d.). Available online at https://thesatanictemple.com/pages/the-satanic-temple-s-guidelines-for-effective-protest (Accessed February 12, 2019).

59. Malcolm Jarry, interview with the author (July 26, 2018).

60. "Atheist group's lawsuit against Orange County School District thrown out," WFTV. com (September 4, 2014). Available online at http://www.wftv.com/news/news/local/atheist-groups-lawsuit-against-orange-county-schoo/nhF7r/ (Accessed February 12, 2019).

61. Andrew Seidel, "What I learned from fighting back against public school Bible distributions," *Friendly Atheist* (May 5, 2015). Available online at http://friendlyatheist.patheos.com/2015/05/05/what-i-learned-from-fighting-back-against-public-school-bible-distributions/ (Accessed February 12, 2019).

62. Malcolm Jarry, interview with the author (July 26, 2018).

63. *Kennedy v. Bremerton School District* No. 16-35801 D.C. No. 3:16-cv-05694-RBL (August 23, 2017). Available online at https://assets.documentcloud.org/documents/3944180/Joe-Kennedy-9th-Circuit-Opinion.pdf, p. 13.

64. Nathan Glover, "Football coach put on leave after Satanists plan invocation at tonight's game," *World Religion News* (October 29, 2015). Available online at https://www.worldreligionnews.com/issues/football-coach-put-on-leave-after-satanists-plan-invocation-at-tonights-game (Accessed February 12, 2019).

65. Lilith Starr, interview with the author (July 27, 2018).

66. Ibid.

67. *Kennedy v. Bremerton School District* 869 F. 3d 813, 827 (9th Cir. 2017). In 2019, the Supreme Court refused to review the decision (Cert. denied, 139 S. Ct. 634 (2019)). However, Alito, Thomas, Gorsuch, and Kavanaugh filed a concurring statement inviting litigants to ask them to overrule *Employment Division v. Smith*, a seminal case ruling that religious liberty does not include exemptions from generally applicable laws.

68. Seidel, "What I learned from fighting back."

69. Damien Ba'al, interview with the author (July 9, 2018).

70. Donny, interview with the author (September 15, 2018).

71. Jill, Jessie, and Brian, interview with the author (July 8, 2018).

72. Simone, interview with the author (July 23, 2018).

73. Elisa Meyer, "YWCA ends menstrual project with Satanists," *World Religion News* (May 22, 2018). Available online at https://www.worldreligionnews.com/religion-news/ywca-ends-menstrual-project-satanist (Accessed February 12, 2019).

74. Hemant Mehta, "After complaint, YWCA cuts ties with Satanists over menstrual hygiene program," *Friendly Atheist* (May 18, 2018). Available online at http://www.

patheos.com/blogs/friendlyatheist/2018/05/18/after-complaint-ywca-cuts-ties-with-satanists-over-menstrual-hygiene-program/ (Accessed February 12, 2019).

75. Jack Matirko, "The Satanic Temple and YWCA settle donation dispute like adults," *For Infernal Use Only* (May 23, 2018). Available online at http://www.patheos.com/blogs/infernal/2018/05/the-satanic-temple-and-ywca-settle-donation-dispute-like-adults/ (Accessed February 12, 2019).

76. Jimmy McCloskey, "Satanists adopt highway, clean it with pitchforks and brand it 'Road to Hell,'" *Metro* (January 31, 2018). Available online at https://metro.co.uk/2018/01/31/satanists-adopt-highway-clean-pitchforks-brand-road-hell-7275873/?ito=cbshare (Accessed February 16, 2018).

77. Justin L. Mack, "Why The Satanic Temple Indiana adopted a stretch of highway in Boone County," *The Indianapolis Star* (July 12, 2018). Available online at https://www.indystar.com/story/news/2018/07/12/indiana-satanists-adopt-highway-inverted-crossroads-effort/778550002/ (Accessed February 12, 2019).

78. WILX, "Satanic Temple adopts highway upsetting residents," (September 13, 2018). Available online at https://www.wilx.com/content/news/Satanic-Temple-adopts-highway-upsetting-residents-493215771.html (Accessed February 12, 2019).

79. Dex Desjardins, interview with the author (September 15, 2018).

80. Susan Wright, "Satanic Temple Valentine's Day fundraiser hopes to raise funds for abortion lawsuits," *RedState.com* (February 12, 2017). Available online at http://www.redstate.com/sweetie15/2017/02/12/satanic-temple-valentines-day-fundraiser-hopes-raise-funds-abortion-lawsuits/ (Accessed February 17, 2017).

81. MomsOnAmission, "Satan wants your blood!? What???," *YouTube.com* (September 28, 2018). Available online at https://www.youtube.com/watch?v=etQKv2Wjf1Q&feature=youtu.be (Accessed February 12, 2019).

82. Peter Berger, *The Sacred Canopy: Elements of a Sociological Theory of Religion* (New York: Anchor Books, 1969), p. 39.

83. Joshua Gunn, *Modern Occult Rhetoric: Mass Media and the Drama of Secrecy in the Twentieth Century* (Tuscaloosa, Ala.: University of Alabama Press, 2005), p. 194.

84. Lilith Starr, interview with the author (July 27, 2018).

85. The Satanic Temple, "TST black mass ritual" (August 13, 2018).

Chapter 7

1. Michael Muhammad Knight, "Muslims should support Satanists," *Vice.com* (May 13, 2014). Available online at https://www.vice.com/en_us/article/gq8jj9/muslims-for-satan (Accessed February 16, 2019).

2. Cherian George, *Hate Spin: The Manufacture of Religious Offense and Its Threat to Democracy* (Cambridge, Mass.: MIT Press, 2017), p. 207.

3. Nathaniel Samuel Murrell, *Afro-Caribbean Religions: An Introduction to Their Historical, Cultural, and Sacred Traditions* (Philadelphia: Temple University Press, 2010), p. 147.

4. James T. Pokines, "A Santeria/Palo Mayombe cauldron containing a human skull and multiple artifacts recovered in western Massachusetts, U.S.A.," *Forensic Science International* 248 (2015): e1–e7.

5. Suzanne Owen, "The world religions paradigm time for a change," *Arts and Humanities in Higher Education* 10, no. 3 (2011): pp. 253–268.

6. Jonathan Z. Smith, *Map Is Not Territory: Studies in the History of Religion* (Chicago: University of Chicago Press, 1993), p. 295.

7. Robert Orsi, *Between Heaven and Earth: The Religious Worlds People Make and the Scholars Who Study Them* (Princeton, N.J.: Princeton University Press, 2005), p. 188.

8. Harvard Chaplains, "Harvard chaplains speak out against a 'black mass,'" (May 10, 2014). Available online at https://chaplains.harvard.edu/harvard-chaplains-speak-out-against-%E2%80%9Cblack-mass%E2%80%9D (Accessed February 12, 2019).

9. David Barnes, "A beautiful night to be Catholic in the Archdiocese of Boston," *A Shepherd's Post* (May 13, 2014). Available online at http://shepherdspost.blogspot.com/2014/05/a-beautiful-night-to-be-catholic-in.html (Accessed February 12, 2019).

10. Jack Matirko, "The *Satanic Temple v. Scottsdale* will set 9th Circuit precedent," *For Infernal Use Only* (August 11, 2018). Available online at http://www.patheos.com/blogs/infernal/2018/08/the-satanic-temple-v-scottsdale-will-set-9th-circuit-precedent/#LAXPPHSJ9ZslXILZ.01 (Accessed February 12, 2019).

11. "Councilman DiCiccio: Satanists to get big win if Phoenix mayor and council sneak last minute proposal banning prayer," *Arizona Progress Gazette* (n.d.). Available online at http://arizonaprogressgazette.com/councilman-diciccio-satanists-to-get-big-win-if-phoenix-mayor-and-council-sneak-last-minute-proposal-banning-prayer/ (Accessed February 12, 2019).

12. Malcolm Jarry, interview with the author (July 18, 2018).

13. Stephen R. Prothero, *God Is Not One: The Eight Rival Religions That Run the World* (New York: HarperOne, 2011), p. 5.

14. Gavin Baddeley, *Lucifer Rising* (London: Plexus, 1999), p. 66.

15. Diana Eck, "What is pluralism?" *Pluralism.org* (2006). Available online at http://pluralism.org/what-is-pluralism/ (Accessed February 12, 2019).

16. Diana. Eck, *A New Religious America: How A "Christian Country" Has Become the World's Most Religiously Diverse Nation* (New York: HarperCollins, 2001), p. 58.

17. Russell T. McCutcheon, *Critics Not Caretakers: Redescribing the Public Study of Religion* (Albany: State University of New York Press, 2001), pp. 160–161.

18. Ibid. p. 163.

19. Tim Murphy, "Notes from the field: Religious defamation and radical pluralism as challenges to the scholar of religion," *The Council of Societies for the Study of Religion Bulletin* 34, no. 4 (November 2005): p. 80.

20. Eck, *A New Religious America*, p. 70.

21. Edward J. Moody, "Magical Therapy: An Anthropological Investigation of Contemporary Satanism," in Irving I. Zaretsky and Mark P. Leone, eds. *Religious Movements in Contemporary America* (Princeton, N.J.: Princeton University Press, 1974), p. 356.

22. Massimo Introvigne (*Satanism: A Social History*. Leiden: Brill, 2016), p. 1035) refers to "the affair of the poisons" (1677–1682) as the "first incarnation" of modern Satanism. This was an episode in which French fortune-teller Catherine La Voisin devised a black mass ceremony at the request of her clients, who hoped to win money, love, and other favors from the devil. Anton LaVey (*The Satanic Bible* [New York: Avon, 1969], p. 102) dismissed the entire episode as "organized fraud." La Voisin's rituals strike me

as a form of ostension in which she was trying to please her clients by performing legends they had heard about black masses. On ostension, see note 27.

23. David Frankfurter, *Evil Incarnate: Rumors of Demonic Conspiracy and Satanic Abuse in History* (Princeton, N.J.: Princeton University Press, 2006).

24. Ruben Van Luijk, *Children of Lucifer: The Origins of Modern Religious Satanism* (New York: Oxford University Press, 2016), p. 44.

25. Linda Dégh and Andrew Vazsonyi, "Legend and Belief," in Dan Ben-Amos, ed., *Folklore Genres* (Austin: University of Texas Press, 1976 [1971]), p. 94.

26. On the sources of *La-bas* see Introvigne, *Satanism: A Social History*, pp. 146–148.

27. Linda Dégh and Andrew Vázsonyi. "Does the word 'dog' bite? Ostensive action: A means of legend-telling," *Journal of Folklore Research* 20, no. 1 (1983): pp. 5–34.

28. Nikolas Schreck, *The Satanic Screen: An Illustrated Guide to the Devil in Cinema* (London: Creation, 2001), p. 15; Gerald Gardner (*Witchcraft Today* [New York: Kensington, 2004], p. 28) described a visit to Rome in 1952 where he was invited to witness a black mass for about twenty pounds. Gardner declined but suspected it was a show put on for tourists.

29. Anton LaVey, *The Satanic Rituals* (New York: Avon, 1972), p. 34.

30. LaVey, *The Satanic Bible*, p. 101.

31. Jeff Wilson, "Blasphemy as Bhavana: Anti-Christianity in a new Buddhist movement," *Nova Religio* 22, no. 3 (2019): 8–35.

32. Lucien Greaves, "What is a black mass," *The Lucien Greaves Archive* (n.d.). Available online at https://luciengreaves.com/letters-to-satan/#what-is-a-black-mass? (Accessed February 16, 2019).

33. Malcolm Jarry, electronic communication with the author (March 4, 2019).

34. David Guinan, interview with the author (March 6, 2019).

35. President of the Harvard Extension Cultural Studies Club, "The secret history of the black mass" (n.d.).

36. Hillary White, "Thousands of Boston Catholics process and pray against Harvard's Satanic 'black Mass,'" *Lifesitenews.com* (May 13, 2014). Available online at https://www.lifesitenews.com/news/thousands-of-boston-catholics-process-and-pray-against-harvards-satanic-bla (Accessed February 12, 2019).

37. Aurora C. Griffin and Luciana E. Milano, "Hatred at Harvard," *The Harvard Crimson* (May 12, 2014). Available online at https://www.thecrimson.com/article/2014/5/12/hatred-at-harvard (Accessed February 12, 2019).

38. David Guinan, interview with the author (March 5, 2019).

39. Elizabeth Scalia, "Yes we will use a 'consecrated host' at Harvard 'black mass,'" *The Anchoress* (May 7, 2014). Available online at http://www.patheos.com/blogs/theanchoress/2014/05/07/no-comment-from-venue-re-harvard-black-mass/ (Accessed February 12, 2019); "BREAKING: Black mass Satanic Temple walks back: Do they mean it? STAY TUNED," *The Anchoress* (May 7, 2014). Available online at http://www.patheos.com/blogs/theanchoress/2014/05/07/satanic-temple-corrects-we-wont-use-consecrated-host/ (Accessed February 12, 2019).

40. C. J. Doye, "Catholic Action League condemns Harvard for allowing black mass," *Catholicactionleague.org* (May 10, 2014). Available online at http://www.

catholicactionleague.org/Archives/2014/Archive_2014.htm (Accessed February 12, 2019).

41. Aurora Griffin, "How we stopped a black mass at Harvard," *The Catholic Herald* (August 19, 2016). Available online at http://www.catholicherald.co.uk/issues/august-19th-2016/how-we-stopped-a-black-mass-at-harvard/ (Accessed February 12, 2019).

42. Francis X. Clooney, S.J. "Fr. Amorth's yoga and the devil," *America Magazine* (December 10, 2011). Available online at https://www.americamagazine.org/content/all-things/fr-amorths-yoga-and-devil (Accessed February 12, 2019).

43. Drew Faust, "Statement on black mass," *harvard.edu* (May 12, 2014). Available online at http://www.harvard.edu/president/news/2014/statement-on-black-mass (Accessed February 12, 2019).

44. Roberto Scalese, "Harvard black mass, first moved, then canceled, may have happened in Chinese restaurant," *Boston.com* (May 12, 2014). Available online at http://www.boston.com/news/local-news/2014/05/12/harvard-black-mass-first-moved-then-canceled-may-have-happened-in-chinese-restaurant (Accessed February 12, 2019).

45. Malcolm Jarry, electronic communication with the author (February 16, 2019).

46. Malcolm Jarry, interview with the author (July 18, 2018).

47. Jacqueline Tempera, "Archdiocese plans counter to Harvard group's black mass," *Boston Globe* (May 10, 2014). Available online at http://www.bostonglobe.com/metro/2014/05/09/catholic-archdiocese-hold-services-simultaneously-with-black-mass-harvard/iYejIvqeBaObTFPeAjfL7I/story.html (Accessed February 12, 2019).

48. Griffin and Milano, "Hatred at Harvard."

49. Tempera, "Archdiocese plans counter to Harvard group's black mass."

50. Roger Landry, letter to Drew Faust (May 8, 2014). Available online at http://catholicpreaching.com/letter-to-harvard-president-drew-g-faust-about-the-satanic-mass-to-take-place-on-the-campus-of-harvard/ (Accessed February 12, 2019).

51. President of the Harvard Extension Cultural Studies Club, "The Secret History of the Black Mass."

52. Knight, "Muslims should support Satanists."

53. President of the Harvard Extension Cultural Studies Club, "The Secret History of the Black Mass."

54. The ARDA, "State membership report," *TheARDA.com* (2010). Available online at http://www.thearda.com/rcms2010/r/s/25/rcms2010_25_state_name_2010.asp (Accessed February 12, 2019).

55. Knight, "Muslims should support Satanists."

56. David Guinan, interview with the author (March 6, 2019).

57. George, *Hate Spin*, p. 2.

58. Archdiocese of Boston, Facebook comment (May 7, 2014). Available online at https://www.facebook.com/BostonCatholic/posts/10152046898552606 (Accessed February 16, 2019).

59. Joe Doyle, "Catholic Action League reacts to cancellation of Harvard's black mass," *Catholicism.com* (May 15, 2014). Available online at http://catholicism.

org/catholic-action-league-reacts-to-cancellation-of-harvards-black-mass.html (Accessed February 12, 2019).

60. Aurora Griffin, "How we stopped a black mass at Harvard." Griffin asserts that Satanists threatened to rape and murder her as she attempted to enter the holy hour at St. Paul's and that during the holy hour, she heard the sound of Satanists attempting, but failing, to break into the church through the basement and disrupt the ceremony. I could find no independent confirmation of these details. Malcolm Jarry (electronic communication with the author, February 17, 2019) found Griffin's account of what happened inaccurate and galling. Jarry noted that everyone involved with the black mass was with him in the Hong Kong while Griffin was allegedly being threatened. The controversy had attracted bystanders from Boston's "punk rock" scene who may have intimidated Griffin. As for the claim of Satanists attempting to break into St. Paul's, this was likely Griffin's imagination.

61. Kaitlyn Schallhorn, "Harvard students organize satanic mass, local Catholic Church condemns," *CampusReform.org* (May 6, 2014). Available online at https://www.campusreform.org/?ID=5601 (Accessed February 12, 2019).

62. Rebecca Hamilton, "Satanic statues in Okieland and black masses at Harvard, oh my!!," *Public Catholic* (May 7, 2014). Available online at http://www.patheos.com/blogs/publiccatholic/2014/05/satanic-statues-in-okieland-and-black-masses-at-harvard-oh-my/ (Accessed February 12, 2019).

63. Francis X. Clooney, electronic communication with the author (June 20, 2018). Malcolm Jarry recalls that someone from Drew Faust's office *did* attend the meeting.

64. Macolm Jarry, electronic communication with the author (March 4, 2019).

65. Quoted in "Justice Elena Kagan's wonderful dissent in *Greece v. Galloway*," *Chicago Tribune* (May 6, 2014). Available online at https://www.chicagotribune.com/news/opinion/zorn/ct-kagan-zorn-0506-story.html (Accessed February 16, 2018).

66. Brian Resnick, "In public prayer case, Scalia asks 'What about devil worshippers?' A Satanist responds," *The Atlantic* (November 6, 2013). Available online at http://www.theatlantic.com/politics/archive/2013/11/in-public-prayer-case-scalia-asks-what-about-devil-worshippers-a-satanist-responds/454029/ (Accessed January 21, 2017). Douglas Laycock (electronic communication with the author, February 26, 2019) wrote a brief response to Greaves's assessment: "This discussion was unprincipled and it threw some people under the bus. But it was *not* naïve. It was based on counting to five and dealing with the situation we faced. The only way to be completely nonsectarian was to have no prayer at all, and there were clearly not five votes for that. There may not have been any votes for that."

67. Lauren Markoe and Cathy Lynn Grossman, "Supreme Court approves sectarian prayer at public meetings," *Washington Post* (May 5, 2014). Available online at https://www.washingtonpost.com/national/religion/supreme-court-approves-sectarian-prayer-at-public-meetings/2014/05/05/62c494da-d487-11e3-8f7d-7786660fff7c_story.html (Accessed February 12, 2019).

68. Robin Abcarian, "After Supreme Court prayer decision, Satanist offers his own prayer," *Los Angeles Times* (May 5, 2014). Available online at http://www.latimes.com/local/

abcarian/la-me-ra-abcarian-scotus-20140505-column.html (Accessed February 12, 2019). It is debatable whether this invocation really falls within Kennedy's parameters. The reference to "delusions of old" could certainly be interpreted as an oblique condemnation of Christianity and other theistic religions. The reference of the Christian story of The Fall strengthens this implication.

69. Alternative models do not conform to traditional standards of beauty. This often includes models who have prominent tattoos and piercings or who model gothic or fetish clothing.

70. Michelle Shortt, interview with the author (September 30, 2018).

71. Dustin Gardiner, "Satanists to give prayer at Phoenix City Council meeting," *AZCentral.com* (January 28, 2016). Available online at http://www.azcentral.com/story/news/local/phoenix/2016/01/28/satanists-give-prayer-phoenix-city-council-meeting/79486460/ (Accessed February 12, 2019).

72. "'Freedom to offend': Satanic Temple to Deliver City Council invocation," *Sputniknews.com* (February 13, 2016). Available online at http://sputniknews.com/us/20160213/1034683216/arizona-satanic-temple-city-council.html#ixzz40N5euTZS (Accessed February 12, 2019).

73. "Strategic level spiritual warfare" refers to an evangelical practice of using prayers to combat evil "territorial spirits" believed to control cities and other large geographical area. Sean McCloud, *American Possessions—Fighting Demons in the Contemporary United States* (New York: Oxford University Press, 2015)) has written on the role of strategic level spiritual warfare in shaping how the third-wave evangelical movement thinks about structure and agency.

74. *Sputniknews.com*, "'Freedom to offend.'"

75. Nick Wing, "Phoenix City Council votes to end prayer rather than let Satanists lead it," *Huffington Post* (February 5, 2016). Available online at https://www.huffingtonpost.com/entry/phoenix-satanists_us_56b4e2b2e4b04f9b57d9639f (Accessed February 12, 2019).

76. Cheryl Chumley, "Satanists stymied from opening meeting in prayer," *WND.com* (February 4, 2016). Available online at http://www.wnd.com/2016/02/satanists-stymied-from-opening-meeting-in-prayer/#hesfPaSGRLmQgdhr.99 (Accessed February 12, 2019).

77. Julia Bryant, "Satanic Temple pushes Phoenix to ban prayer at City Council meetings," *Law Street* (February 10, 2106). Available online at https://lawstreetmedia.com/news/satanic-temple-pushes-phoenix-ban-prayer-city-council-meetings/ (Accessed February 12, 2019).

78. Parker Leavitt, "What Satanists plan to say in Scottsdale City Council prayer," *AZCentral.com* (March 23, 2016). Available online at http://www.azcentral.com/story/news/local/scottsdale/2016/03/23/satanists-plan-scottsdale-city-council-prayer/81887466/ (Accessed February 12, 2019).

79. KUSA Staff, "Phoenix council votes to bring prayer back to meetings," *9news.com* (March 3, 2016). Available online at https://www.9news.com/article/news/nation-now/phoenix-council-votes-to-bring-prayer-back-to-meetings/65825726 (Accessed February 16, 2019).

80. Associated Press, "Arizona city bars Satanic Temple prayer at council meeting," *Foxnews.com* (May 24, 2016). Available online at https://www.foxnews.com/us/arizona-city-bars-satanic-temple-prayer-at-council-meeting (Accessed February 12, 2019).

81. Joshua Gill, "Satanic Temple sues Arizona city over alleged discrimination," *The Daily Caller* (February 27, 2018). Available online at http://dailycaller.com/2018/02/27/satanic-temple-sues-arizona-city-over-alleged-discrimination/ (Accessed February 12, 2019).

82. Milton Watkins, "Okaloosa County schoolboard meeting chaos," *YouTube.com* (October 13, 2015). Available online at https://www.youtube.com/watch?v=HKt6F2tUN9Q (Accessed February 12, 2019).

83. Hayley Minogue, "The Satanic Temple of West Florida will deliver invocation," *WKRG.com* (July 7, 2016). Available online at https://www.wkrg.com/gulf-coast-cw/cw-contests/the-satanic-temple-of-west-florida-will-deliver-invocation/957240025 (Accessed February 12, 2019).

84. David Suhor, interview with the author (January 17, 2019).

85. Jasmine Anderson, "Satanic prayer disrupted at council meeting," *weartv.com* (July 15, 2016). Available online at https://weartv.com/news/local/satanic-prayer-at-council-meeting-disrupted-by-crowd (Accessed February 12, 2019); Shamalamagram, "Full version Satanic Temple invocation and protest interruption at Pensacola Florida city council," *YouTube.com* (August 7, 2016). Available online at https://www.youtube.com/watch?v=jNjlfWVkdWA&t=4s&fbclid=IwAR3kmT1AIbhyEFPm8jzkZnRTMQTfZQHPSBOJv-KuER0VYska7m3htJQXjQU (Accessed February 12, 2019).

86. Anderson, "Satanic prayer disrupted at council meeting."

87. CBN News, "What a group of Christians did to counter a satanic prayer at a public meeting," *CBN News* (July 20, 2016). Available online at http://www1.cbn.com/cbnnews/us/2016/july/what-a-group-of-christians-did-to-counter-a-satanic-invocation-at-a-public-meeting (Accessed February 12, 2019).

88. Pensacola News Journal, "Satanist disturbed by city of Pensacola invocation policy," *Pensacola News Journal* (February 10, 2017). Available online at http://www.pnj.com/story/news/local/pensacola/2017/02/10/satanist-disturbed-city-invocation-policy/97737970/ (Accessed February 12, 2019).

89. Jim Little, "Satanist removal: ECUA officials stand behind their right to pray before meetings," *Pensacola News Journal* (August 25, 2017). Available online at https://www.pnj.com/story/news/2017/08/25/satanist-removal-ecua-officials-stand-behind-their-right-pray-before-meetings/602370001/ (Accessed February 16, 2019).

90. Heather Clark, "Florida member of The Satanic Temple convicted of trespassing for disrupting government meeting," *Christian News* (August 10, 2018). Available online at https://christiannews.net/2018/08/10/florida-member-of-the-satanic-temple-convicted-of-trespassing-for-disrupting-government-meeting/ (Accessed February 12, 2019).

91. Associated Press, "Satanist acquitted of disrupting government meeting," *The Seattle Times* (April 5, 2019). Available online at https://www.seattletimes.com/nation-world/nation/satanist-acquitted-of-disrupting-government-meeting/   (Accessed May 16, 2019).

92. Jenny Neyman, "Assembly hears invocation from Satanic Temple," *KBBI.org* (August 15, 2016). Available online at http://kbbi.org/post/assembly-hears-invocation-satanic-temple (Accessed February 16, 2019); Gary Nguyen, "Alaskan council meeting opened with prayer hailing Satan," *World Religion News* (August 18, 2016). Available online at http://www.worldreligionnews.com/religion-news/alaskan-council-meeting-opened-with-prayer-hailing-satan (Accessed February 12, 2019).

93. Rodney Pelletier, "Alaskan district meeting opens with prayer to Satan," *Church Militant.com* (August 15, 2016). Available online at http://www.churchmilitant.com/news/article/alaskan-district-meeting-opens-with-prayer-to-satan (Accessed February 12, 2019).

94. Daysha Eaton, "Assembly considers moment of silence after satanic prayer, protest, counterprotest," *KBBI.org* (August 23, 2016). Available online at http://kbbi.org/post/assembly-considers-moment-silence-after-satanic-prayer-protest-counterprotest (Accessed February 12, 2019).

95. Hemant Mehta, "Alaskan borough's new invocation rule leads to Satanist and Pastafarian speakers," *Friendly Atheist* (January 1, 2019). Available online at https://friendlyatheist.patheos.com/2019/01/01/alaskan-boroughs-new-invocation-rule-leads-to-satanist-and-pastafarian-speakers/ (Accessed February 12, 2019).

96. Dan Atkinson, "Satanists fired up over city council's invocation refusal," *Boston Herald* (July 16, 2013). Available online at http://www.bostonherald.com/news/local_coverage/2016/10/satanists_fired_up_over_city_council_s_invocation_refusal (Accessed February 12, 2019).

97. Max Douglas, "Satanic Temple Boston complains after denial of satanic invocation," *Church Militant.com* (October 14, 2016). Available online at https://www.churchmilitant.com/news/article/satanic-temple-boston-complains-after-denial-of-satanic-invocation (Accessed February 12, 2019).

98. Jonathan Choe, "Satanic Temple may sue over Boston city council invocation," *necn.com* (October 19, 2017). Available online at https://www.necn.com/news/new-england/Satanic-Temple-May-Sue-Over-Boston-City-Council-Invocation-451705243.html (Accessed February 12, 2019).

99. "Satanic Temple or flying spaghetti monster: Austin council invocations," *klbj.com* (November 28, 2016). [Website defunct].

100. Hemant Mehta, "Satanists say the Boston city council won't allow them to deliver an invocation," *Friendly Atheist* (February 16, 2019). Available online at https://friendlyatheist.patheos.com/2019/02/16/satanists-say-the-boston-city-council-wont-allow-them-to-deliver-an-invocation/ (Accessed February 17, 2019).

101. *The Satanic Temple and Michelle Shortt v. City of Scottsdale*. U.S. District Court, District of Arizona (February 22, 2018). Available online at https://www.rluipa-defense.com/

wp-content/uploads/sites/9/2018/03/372494707-The-Satanic-Temple-v-City-of-Scottsdale-Complaint-1.pdf (Accessed February 12, 2019).

102. Jack Matirko, "Arizona town changes invocation policy after Satanic Temple invitation," *For Infernal Use Only* (January 30, 2019). Available online at https://www.patheos.com/blogs/infernal/2019/01/arizona-town-changes-invocation-policy-after-satanic-temple-invitation/ (Accessed February 12, 2019).

103. Hemant Mehta, "Phoenix city council will replace invocation with moment of silence to spite Satanic Temple," *Friendly Atheist* (February 3, 2016). Available online at http://www.patheos.com/blogs/friendlyatheist/2016/02/03/phoenix-city-council-will-replace-invocation-with-moment-of-silence-to-spite-satanic-temple/?repeat=w3tc (Accessed February 12, 2019).

104. Thomas Essel, "The sage of Chaz Stevens, or how not to be an activist," *Danthropology* (January 12, 2016). Available online at http://www.patheos.com/blogs/danthropology/2016/01/the-saga-of-chaz-stevens-or-how-not-to-be-an-activist/. (Accessed February 12, 2019). In February 2016, Stevens mailed a butt plug and a Barry White CD to Phoenix councilman Sal DiCiccio, who had been the most outspoken against TST: Miriam Wasser, "Phoenix city councilman getting butt plug following Satanist scrap," *Phoenix New Times* (February 9, 2016). Available online at https://www.phoenixnewtimes.com/news/phoenix-city-councilman-getting-butt-plug-following-satanist-scrap-8039529 (Accessed February 12, 2019).

105. Michelle Shortt, interview with the author (September 30, 2018).

106. The Satanic Temple-Arizona Chapter, "heaven sent-satanic invocation commentary," *YouTube.com* (August 29, 2018). Available online at https://www.youtube.com/watch?v=rXa1up9dPWM&feature=youtu.be (Accessed February 12, 2019).

107. In *Santa Fe Independent School District v. Doe* (2000), which tested prayer at football games, the plaintiff was sent death threats and their dog was killed. Douglas Laycock, "Government-sponsored religious displays: Transparent rationalizations and expedient post-modernism," *Case Western Reserve Law Review* 61, no. 4 (Summer 2011): p. 1224.

108. Noah Feldman, "James Madison would've backed Phoenix's Satanist," *Bloomberg.com* (February 8, 2016). Available online at https://www.bloomberg.com/opinion/articles/2016-02-08/james-madison-would-ve-backed-phoenix-s-satanists (Accessed February 12, 2019).

109. Fox 10 Phoenix, "FULL Satanic prayer vote Phoenix city council (FNN)," *YouTube.com* (February 3, 2016). Available online at https://www.youtube.com/watch?v=sC_ZIiL5zMg&t=541s (Accessed February 12, 2019).

110. John Horvat II, "A call to protest the growing threat from Satanism," *Crisis Magazine* (July 19, 2017). Available online at https://www.crisismagazine.com/2017/a-call-to-protest-satanism?utm_source=feedburner&utm_medium=feed&utm_campaign=Feed%3A+CrisisMagazine+%28Crisis+Magazine%29 (Accessed February 11, 2019).

111. Jon Winningham, interview with the author (September 12, 2018).

Chapter 8

1. James Madison "Memorial and Remonstrance Against Religious Assessments," in Vincent Philip Munoz, ed., *Religious Liberty and the American Supreme Court: The Essential Cases and Documents* (New York: Rowman and Littlefield, 2015), p. 608.

2. Quoted in Arthur Lyons, *Satan Wants You: The Cult of Devil Worship in America* (New York: Mysterious Press, 1988), p. 185.

3. Massimo Introvigne, *Satanism: A Social History* (Leiden: Brill, 2016), pp. 11–13.

4. Ted Peters, "Satanism: Bunk or blasphemy?," *Theology Today* 51, no. 3 (1994): pp. 381–393.

5. Sutkeh, interview with the author (February 3, 2019).

6. Jonathan Edwards, *A History of the Work of Redemption* (New York: Shepard Kollock, 1786), p. 319.

7. Christopher Bader, Joseph O. Baker, and Frederick Carson Mencken, *Paranormal America: Ghost Encounters, UFO Sightings, Bigfoot Hunts, and Other Curiosities in Religion and Culture* (Waco, Tx.: Baylor University Press, 2017), p. 192.

8. W. Scott Poole, *Satan in America: The Devil We Know* (New York: Rowan and Littlefield, 2010), p. 189., p. 216.

9. Randall H. Alfred, "The Church of Satan," in James R. Lewis and Jesper Aagaard Petersen, eds., *The Encyclopedic Sourcebook of Satanism* (Amherst, N.Y.: Prometheus Books, 2008), p. 488.

10. Anton Szandor LaVey, *Satan Speaks!* (Venice, Calif.: Feral House, 1998), p. 4.

11. Blanche Barton, *The Secret Life of a Satanist: The Authorized Biography of Anton LaVey* (Los Angeles: Feral House, 1990), p. 213.

12. Kathleen S. Lowney, "Teenage Satanism as Oppositional Youth Subculture," in James R. Lewis, and Jesper Aagaard Petersen, eds., *The Encyclopedic Sourcebook of Satanism* (Amherst, N.Y.: Prometheus Books, 2008), p. 515.

13. Quoted in Denis R. Janz, editor, *A Reformation Reader: Primary Texts with Introductions* (Minneapolis, Minn.: Fortress Press, 1999), pp. 378–379.

14. William Wells Brown, *My Southern Home: The South and Its People* (Chapel Hill: University of North Carolina Press, 2011), p. 60.

15. Ruben van Luijk, *Children of Lucifer: The Origins of Modern Religious Satanism* (New York: Oxford University Press, 2016), p. 370.

16. Barton and LaVey, *The Secret Life of a Satanist*, p. 199. Van Luijk (*Children of Lucifer*, p. 556) notes that this quote by LaVey was influenced by the dictum that when fascism comes to America, it will be in the form of "Americanism." Van Luijk suggests that LaVey predicted a coming right-wing uprising in America and hoped to position the Church of Satan to benefit from this shift.

17. Seraphina, interview with the author (July 1, 2018).

18. Field notes, San Marcos, Texas (June 15, 2018).

19. "Spokesman for the Satanic Temple speaks in Little Rock," *youtube.com* (August 16, 2018). Available online at https://www.youtube.com/watch?v=yXq835Omy7c (Accessed February 11, 2019).

20. David Guinan, interview with the author (March 6, 2019).

21. R. Laurence Moore, *Religious Outsiders and the Making of Americans* (New York: Oxford University Press, 1986), p. 205.
22. Catherine L. Albanese, "Exchanging Selves, Exchanging Souls: Contact, Combination, and American Religious History," in Thomas A. Tweed, ed., *Retelling US Religious History* (Berkeley: University of California Press, 1997), p. 225.
23. Claire Ballor, "Dallas Satanist, Forney youth minister chat at dueling Planned Parenthood protests," *The Dallas Morning News* (February 11, 2017). Available online at https://www.dallasnews.com/news/southern-dallas/2017/02/11/dallas-satanist-forney-youth-minister-take-time-chat-dueling-planned-parenthood-protests (Accessed February 11, 2019).

Bibliography

Albanese, Catherine L. *America, Religions, and Religion*. Belmont, Calif.: Thomson/ Wadsworth, 2007.

Albanese, Catherine L. "Exchanging Selves, Exchanging Souls: Contact, Combination, and American Religious History." In Thomas A. Tweed, ed., *Retelling U.S. Religious History*. Berkeley: University of California Press, 1997, 200–226.

Alfred, Randall H. "The Church of Satan." In James R. Lewis and Jesper Aagaard Petersen, eds., *The Encyclopedic Sourcebook of Satanism*. Amherst, N.Y.: Prometheus Books, 2008, 478–502.

Anderson, Benedict. *Imagined Communities: Reflections on the Origin and Spread of Nationalism*. New York: Verso, 2016.

Aquino, Michael. *The Church of Satan*. Vol. 1, 8th.ed. Michael Aquino, 2013.

Ba'al, Damien. *The Satanic Narratives: A Modern Satanic Bible*. St. Louis, Mo.: HLA, 2015.

Baddeley, Gavin. *Lucifer Rising*. London: Plexus, 1999.

Bader, Christopher, Joseph O. Baker, and Frederick Carson Mencken. *Paranormal America: Ghost Encounters, UFO Sightings, Bigfoot Hunts, and Other Curiosities in Religion and Culture*. New York: New York University Press, 2017.

Bagger, Matthew. *The Uses of Paradox Religion, Self-Transformation, and the Absurd*. New York: Columbia University Press, 2012.

Barber, Malcolm. *The New Knighthood: A History of the Order of the Temple*. New York: Cambridge University Press, 2012.

Barton, Blanche. *The Church of Satan*. New York: Hell's Kitchen Productions, 1990.

Barton, Blanche, and Anton Szandor LaVey. *The Secret Life of a Satanist: The Authorized Biography of Anton LaVey*. Los Angeles: Feral House, 1990.

Bellah, Robert N. *Religion in Human Evolution: From the Paleolithic to the Axial Age*. Cambridge, Mass.: Harvard University Press, 2011.

Berger, Peter. *The Sacred Canopy: Elements of a Sociological Theory of Religion*. New York: Anchor Books, 1969.

Bivins, Jason. *Religion of Fear: The Politics of Horror in Conservative Evangelicalism*. Oxford: Oxford University Press, 2008.

Bromley, David G. "Satanism: The New Cult Scare." In James T. Richardson, Joel Best, and David G. Bromley, eds., *The Satanism Scare*. Hawthorne, N.Y.: Aldine De Gruyter, 1991, 49–74.

Bromley, David G., and Susan G. Ainsley. "Satanism and Satanic Churches: The Contemporary Incarnations." In Timothy Miller, ed., *America's Alternative Religions*. Albany: State University of New York Press, 1995, 401–409.

Brown, William Wells. *My Southern Home: The South and Its People*. Chapel Hill: University of North Carolina Press, 2011.

Bryant A.G., and J. J. Swartz. "Why Crisis Pregnancy Centers Are Legal but Unethical." *AMA Journal of Ethics* 20:1 (2018): 269–277.

Campbell, Bradley, and Jason Manning. *The Rise of Victimhood Culture: Microaggressions, Safe Spaces, and the New Culture Wars*. New York: Palgrave MacMillan, 2018.

Coles, Bryn Alexander, and Melanie West. 2016. "Trolling the Trolls: Online Forum Users Constructions of the Nature and Properties of Trolling." *Computers in Human Behavior* 60: 232–244.

Crowe, Gretchen R. "Under Threat of Satanic Ritual, Church Counters with Prayer." *Our Sunday Visitor*, May 25, 2014, 2.

Curtis, Finbarr. *The Production of American Religious Freedom*. New York: New York University Press, 2017.

Cusack, Carole M. *Invented Religions: Imagination, Fiction and Faith*. Farnham, Surrey, UK: Ashgate, 2010.

Davies, Owen. *Grimoires: A History of Magic Books*. Oxford: Oxford University Press, 2009.

De Young, Mary. *The Day Care Ritual Abuse Moral Panic*. Jefferson, N.C.: McFarland, 2004.

Dégh, Linda, and Andrew Vázsonyi. "Does the Word 'Dog' Bite? Ostensive Action: A Means of Legend-Telling." *Journal of Folklore Research* 20:1 (1983): 5–34.

Dégh, Linda and Andrew Vazsonyi. "Legend and Belief." In Dan Ben-Amos, ed., *Folklore Genres*. Austin: University of Texas, Press, 1976 [1971], 93–123.

Dery, Mark, and Bruce Sterling. *I Must Not Think Bad Thoughts: Drive-by Essays on American Dread, American Dreams*. Minneapolis: University of Minnesota Press, 2012.

Dyrendal, Asbjørn. "Darkness Within: Satanism as a Self-Religion." In Jesper Aagaard Petersen, ed., *Contemporary Religious Satanism: A Critical Anthology*. Farnham, UK: Ashgate, 2009, 59–73.

Dyrendal, Asbjørn. "Devilish Consumption: Popular Culture in Satanic Socialization." *Numen*. 55:1 (2008): 68–98.

Dyrendal, Asbjørn, James R. Lewis, and Jesper Aagaard Petersen. *The Invention of Satanism*. New York: Oxford University Press, 2015.

Eck, Diana. *A New Religious America: How A "Christian Country" Has Become the World's Most Religiously Diverse Nation*. New York: HarperCollins, 2001.

Edwards, Jonathan. *A History of the Work of Redemption*. New York: Shepard Kollock, 1786.

Faxneld, Per. "Secret Lineages and De Facto Satanists: Anton LaVey's Use of Esoteric Tradition." In Egil Asprem and Kennet Granholm, eds., *Contemporary Esotericism*. Sheffield, UK: Equinox, 2013, 72–90.

Faxneld, Per, and Jesper Aagaard Petersen. *The Devil's Party: Satanism in Modernity*. New York: Oxford University Press, 2013.

Feltmate, David. *Drawn to the Gods: Religion and Humor in The Simpsons, South Park, and Family Guy*. New York: New York University Press, 2017.

France, Anatole. *The Revolt of the Angels*. Translated by Wilifred Jackson. New York: Dodd, Mead, 1914.

Frankfurter, David. *Evil Incarnate: Rumors of Demonic Conspiracy and Satanic Abuse in History*. Princeton, N.J.: Princeton University Press, 2006.

Frankfurter, David. "Review of *The Invention of Satanism*. Asbjorn Dyrendeal, James Lewis, and Jesper Peterson." *Journal of Religion and Violence* 5:1 (2017): 111–115.

Gardner, Gerald. *Witchcraft Today*. New York: Kensington, 2004.

George, Cherian. *Hate Spin: The Manufacture of Religious Offense and Its Threat to Democracy*. Cambridge, Mass.: MIT Press, 2017.

Gilmore, Peter H. "LaVey, Anton Szandor." In James R. Lewis, ed. *Satanism Today: An Encyclopedia of Religion, Folklore, and Popular Culture*. Santa Barbara: ABC-CLIO. 2001, 144–147.

Ginzburg, Carlo. *Ecstasies: Deciphering the Witches' Sabbath*. Translated by Raymond Rosenthal. New York: Pantheon, 1991.

Ginzburg, Carlo. *The Night Battles*. Translated by John and Anne Tedeschi. Baltimore, Md.: Johns Hopkins University Press, 1983.

Gunn, Joshua. *Modern Occult Rhetoric: Mass Media and the Drama of Secrecy in the Twentieth Century*. Tuscaloosa: University of Alabama Press, 2005.

Haldane, John, and Patrick Lee. "Aquinas on Human Ensoulment, Abortion and the Value of Life." *Philosophy* 78:2 (2003): 255–278.

Hamburger, Philip. *Separation of Church and State*. Cambridge, Mass.: Harvard University Press, 2002.

Harvey, Graham. "Satanism: Performing Alterity and Othering." In James R. Lewis and Jesper Aagaard Petersen, eds., *The Encyclopedic Sourcebook of Satanism*. Amherst, N.Y.: Prometheus Books, 2008: 610–632.

Huizinga, Johan. *Homo Ludens: A Study of the Play-Element in Culture*. Boston: Beacon Press, 2014.

Hurd, Elizabeth Shakman. *Beyond Religious Freedom: The New Global Politics of Religion*. Princeton, N.J.: Princeton University Press, 2015.

Introvigne, Massimo. *Satanism: A Social History*. Leiden: Brill, 2016.

Jones, Robert P. *The End of White Christian America*. New York: Simon and Schuster, 2016.

Laborde, Cécile. "Religion in the Law: The Disaggregation Approach." *Law and Philosophy* 34:6 (2015): 581–600.

Lasn, Kalle. *Culture Jam: The Uncooling of America*. New York: Eagle Brook, 1999.

LaVey, Anton S. *Satan Speaks!* Venice, Calif: Feral House, 1998.

LaVey, Anton S. *The Satanic Bible*. New York: Avon, 1969.

LaVey, Anton S. *The Satanic Rituals*. New York: Avon, 1972.

Laycock, Douglas. "Government-Sponsored Religious Displays: Transparent Rationalizations and Expedient Post-Modernism." *Case Western Reserve Law Review* 61:4 (Summer 2011): 1211–1252.

Laycock, Joseph. "Laughing Matters: 'Parody Religions' and the Command to Compare." *Bulletin for the Study of Religion* 42:3 (2013): 19–26.

Lewis, James R. "Conversion to Satanism: Constructing Diabolical Identities." In Per Faxneld and Jesper Aagaard Petersen, eds., *The Devil's Party: Satanism in Modernity*. New York: Oxford University Press, 2013, 145–166.

Lewis, James R. *Legitimating New Religions*. Piscataway, N.J.: Rutgers University Press, 2004.

Lewis, James R. "Review of Chris Mathews, *Modern Satanism: Anatomy of a Radical Subculture*." *Alternative Religion and Spirituality Review* 1:1 (2010): 109–113.

Lewis, James R. *Satanism Today: An Encyclopedia of Religion, Folklore, and Popular Culture*. Santa Barbara, Calif.: ABC-CLIO, 2001.

Lewis, James R. "Who Serves Satan? A Demographic and Ideological Profile." *Marburg Journal of Religion* 6:2 (2001): 1–25.

Lowney, Kathleen S. "Teenage Satanism as Oppositional Youth Subculture." In James R. Lewis, and Jesper Aagaard Petersen, eds., *The Encyclopedic Sourcebook of Satanism*. Amherst, N.Y.: Prometheus Books, 2008, 503–530.

Lukianoff, Greg, and Jonathan Haidt. *The Coddling of the American Mind: How Good Intentions and Bad Ideas Are Setting Up a Generation for Failure*. New York: Penguin, 2018.

Lyons, Arthur. *Satan Wants You: The Cult of Devil Worship in America*. New York: Mysterious Press, 1988.

Lyons, Arthur. *The Second Coming: Satanism in America*. New York: Dodd, Mead, 1970.

Main, Thomas J. *The Rise of the Alt-Right*. Washington, DC: Brookings Institution Press, 2018.

Marcus, Greil. *Lipstick Traces: A Secret History of the Twentieth Century*. Cambridge, Mass.: Harvard University Press, 1990.

Marcuse, Herbert, and Andrew Feenberg, eds., *The Essential Marcuse: Selected Writings of Philosopher and Social Critic Herbert Marcuse*. Boston: Beacon Press, 2007.

Martin, Craig. *Masking Hegemony: A Genealogy of Liberalism, Religion, and the Private Sphere*. London: Equinox, 2010.

Martin, Michelle, "Archbishop Urges Prayer to Combat Black Mass." *Our Sunday Visitor*, September 7, 2014, 4A.

Mathews, Chris. *Modern Satanism: Anatomy of a Radical Subculture*. Westport, Conn: Praeger, 2009.

McCloud, Sean. *American Possessions—Fighting Demons in the Contemporary United States*. New York: Oxford University Press, 2015.

McCutcheon, Russell T. *Critics Not Caretakers: Redescribing the Public Study of Religion*. Albany: State University of New York Press, 2001.

McCutcheon, Russell. "'They Licked the Platter Clean': On the Co-Dependency of the Religious and The Secular." *Method & Theory in the Study of Religion* 19: 3/4 (2007): 173–199.

McLeod, Kembrew. *Freedom of Expression®: Resistance and Repression in the Age of Intellectual Property*. Minneapolis: University of Minnesota Press, 2007.

Modern, John Lardas. "My Evangelical Conviction." *Religion* 42 (June 2012): 439–457.

Moellering, Ralph A. "The New Quest for the Sacred: The Witchcraft Craze and the Lure of the Occult." *The Springfielder* 35:4 (1972): 274–278.

Moody, Edward J. "Magical Therapy: An Anthropological Investigation of Contemporary Satanism." In Irving I. Zaretsky and Mark P. Leone, eds. *Religious Movements in Contemporary America*. Princeton, N.J.: Princeton University Press, 1974, 355–382.

Moore, R. Laurence. *Religious Outsiders and the Making of Americans*. New York: Oxford University Press, 1986.

Morreall, John. *Taking Laughter Seriously*. Albany: State University of New York Press, 1998.

Munoz, Vincent Philip. *Religious Liberty and the American Supreme Court: The Essential Cases and Documents*. New York: Rowman and Littlefield, 2015.

Murphy, Tim. "Notes from the Field: Religious Defamation and Radical Pluralism as Challenges to the Scholar of Religion." *The Council of Societies for the Study of Religion Bulletin* 34:4 (Nov. 2005): 79–83.

Murrell, Nathaniel Samuel. *Afro-Caribbean Religions: An Introduction to Their Historical, Cultural, and Sacred Traditions*. Philadelphia: Temple University Press, 2010.

Newton, Michael. *Raising Hell: An Encyclopedia of Devil Worship and Satanic Crime*. New York: Avon Books, 1993.

Orsi, Robert. *Between Heaven and Earth: The Religious Worlds People Make and the Scholars Who Study Them*. Princeton, N.J.: Princeton University Press, 2005.

Owen, Suzanne. 2011. "The World Religions Paradigm Time for a Change." *Arts and Humanities in Higher Education* 10:3: 253–268.

Paine, Thomas. *The Age of Reason.* New York: Truth Seeker, 1898.

Peters, Ted. "Bunk or Blasphemy?" *Theology Today* 51:3 (1994): 381–393.

Petersen, Jesper Aagaard. "The Carnival of Dr. LaVey: Articulations of Transgression in Modern Satanism." In Per Faxneld and Jesper Aagaard Petersen, eds., *The Devil's Party: Satanism in Modernity.* New York: Oxford University Press, 2013, 167–188.

Petersen, Jesper Aagaard. "Contemporary Satanism." In Christopher Partridge, ed., *The Occult World.* New York: Routledge, 2015, 396–404.

Petersen, Jesper Aagaard. "From Book to Bit: Enacting Satanism Online." In Egil Asprem and Kennet Granholm, eds., *Contemporary Esotericism.* Sheffield, UK: Equinox, 2013, 134–158.

Petersen, Jesper Aagaard. "Introduction: Embracing Satan." In Jesper Aagaard Petersen, ed., *Contemporary Religious Satanism: A Critical Anthology.* Farnham, UK: Ashgate, 2009: 1–26.

Petersen, Jesper Aagaard. "Modern Satanism: Dark Doctrines and Black Flames." In James R. Lewis and Jesper Aagaard Petersen, eds., *Controversial New Religions.* New York: Oxford, 2014, 423–457.

Petersen, Jesper Aagaard. "Satanists and Nuts: The Role of Schisms in Modern Satanism." In James R. Lewis and Sarah M. Lewis, eds., *Sacred Schisms: How Religions Divide.* Cambridge: Cambridge University Press, 2009, 218–247.

Petersen, Jesper Aagaard. "'Smite Him Hip and Thigh': Satanism, Violence, and Transgression." In James R. Lewis, ed., *Violence and New Religious Movements.* New York: Oxford University Press, 2011, 351–378.

Petersen, Jesper Aagaard, and Asbjorn Dyrendal. "Satanism." In Olav Hammer and Mikael Rothstein, eds., *The Cambridge Companion to New Religious Movements.* Cambridge: Cambridge University Press, 2012, 215–230.

Pokines, James T. "A Santeria/Palo Mayombe Cauldron Containing a Human Skull and Multiple Artifacts Recovered in Western Massachusetts, U.S.A." *Forensic Science International* 248 (2015): e1–e7.

Poole, W. Scott. *Satan in America: The Devil We Know.* New York: Rowan and Littlefield, 2010.

Prothero, Stephen R. *God Is Not One: The Eight Rival Religions That Run the World.* New York: HarperOne, 2011.

Prothero, Stephen R. *Religious Literacy: What Every American Needs to Know—and Doesn't.* San Francisco: HarperSanFrancisco, 2007.

Prothero, Stephen R. *Why Liberals Win the Culture Wars (Even When They Lose Elections): The Battles That Define America from Jefferson's Heresies to Gay Marriage.* New York: HaperOne, 2016.

Queen, Christopher S., and Sallie B. King. *Engaged Buddhism: Buddhist Liberation Movements in Asia.* Albany: State University of New York Press, 1996.

Reichley, A. James. *Religion in American Public Life.* Washington, DC: Brookings Institution, 1985.

Robin, Corey. *The Reactionary Mind: Conservatism from Edmund Burke to Sarah Palin.* Oxford: Oxford University Press, 2011.

Roberts, Susan. *Witches U.S.A.* New York: Dell, 1971.

Rountree, Kathryn. *Embracing the Witch and the Goddess: Feminist Ritual-Makers in New Zealand.* London: Routledge, 2004.

Russell, Jeffrey Burton. *The Devil, Perception of Evil: Perceptions of Evil from Antiquity to Primitive Christianity*. Ithaca, N.Y.: Cornell University Press, 1982.

Sagan, Carl. *The Demon-Haunted World: Science as a Candle in the Dark*. New York: Random House, 1995.

Santino, Jack. *The Hallowed Eve Dimensions of Culture in a Calendar Festival in Northern Ireland*. Lexington: University of Kentucky Press, 2015.

Schock, Peter A. *Romantic Satanism: Myth and the Historical Moment in Blake, Shelley, and Byron*. Houndmills, Basingstoke, Hampshire: Palgrave Macmillan, 2003.

Schreck, Nikolas. *The Satanic Screen: An Illustrated Guide to the Devil in Cinema*. London: Creation, 2001.

Seligman, Adam B., Robert P. Weller, Michael J. Puett, and Bennett Simon. *Ritual and Its Consequences: An Essay on the Limits of Sincerity*. New York: Oxford University Press, 2008.

Senholt, Jacob. "Secret Identities in the Sinister Tradition: Political Esotericism and the Convergence of Radical Islam, Satanism and National Socialism in the Order of Nine Angles." In Per Faxneld and Jesper Petersen, eds., *The Devil's Party: Satanism in Modernity*. New York: Oxford University Press, 2012, 250–274.

Shaw, George Bernard. *Man and Superman: A Comedy and a Philosophy*. New York: Brentano's, 1922.

Shelley, Percy Bysshe. *A Defense of Poetry*. Charleston, S.C.: BiblioLife, 2009.

Smith, Jonathan Z. *Map Is Not Territory: Studies in the History of Religion*. Chicago: University of Chicago Press, 1993.

Smith, Jonathan Z. *Relating Religion: Essays in the Study of Religion*. Chicago: University of Chicago Press, 2004.

Smith, Jonathan Z. "Religion, Religions, Religious." In Mark C. Taylor, ed., *Critical Terms for Religious Studies*. Chicago: University of Chicago Press, 1998, 269–285.

Solomon, Norman. *Judaism a Very Short Introduction*. New York: Oxford University Press, 2014.

Stallybrass, Peter, and Allon White. *The Politics and Poetics of Transgression*. Ithaca, N.Y.: Cornell University Press, 1995.

Stark, Rodney, and Williams Sims Bainbridge. *The Future of Religion: Secularization, Revival, and Cult Formation*. Los Angeles: University of California Press, 1985.

Stewart, Katherine. *The Good News Club: The Christian Right's Stealth Assault on America's Children*. New York: PublicAffairs, 2012.

Sullivan, Winnifred Fallers. *The Impossibility of Religious Freedom*. Princeton, N.J.: Princeton University Press, 2005.

Sullivan, Winnifred Fallers, Elizabeth Shakman Hurd, Saba Mahmood, and Peter G. Danchin, eds. *Politics of Religious Freedom*. Chicago: University of Chicago Press, 2015.

Sutcliffe, Steven, and Carole M. Cusack. *The Problem of Invented Religions*. New York: Routledge, 2016.

Swidler, Ann. "Culture in Action: Symbols and Strategies." *American Sociological Review* 51:2 (1986): 273–286.

Thavis, John. *The Vatican Prophecies*. New York: Viking, 2015.

Truzzi, Marcello. "The Occult Revival as Popular Culture: Some Random Observations on the Old and the Nouveau Witch." *The Sociological Quarterly* 13:1 (1972): 16–36.

Tylor, Edward Burnett. *Primitive Culture: Researchers into the Development of Mythology, Philosophy, Religion, Language, Art, and Custom*. New York: G. P. Putnam's Sons, 1920 [1871].

Urban, Hugh B. *The Church of Scientology: A History of a New Religion*. Princeton, N.J.: Princeton University Press, 2013.

Urban, Hugh B. *New Age, Neopagan, and New Religious Movements: Alternative Spirituality in Contemporary America*. Oakland: University of California Press, 2015.

Van Luijk, Ruben. *Children of Lucifer: The Origins of Modern Religious Satanism*. New York: Oxford University Press, 2016.

Van Luijk, Ruben. "Sex, Science, and Liberty: The Resurrection of Satan in Nineteenth-Century (Counter) Culture." In Per Faxneld and Jesper Aagaard Petersen, eds., *The Devil's Party: Satanism in Modernity*. New York: Oxford University Press, 2013, 41–52.

Wenger, Tisa J. *Religious Freedom: The Contested History of an American Ideal*. Chapel Hill: University of North Carolina Press, 2018.

Wexler, Jay. *Holy Hullabaloos: A Road Trip to the Battlegrounds of the Church/State Wars*. Boston: Beacon Press, 2009.

Wilcox, Melissa M. *Queer Nuns: Religion, Activism, and Serious Parody*. New York: New York University Press, 2018.

Wilson, Jeff. "Blasphemy as Bhavana: Anti-Christianity in a New Buddhist Movement." *Nova Religio* 22:3 (2019): 8–35.

Wright, Lawrence. *Saints & Sinners: Walker Railey, Jimmy Swaggart, Madalyn Murray O'Hair, Anton LaVey, Will Campbell, Matthew Fox*. New York: Knopf, 1993.

Index

abortion, 16, 23, 25, 28, 41, 46, 89, 91,
    105–111, 113, 143–145, 153,
    160–161, 180, 193, 230
affair of the poisons, the, 233
After-School Satan Club, 50–57, 80, 129
alt-right, 61, 63, 64, 67, 73, 212
Altizer, Thomas, 97
America Needs Fatima, 56, 59, 102
American Atheists, 32
American Civil Liberties Union, 4–5, 13,
    108, 180
American Society for the Defense of
    Tradition, Family and Property
    (TFP), 15, 18, 56, 59, 131, 137, 185
Americans United For the Separation of
    Church and State, 42
Anderson, Benedict, 87
Anglin, Andrew, 63
anti-semitism, 70
antifa, 76
appropriating the discourse of evil, 25, 133
Aquino, Michael, 84–85, 227
Atomwaffen Division, 65
audience cults, 85, 217

Baphomet, 10–13, 38, 44–45, 71, 80, 91,
    101, 193
Beck, Glenn, 45
Bellah, Robert, 115
black mass, 18, 26, 35, 41, 84, 88, 97, 99,
    115, 121, 126, 135, 151, 154, 157–158,
    160–166, 180, 234
Blaine Amendments, 9–10
Boston Marathon bombing, 34
Brietbart, 76
Brown, William Wells, 191
Bugbee, Shane, 30, 69, 116, 138
Burwell v. Hobby Lobby, 105–107, 125–126
Bush, George W., 28, 97

California Board of Psychology, 50
Camp Quest, 53

Campus Reform, 170
Carlson, Tucker, 37, 59, 86
Catholic Action League, 164, 169
Catholic League, 15
Cernovich, Mike, 63
Chick, Jack, 32
Child Evangelism Fellowship, 51–52
Christian nation, 20
Church Militant, 23, 45, 113, 126, 179
Church of Satan, 14, 16, 25, 30–31, 36,
    38, 54, 64, 83–85, 87, 89–94, 96, 98,
    103, 114–115, 117, 134–136, 162,
    199–200, 227
CNN, 45
Crisis pregnancy centers, 28, 143, 203
Crossroads Assembly, 82, 102
culture jamming, 25, 131, 139–146
culture wars, 19–23

de Las Casas, Bartolomé, 190
Debord, Guy, 140, 168
détournement, 140, 143–144
diversity committee, 79

FAUST: The Satanic Federation, 82
Feldman, Corey, 62
Feral House, 64
First Great Awakening, 188
Foucault, Michel, 23, 104, 133
Fox news, 8, 24, 37, 59, 86
France, Anatole, 42, 98, 101, 189
Freedom From Religion Foundation,
    41–43, 58, 60, 147, 148, 149, 174,
    177, 183
Freedom of Information Act, 8, 43,
    158, 181
freedom of speech, 67, 76–77

Gatto, John Taylor, 53
Gilmore, Peter, 16, 30, 87, 89, 91–92, 135
Global Order of Satan, 65–67, 188
Good News Club, 52, 54–57

Good News Club v. Milford Central
    School, 51, 54
Graham, Franklin, 54
Greece v. Galloway, 16, 157, 172–174,
    180, 184
Grove City v. Summum, 197–198

Hail Satan? (film), 68, 189
Harris v. McRae, 109
Harvard University, 18, 26, 41, 127, 135,
    155, 157, 158, 159, 160, 161–166, 170,
    180, 236
hate speech, 72, 157, 161–170, 185
hate spin, 166–170, 184, 186
headquarters of The Satanic
    Temple, 62, 92
hegemony, 23–24, 76, 127,
    133, 150, 194
HelLA, 67
highway adoption, 150, 152
Hobby Lobby. See Burwell v. Hobby Lobby
Hoffman, Abbie, 140
holiday displays, 41–44
hosts, consecrated, 18, 135, 154, 162,
    164–165, 169, 171
House Office of Faith-Based and
    Community Initiatives, 28
Huizinga, John, 115
humor, incongruity theory of, 33
Huysman, Joris-Karl, 84, 101, 115,
    162–163, 171–172

ignorant familiarity, 24
Illuminati, 86
Ingraham v. Wright, 39
invented religion, 115
ISIS, comparisons to, 176, 177, 185
Islam, 46, 59, 66, 80, 167–168
Islamic terrorism, 46
ISSTD (International Society for
    the Study of Trauma and
    Dissociation), 49

Jehovah's Witnesses, 24
Job, Book of, 186
Johnson Amendment, 129
Jones, Alex, 63, 73
Jordan, Gigi, 50

Kennedy, Joe, 148–149
Knights of the KKK, 71

Lamers, Martin, 85, 220
LaVey, Anton, 14, 25, 30, 64–65, 83, 85,
    89–99, 102–103, 115, 136, 138, 141,
    153, 159, 162, 189, 192, 199–200
Le Bas. See Huysman, Joris-Karl
League of Revel Eve: Satanic Collective of
    New York City (LORE:SYNC), 82, 101
legitimation strategies, 38
Levi, Eliphaz, 11, 38, 80, 193
Liberty Counsel, 43, 51, 54–55, 208
Lifesitenews, 24, 113, 129, 145
Lovecraft, H.P., 88
Lucien's Law, 139, 146–150, 183

Madison, James, 184, 187
Marcuse, Herbert, 76
Marxism, 76
Massachusetts Commission Against
    Discrimination, 63, 181
McCreary County v. ACLU of Kentucky, 2
Mehta, Hemant, 43, 135
Menstratin' with Satan, 150–151
Might is Right, 30, 69, 84
millennialism, 189
Milton, John, 88, 96, 100–101
Minnesota Left Hand Path Community,
    46, 58–59, 81

National Council, 47, 66–68, 73, 78–79,
    81, 89, 128, 139, 180, 194
National Right to Life Committee,
    109–110
Negativland, 139–140, 142
Neo-Nazis, 37, 63–65, 72–74
Netflix, 80–81
new religions studies, 22
non-disclosure agreements, 72–73

Obama, Barack, 28
Obergefell v. Hodges, 41
ordination program, 63, 80
Ordo Sororitatis Satanicae, 81, 223

Paradise Lost. See Milton, John
Parfrey, Adam, 64, 69, 70, 74

Pastafarianism, 115–116
Philadelphia Insurance Companies, 57
philanthropy, Satanic, 150–153
pink mass, 34–36
Planned Parenthood, 106, 108, 110,
    143–145, 179, 194
Pluralism Project, 155, 161
pluralism, religious, 26, 158–161, 169, 172,
    185, 186
prayer invocations, 16, 157–158, 172–181
pregnancy crisis centers, 28
*Prescott v. Oklahoma Capitol Preservation
    Commission*, 4
Process Church of Final Judgment, 49
Protect Children Project, 39–41
Protestant Reformation, 89
public forums, 41–43, 51, 58, 60, 148
purity spiral, 74

Quran, 52, 167

racism, 65, 67, 69–71, 78
Radio Free Satan, 30
rally for religious liberty, Little Rock,
    Arkansas, 13, 71–72, 81
Rand, Ayn, 93
Randazza, Marc, 61, 63–65, 67, 70, 73–74
Reason Alliance, 41, 56
recovered memories, 29
religious freedom, 23–24, 39, 42, 45, 75,
    125–127
Religious Freedom Restoration Act
    (RFRA), 25, 107, 109–111
Return to Order, 56
Revolt of the Angels. See France, Anatole
Rivera, Geraldo, 29
Roe v. Wade, 106, 110
Romanticism, 82, 88–90, 93, 99–100
Rosemary's Baby, 84

same-sex marriage, 41
*Santa Fe Independent School District
    v. Doe*, 240
Satanhaus, 81
Satanic Australia, 153, 188
Satanic New Zealand, 153
Satanic Panic, 14, 29–30, 32, 49, 95, 97,
    115, 136, 187, 189

Satanic ritual abuse, 29, 54
Scientology, 22, 104, 130
Scott, Rick, 31
secularization narrative, 97
self religion, 15
serious parody, 25, 114–117
Seven Tenets, the, 37–38, 93, 119–120,
    127–129, 150, 192
sexism, 69–70
Situationists, The. *See* Debord, Guy
SMART (Stop Mind Control
    And Ritual Abuse Today),
    30–31, 70
Smith, Jonathan Z., 118, 130, 156
Snaketivity, 42
social Darwinism, 89–90, 93, 97–99
Socialism, 90
socially engaged Satanism, 14–19
soul contracts, 44, 72
Southern Poverty Law Center, 65
Subversive Autonomous Satanic Ritual,
    68, 145
Supreme Court, 24
Swidler, Ann, 88–89

tax-exempt status, 129, 220, 227
Temple of Set, 84–85
The Chilling Adventures
    of Sabrina, 80
The Satanic Bible, 30, 84–85, 92–95
*The Satanic Children's Big Book of
    Activities*, 147–148
The Satanic Temple headquarters, 49
The Witch (film), 142
Thomas More Society, 112
Torcaso v. Watkins, 117
trolling, 103, 124
Trump, Donald, 21, 77, 79, 97
Twitter, 62–63, 67, 93
two-tier model of religion, 22, 24

unbaptism, 121–123
United Aspects of Satan, 81, 149
United States v. Seeger, 117–118
US Conference of Bishops, 110

Van Orden v. Perry, 2–4, 6, 12
viewpoint discrimination, 51

Webster v. Reproductive Health Services, 108
Werner, Brian, 94, 102, 138
Westboro Baptist Church, 34, 36, 114
white supremacists, 71
WITCH, 141

women's march (2016), 22
World Changers of Florida, Inc., 147
world religion paradigm, 156

Yiannopoulos, Milo, 76–77